Acknowledgements

We owe a tremendous debt to the companies and managers who agreed to take part in our study. They submitted good-naturedly to lengthy interviews, and were kind enough to share with us their views on their companies, developments in their industries, and the significance of the Single European Market. We would like to thank them all.

Roland Calori would also like to thank the French companies – L'Oreal, Peugeot and Otis – which fund the European Research Chair at Groupe ESC Lyon.

In addition Peter Lawrence would like to thank the Research Committee of the University of Loughborough for a grant which made fieldwork in Britain and the Netherlands possible. He would also like to thank Janet Brittain and Judith Poulton for a painstaking and quality preparation of the manuscript.

R.C. and P.L.

List of Contributors

Tugrul Atamer is Professor of Business Policy at the Groupe ESC Lyon in France. He studied at the Institut d'Administration des Entreprises (University of Grenoble, France), where he obtained his doctorate in management, and he has been Assistant Professor at the University of Rennes (France). He is also a professional consultant and his main interests are in international strategy, particularly in strategic alliances.

Jean-Louis Barsoux is Research Fellow at Templeton College, Oxford, working on a project comparing management in Britain and Germany. He has a BA and PhD in management from Loughborough University, and is joint author of *Management in France* (Cassell, 1990) and *The Challenge of British Management* (Macmillan, 1990).

Roland Calori is Professor of Business Policy, head of the Business Policy Department at the Groupe ESC Lyon in France. He studied at the Ecole des Hautes Etudes Commerciales in Paris and has a doctorate from the Institut d'Administration des Entreprises (University of Aix en Provence, France). He is also a professional consultant in strategic management and has published several articles in international journals on managing strategic change and diversity. He is currently working on mergers and acquisitions in Europe.

Peder Smed Christensen has a BA in Economics, a BA in French, an MBA, and a PhD in Strategic Management and is currently Assistant Professor of Strategic Management at the Institute of Management, Aarhus University, Denmark. Dr Christensen earlier worked as a systems analyst for Great Western Bank, Los Angeles.

Gianluca Colombo has a degree in Business Administration from Bocconi University in Milan, Italy. He is Associate Professor of Business Administration at Bocconi University, and of Business Policy on the MBA course. He is Vice-president of the CESAD Research Center for administrative and management studies at Bocconi University, and is active as a management consultant.

Giovanni Comboni is Assistant Professor of Business Policy at SDA Bocconi, Milan, Italy. He studied at the University of Milan, and was awarded an MBA at SDA Bocconi. He works as a management consultant, and his main interests are in communication and business start-ups.

Paola Dubini is Lecturer in Business Administration at L. Bocconi University

The Business of Europe

Managing Change

Edited by

Roland Calori and Peter Lawrence

SAGE Publications
London · Newbury Park · New Delhi

Editorial arrangement © Roland Calori and Peter Lawrence, 1991
Introduction © Jacques van der Meer, 1991
Chapter 1 © Egbert Kahle, 1991
Chapter 2 © Murray Steele, 1991
Chapter 3 © Jenny Piesse, 1991
Chapter 4 © Alessandro Sinatra and Paola Dubini, 1991
Chapter 5 © Gianluca Colombo and Giovanni Comboni, 1991
Chapter 6 © Roland Calori, 1991
Chapter 7 © Roland Calori, 1991
Chapter 8 © Jean-Louis Barsoux and Peter Lawrence, 1991
Chapter 9 © Tugrul Atamer and Gerry Johnson, 1991

First published 1991   First paperback edition 1992

SAGE Publications Ltd
6 Bonhill Street
London EC2A 4PU

SAGE Publications Inc
2455 Teller Road
Newbury Park, California 91320

SAGE Publications India Pvt Ltd
32, M-Block Market
Greater Kailash-I
New Delhi 110 048

British Library Cataloguing in Publication data

The business of Europe: Managing change.
  I. Calori, Roland   II. Lawrence, Peter
  382

ISBN 0-8039-8492-8
ISBN 0-8039-8746-3 pbk

Library of Congress catalog card number 90-053712

Typeset by Photoprint, Torquay, Devon
Printed in Great Britain by Billing and Sons Ltd, Worcester

Contents

in Milan, Italy, and instructor of strategy and entrepreneurship at SDA Bocconi Business School. She has been visiting Assistant Professor of Management at Stern School of Business – New York University.

Gerry Johnson is Director of Research and Professor of Strategic Management at the Cranfield School of Management. He studied anthropology at University College, London, and later gained a PhD in strategic management at Aston University. He has worked as a marketing executive with Unilever and Reed International and as a management consultant with Urwick, Orr and Partners. Together with Kevin Scholes he is the author of the widely used book *Exploring Corporate Strategy*.

Egbert Kahle, born 1943, studied business management and sociology at the Universities of Hanover and Göttingen. He was awarded the degree of Dipl.-Kfm in 1969 and that of Dr. rer.pol. for a thesis on problem-solving behaviour in 1973 in Göttingen, becoming full Professor of Organization and Decision Theory in 1982 at the University of Lüneburg. He has written five books and 40 articles, mostly on decision theory and production planning.

Peter Lawrence is Senior Lecturer in Management at Loughborough University in England. He studied at the Universities of London, Cambridge and Essex and has held posts at the Universities of Strathclyde, Konstanz and Southampton. His main interests are in management work and comparative management, and he has held fellowships in several continental European universities and in Israel.

Jacques van der Meer is a consultant in strategic management with van Spaendonck Adviesgroep in Tilburg in the Netherlands. He holds a degree in business economics from Erasmus University in Rotterdam, and was awarded a PhD for his dissertation on effective R&D-based strategy by the University of Twente at Enschede. Teaching and writing in the areas of business policy and innovation, he worked as Lecturer at the School of Management of Rotterdam University, and as Professor at Groupe ESC Lyon.

Jenny Piesse is Lecturer in Financial Economics at Brunel University in England. She studied at Columbia University, then worked as an economic consultant for Chase Econometrics in New York and San Francisco. She has taught at various business schools, including a five-year appointment at the Manchester Business School. She is engaged in research on the organisation of financial institutions.

Melchior Salgado is Assistant in Business Policy at the Groupe ESC Lyon in France. He has a Diplôme d'Etudes Approfondies from the University of Lyon II. His main interests are in comparative management. He is currently working on comparisons between Spain and France for his doctoral thesis.

Hans Meyer zu Selhausen, born 1940, studied business management and banking and was awarded the degree of Dr. oec.publ. for his work on capital planning in a credit bank in Munich in 1970, and the degree of Dr. rer. pol. habil. for a thesis on quantitative marketing models in banking in 1975, also in Munich. Since 1975 he has been a full Professor of Business Management at the University of Munich. He has written two books and more than 20 articles on banking.

Alessandro Sinatra is Professor of Business Policy at L. Bocconi University and is responsible for the Business Policy Department at SDA Bocconi Business School. As international consultant for strategy, he has worked in Europe and in the US on competitive strategies.

Murray Steele is currently Visiting Senior Lecturer in Business Strategy at Cranfield School of Management, where he has worked in most areas of the School's activities including being Course Director of the Senior Managers' Programme, Deputy Director of the MBA Programme and Chairman of the School's Alumni Association. He holds bachelors and masters degrees in engineering from the University of Glasgow, as well as an accountancy diploma and an MBA. He is a non-executive member of the Management Committee of the Airline Division of British Aerospace, as well as Chairman and Finance Director of Henley Hotels plc.

A Note on Who Did What

Most chapters in this book are a synthesis of what senior practitioners consider to be crucial developments in their industry during the 1990s. In that respect, the book has been realised by the managers who participated in our study. The main contributing researchers, in alphabetical order, are:

Tugrul Atamer
Groupe ESC Lyon (France), carried out part of the field study in France and is co-author of the Conclusions.

Jean-Louis Barsoux
University of Loughborough (UK), helped with the evaluation of interview material and wrote the chapter on comparisons between countries with Peter Lawrence.

Roland Calori
Groupe ESC Lyon, co-ordinated the project and conducted part of the field study in France. He has written the 'transverse' chapters looking at all the industries across countries.

Peder Christensen
Aarhus University (Denmark), did all of the fieldwork in Denmark.

Gianluca Colombo
SDA Bocconi (Milan, Italy), did part of the field study in Italy and is co-author of the chapter on the car industry.

Giovanni Comboni
SDA Bocconi (Milan, Italy), did part of the field study in Italy and is co-author of the chapter on the car industry.

Paola Dubini
SDA Bocconi, conducted part of the field study in Italy and is co-author of the chapter on publishing.

Gerry Johnson
Cranfield School of Management (UK), undertook part of the field study in the UK and is co-author of the concluding chapter.

Egbert Kahle
Lüneburg University (Germany), did part of the field study in West Germany

	and is author of the first chapter setting the scene on Europe.
Peter Lawrence	University of Loughborough (UK), conducted part of the interviews in the UK and the Netherlands, and has co-authored the chapter on comparisons between countries. He has edited the final version of this book.
Jacques van der Meer	Groupe ESC Lyon, did part of the field study in Holland and is author of the Introduction.
Jenny Piesse	Kingston Polytechnic (UK), and later of Brunel University (UK), did part of the field study in the UK and wrote the chapter on banking.
Melchior Salgado	Groupe ESC Lyon, did all the interviews in Spain.
Alessandro Sinatra	SDA Bocconi, did part of the field study in Italy and is co-author of the chapter on publishing.
Murray Steele	Cranfield School of Management, conducted part of the field study in the UK and wrote the chapter on the brewing industry.

The following colleagues also assisted in the field studies:

Siobhan Alderson	Cranfield School of Management, in the UK.
Giancarlo Forestieri	SDA Bocconi, in Milan, Italy.
Hans Meyer zu Selhausen	University of Munich, Germany.
Paola Tanzi	SDA Bocconi, in Milan, Italy.
Federico Visconti	SDA Bocconi, in Milan, Italy.

Introduction

Jacques B.H. van der Meer

Humans are remarkable creatures. First they expend a tremendous effort to create borders and defend their territory. This makes them feel relatively secure and able to protect their culture, economic interests, and national heritage. Then they realise that this quasi-comfortable niche can actually be an impediment to further economic growth and national welfare. So they once more invest enormous effort, and money, to do away with the previously comforting frontiers. Europe is now in the process of dissolving its internal frontiers. After numerous wars, more than a generation in the shadow of nuclear deterrence, and endless political debate, Europe now realises that maintaining internal divisions and emphasising national social-economic interests carries tremendous opportunity costs in an economic system that is no longer national but global. The call for a joint economic and political stand became stronger as Europe's economic competitors, the US and especially Japan, got richer, and that in an era where growth and innovation within European economies stagnated. One could say that paradoxically non-Europeans have contributed decisively to European unification.

With borders vanishing, some hitherto comfortably secured national industries have become anxious about the overall effects of a pan-European competitive arena. Other elements also contribute to this anxiety. It is for instance quite unclear whether Europe should be taken to mean the EC, or the whole of Western Europe, or the stretch of land from the Atlantic to the Urals. When this book was being written, one could hardly keep track of the process of liberalisation in the former Eastern Bloc economies. Whatever the definition of Europe, there is an undeniable continent-wide tendency towards unification. At the same time, Europe still consists of countries with different languages, cultures, histories, customs, not to mention different tastes and preferences, levels of wealth, and bodies of legislation. Europeans therefore do not feel European. They feel Italian, Spanish or Dutch. Europe in itself is a paradox.

The emergence of a new management challenge coincides with the publication of what one might call 'management cookbooks'. European integration has fuelled the publication of books that attempt to outdo each other in prescribing instant 'Competitive management strategies for 1992'. Although such books may serve to relieve the aforementioned managerial anxiety, most of them fail to address the complex, and often contradictory, issues of management in Europe in the 1990s.

A conversation that one of the authors overheard in the departure lounge at Heathrow airport may highlight in a small way the problematic nature of 'Europe 1992'. The discussion is between an American, an Englishman and a German manager, all working for an American company:

American: We just spent three days at HQ in Colorado. Fantastic! The board revealed a fully integrated European strategy for our business over here. What is more, further penetration into the German market is a priority.

Englishman: That is very nice. When you discussed the European strategy how exactly did you define Europe?

American: Hell, you ought to know, you are European.

Englishman: Well, I'm English actually. I come from Hereford.

American: Sure, but don't you think that many problems will be resolved by 1992, with the United States of Europe?

Englishman: Not exactly. Europe will remain what it is, a collection of countries each with different customs, sometimes even within countries. Jolly hard to build a fully integrated European strategy . . .

German: And there are other questions. You implied that Europe is the EC, but it now also includes former Eastern Bloc countries. As to the further penetration of the German market, you must recognise that it is both a mature and fragmented market, with regional differences as well. The characteristics of distribution in Schleswig-Holstein differ importantly from those in Bavaria. Then we don't even speak about the completely different situation on the East German market.

Englishman: Also you must take account of the entirely different conditions we face in the premium and middle-range segments of the market, where the internal cultural differences will be more critical.

American: You Europeans sure want to make everything complicated.

A tough one to crack indeed, especially because many other questions arise. Are German companies still interested in the EC, or are they oriented towards the developments in Eastern Europe? How exactly will the liberalisation of the European capital markets affect companies? How will distribution channels change? Will companies do away with importers? Will Europe trigger a price-war, leading to further cost-efficient, although sometimes capital-intensive, strategies? Who will take over whom? Will the buying behaviour of clients change? What strategies can be expected of the Japanese competitors? What technological developments will affect the industry?

For whom is this book? In times when there are more questions than answers, people either become religious, or confer, in order to make sense of the new situation. The latter is the working assumption in this book. It examines how senior managers, the people in the field, make sense of the developments in their market or industry. What do they consider are the main management issues in Europe of the 1990s? How do managers prepare to be at pole-position by 1992? What strategies and organisational arrangements are being made? How do these deal with the issues at hand? How is the issue of strategic change to be tackled?

This book stands apart in the sense that it is a book by managers as well as for managers. The academics who wrote it have tried to organise and interpret the views of managers but at the same time to keep 'punditry' within bounds. It should be of interest to three types of managers: first, managers of companies that are already operating in some European countries, but who want to develop their market in others and would like to know something of the competition there; secondly, the managers of companies planning to remain either national or local, but who want to know what developments can be expected in their own market; thirdly, since the European Market in the 1990s will also open up opportunities for non-European companies, American and Japanese managers can learn something of how their European counterparts see the evolution of their business.

Europe: convergence or divergence? Europe has already been designated a paradox. Seemingly contradictory forces can be seen to be at work. At the very time when Europe is moving towards greater political unity, individual states share a strong development of national consciousness, stressing the uniqueness of a country's cultural and historical heritage. Or again some traditional but non-European partners of EC states are increasingly concerned that the focus on the single European market will reduce established trade relations, for example those between France and North Africa, Spain and Latin America, or Great Britain and the Commonwealth.

Paradoxes are not only found at the level of external trade. Europe embodies some contradictory issues for management. First is the managers' need for generalisation in an increasingly diversified, sometimes even fragmented, market. Prices are being eroded by increased international competition. This in turn forces managers to reduce cost levels. The obvious way to do this is through standardisation, that is, through the production of homogeneous products for all the European countries. But the dilemma here is that the various national markets may be too diverse, in the sense of different from each other, to be served by such a homogeneous product.

Another dilemma may occur when a firm's competitive advantages are too small for it to enter foreign markets, yet it is compelled to do so by clients that are internationalising and asking for the firm's services at an international level. Clearly, some of the smaller banks are being caught in this way.

Management perceptions and priorities also vary largely over Europe. Numerous Dutch and Danish managers, for example, see environmental legislation as a key issue, although it did not seem from our interviews to concern French or Italian managers yet. Combining the sometimes contradictory views of the more than ninety managers we interviewed has resulted in a vivid image of a complex, but intriguing and dynamic continent. An old world, but with unlimited potential for innovation in management when the right questions are raised.

Background and Contents of this Book

The idea for this study started in May 1989, when Gianluca Colombo of SDA-Bocconi in Milan, Gerry Johnson of the Cranfield School of Management, Peter Lawrence of the University of Loughborough and Roland Calori, Jacques van der Meer and Tugrul Atamer, all of the Groupe ESC de Lyon met at a seminar on the consequences of 'Europe 1992'. This seminar was organised for the students of the ESC Lyon. We felt that the seminar had been worthwhile, but also recognised the need for more research to further understanding in this area.

An idea for joint research emerged quite promptly. This was not so much to study the effects of 1992 as an economic and administrative phenomenon, but to look at a variety of developments in selected industries, including for instance the entry of new competitors, the effects of new technologies, or changes in consumer tastes. We recognised that the most interesting and informed views of these developments existed in the field, with the managers involved. So our main interest was to learn their opinions, and to see what actions companies were taking to deal with the new competitive situation in their industries.

We also decided at the start that this research should be longitudinal, and should have a follow-up. So we intend to revisit the managers in the study during 1992 itself. Reminding them of their perception in the 1989–90 period, we will ask whether their opinions have changed, and what consequences that may have had. This should offer a window on the question: how do organisations learn and adapt to their environment?

The people we talked to were directly involved in the formulation of strategy for their companies; that is to say managing directors/CEOs or managers with a special brief to develop corporate strategy. The managers in our study are drawn from four industries: retail banking, book publishing, brewing and car manufacturing. One simple finding of our study is that there are substantial differences between them, both in general strategic terms, and vis-à-vis 1992. Strategic issues in brewing, for example, can hardly be compared with those in book publishing. What is more, the concerns of an Italian retail banker are quite different from those of other European colleagues in that industry. A successful strategy for England may not be appropriate for France.

We selected these four industries for special reasons. Retail banking pre-1992 is a heavily regulated, quite fragmented service industry. The harmonisation of European legislation, and subsequent deregulation, will definitely open up new possibilities for banks with implications for strategy and organisation.

The brewery industry was chosen for a number of reasons. We were interested in whether the lifting of the *Reinheitsgebot*, the German purity laws, would trigger an invasion of Europe's largest beer market, that of Germany. The regional differences in consumption and taste, market maturity and competitive structures were also interesting issues in the brewing industry. Book publishing was thought to be a rewarding choice. It raises the question of how to develop international strategies in a market that is tightly linked to language, but where the major firms have already taken a decisive advantage, and coexist with a host of small regional competitors.

The last of the four industries, the car industry, was chosen as a role model. This industry was already very internationally oriented with

Table 1

	Retail Banking	Brewing	Car Manufacturing	Book Publishing
Denmark	Unibank Danmark Sparekassen Sydjylland	Albani Faxe Jyske		Centrum Gutenberghus Gyldendal Aarhus University Press
Germany	Bayerische Hypotheken – und Wediselbank, München Commerzbank Stadtsparkasse Hannover Norddeutsche Landesbank	Bavaria Dinckelacker Holsten Wittingen	Opel (GM) BMW Porsche Volkswagen	Bertelsmann Poeschel Verlag Oldenburg Verlag Rowohlt Verlag
France	Credit Agricole Société Générale Lyonnaise de Banque Banque Nationale de Paris	Kronenbourg Société Française de Brasserie Brasseries Semeuse Interbrew Brasseries le Pecheur	PSA Automobiles Renault	Hachette Groupe de la cité Vuibert Flammarion Edition du Seuil Eyrolles
Great Britain	TSB Midland Bank Bank of Scotland National Westminster Abbey National	Grand Metropolitan Greene King Courage Greenall Whitley	Ford Europe Jaguar Rover Group	Penguin Longman Pinter Hodder & Stoughton Stanley Thornes Prentice-Hall
Italy	Monte dei Paschi di Siena Instituto S Paolo di Torino Casse di Risparmio Banca Popolare Credito Emiliano	Dreher Italia Peroni Poretti Wunster	Fiat Auto Alfa Romeo	Mondadori Feltrinelli Messaggerie Libri Jackson
Netherlands	Bank Mees en Hope Algemene Bank Nederland Amro-bank	Heineken Grolsch		Elsevier Wolters Kluwer
Spain	Banesto Banco Popular Espanol Banco Hispano Americano Banco Atlantico	Union Cervecera	Seat	Aguilar Espasa-Calpe

the same competitors in all major European markets. So it raises the key question: what are the strategies and organisational solutions in such a competitive setting? At the same time we must be honest as to the limitations of the four selected industries: none of them are capital goods industries engaged in company-to-company sales, and all four industries are relatively mature.

We have suggested that our study is a little different in that it is truly based upon the ideas and perceptions of European managers themselves, either substantively or as a starting point for discussion. Most of the managers were interviewed in early 1990. We used a standardised but only semi-directive interview schedule. That is to say, we put the same questions, explored the same themes, with each manager, but also took on board other things which they volunteered, and pursued 'targets of opportunity'.

Where other studies typically concentrate on West Germany, the United Kingdom and France as the key countries of the EC, generalising for the other nationalities, this book also considers the perceptions and concerns of managers in Denmark, Italy, the Netherlands and Spain. In short, managers from a total of some 90 companies in seven EC member states have been interviewed. The companies that participated in this research are as shown in Table 1.

The results of the study are presented in the main body of the book. The information that companies have provided is used in a way that should not reveal their identity. The scale of the research project in fact required quite a large team of participants. From the five initiators, the team of researchers eventually grew to nineteen participants, of eight nationalities.

As the aim is to describe how managers perceive the dynamics of Europe in the 1990s, the book is sparing with bibliographical references. Nevertheless, Egbert Kahle of the University of Lüneburg in Germany does give the reader a short review of current literature and thinking on the Single European Market, the managerial consequences of 1992 and on Eastern Europe.

The managers' perceptions of the developments in each of the four industries are synthesised in the four chapters that follow the introduction to Europe mentioned above. These industry-by-industry chapters are followed by four further chapters which attempt to analyse, synthesise and draw conclusions. In this context Roland Calori describes common denominators and divergences between and within the four industries. He raises several questions that have to be addressed in developing competitive European strategy. Then Jean-Louis Barsoux and Peter Lawrence shift the focus on to the individual countries and the differences between them, notwithstanding 1992. And finally Tugrul Atamer and Gerry Johnson offer some conclusions.

Throughout we have tried to do justice to, and be honest about, the complexity and the unknowns. There are no easy answers; indeed there are not even any easy questions.

1

Europe 1992: Issues and Implications

Egbert Kahle

The aim of this first chapter is to give an outline of the situation in Europe and more specifically in the European Community. This comes from three different sources: general data on the European economic and geo-political situation, the assessment of the Single Market and its implications for corporate strategy by some selected authors, and an assessment of recent developments in Eastern Europe.

Europe: Economic and Cultural

In considering Europe 1992 one cannot restrict one's view to the European Community alone. The EC is only a part of Europe, certainly the most important one economically, but the other parts of Europe obviously play an important role and will do so more in the future. The assessment of opportunities and threats opened up by the Single Market in 1992 has to take into consideration the relations

Table 1.1 *European countries by economic affiliation (1990)*

EC	EFTA	COMECON	unattached
Belgium	Austria	Bulgaria	Albania
Denmark	Finland	Czechoslovakia	Malta
France	Iceland	Germany (E)[1]	Yugoslavia
Germany (W+E)[2]	Norway	Hungary	
Greece	Sweden	Poland	
Ireland	Switzerland	Romania	
Italy			
Luxembourg			
Netherlands			
Portugal			
Spain			
UK			

[1] until 3.10.90.
[2] after 3.10.90.

between Community members and other European countries, as well as the developments resulting from the disintegration of COMECON and the radical change in East–West relations.

These general political changes in the European situation make new economic scenarios feasible, where new opportunities and problems arise. The following description of Europe from a geographical, ethnical and economic viewpoint may help to set the scene in a basic way.

Excluding Russia (USSR), which has to be treated separately, Europe consists of 26 countries, plus six economically insignificant mini-countries. Except Malta, all these mini-countries belong economically to the area of the next bigger country, on the Monaco–France model. The European countries can be placed in four groups: EC, EFTA, COMECON and unattached countries (see Table 1.1).

The membership of these various economic federations has changed in the course of time; three members of EFTA (Britain, Ireland and Denmark) went over to the EC, and in October 1990 East Germany, formerly belonging to COMECON, became part of the EC. Again, in September 1990 the Social Democratic Party in Sweden raised at its party congress the possibility of Sweden seeking entry to the EC after 1992: such a development would almost certainly bring in Norway and might induce Finland to join.

The area of Europe is 4.8 million square km and it has somewhat over 460 million inhabitants. Less than half this area, 2.2 million square km (with East Germany included 2.3 million square km), is inhabited by EC members, who make up more than two-thirds of the European population, 323 million without East Germany, 339 million including East Germany. This market of the European Community had a private consumption of 2,400 billion ECU in 1988 and produced a Gross Domestic Product of 3,670 billion ECU in 1987, which was almost as much as the USA and almost twice as much as Japan (Directorate-General, 1988, p.26). Future scenarios of a Europe of 460 million consumers will be discussed later.

This economically tripartite Europe is ethnically and culturally much more subdivided, so that the Single Market is only a formal economic entity. In Europe there are as many, or even more, languages as there are countries; between these languages and the different national cultures there are different degrees of correspondence (see Table 1.2). These language groups do not coincide with the economic partition of Europe outlined above. In some countries more than one language is spoken, not to mention different dialects, so there is a lot of linguistic–cultural difference in Europe generally and within the EC.

The barriers between the countries derived from these language

Table 1.2[1] *European languages spoken in the different economic federations (EC, EF for EFTA, CO for COMECON, U for unattached). The former independent Baltic countries, now striving for independence from the USSR, would add another three languages.*

Romance languages	Teutonic languages	Slavic languages	Celtic languages	Other languages
Catalan (EC)	*Danish* (EC)	*Bulgarian* (CO)	Gaelic (EC)	*Greek* (EC)
French (EC, EF)	*Dutch* (EC)	*Czech* (CO)	Welsh (EC)	*Finnish* (EF)
Italian (EC)	Frisian (EC)	*Polish* (CO)	Scottish (EC)	*Hungarian* (CO)
Portuguese (EC)	*German* (EC,CO,EF)	*Serbo-Croatian* (U)	Breton (EC)	*Albanian* (U)
Romansh (EF)	*Icelandic* (EF)	Slowenian (U)		Basque (EC)
Romanian (CO)	*Norwegian* (EF)			Lapp (EF)
Spanish (EC)	*Swedish* (EF)			

[1] Main languages italicised.

differences vary with the distance or familiarity of languages. So there is a low barrier between the Netherlands and Germany, and an even lower one between Denmark, Sweden and Norway, while linguistic-cultural barriers are quite high between, say, France and Germany, let alone Greece and Belgium or Denmark and Spain.

Furthermore in some countries more than one language is spoken as an official language, and within one language there may be different dialects which, combined with religion and tradition, have resulted in clearly recognisable cultural differences. For example Switzerland is officially multilingual (German, French, Italian, Romansh), so is Spain (Spanish and Catalan), Finland (Finnish and Swedish), and Belgium (French and Flemish). Countries with distinctive regional differences include Italy (the North versus the Mezzogiorno) and Germany (Protestant low Germany versus Catholic Bavaria). On the other hand, many countries have immigrants from various other countries, partly from former colonies (Britain), partly hired in years of labour scarcity (Germany), which increase the cultural variety.

Some of the languages are spoken in more than one country: French in Belgium, France and Switzerland; Italian in Switzerland and Italy; German in Germany, Austria and Switzerland, and English not only in Britain and Ireland, but also as a first foreign language in most of the West European countries, especially in the north of Europe. The preference for English in business relations which is widely accepted should not mislead managers into believing that these multi-lingual and multi-cultural features of Europe will cease to exist. They may be lessened in impact somehow, but there is

Table 1.3   *Percentage of export to EC countries*

	%		%
Denmark	48·5	Greece	68
Great Britain	49·4	Portugal	71
Germany	53·1	Ireland	74
Italy	56·6	Belgium/	
		Luxembourg	74·5
France	60·4	Netherlands	75·1
Spain	63·8		

Source: OECD

all over Europe a revival of local or regional culture and self-consciousness.

Another aspect of Europe and the EC is that the EC is not a single event or treaty (even if it was set up by one), but a process of development, where 1992 is only a milestone, not a terminus. Membership in the EC (and its counterparts) has changed over time, and East Germany has been absorbed by the Community. The EC in a sense started with six countries in 1951 with the formation of the European Coal and Steel Community, and in 1957 the Rome Treaty was signed leading to the establishment of the EC in 1958. The original six countries were France, Germany, Italy, Holland, Belgium and Luxembourg. Denmark, Ireland and Britain joined in 1973; Greece in 1981, and the Twelve was completed in 1986 by Portugal and Spain.

One major point has to be made here: while our interviews and the following implications are related to EC countries, the strong connections with other European countries should not be over-

Table 1.4   *Relative importance of the EC's trade partners*

Rank	Country	Exports to	Imports from[1]
1	USA	71·9	56·2
2	Switzerland	32·8	26·7
3	Sweden	20·2	20·1
4	Austria	20·1	15·2
5	Japan	13·6	34·8
6	Norway	9·5	12·1
7	USSR	9·2	13·1
8	Canada	9·0	6·9
9	Saudi Arabia	7·7	5·6
10	Finland	7·0	7·9

[1] in billion ECU.
Source: Die Zeit, 11.11.88.

looked. These connections differ between the EC member countries as the proportion of intra-EC trade shows (Table 1.3).

If we combine the data in Table 1.3 with the import/export data of the EC's ten most important trading partners (Table 1.4), it is clear that both geographically and economically Europe is more than the EC, and that the EC itself is not isolated but an integrated part of Europe.

It is clear from Tables 1.3 and 1.4 that Denmark, for example, with its strong connection with Sweden and Norway, has a relatively low proportion of intra-EC trade, because some of its main partners are outside the Community. The opposite applies to Switzerland and Austria in relation to West Germany; these two countries do more than two-thirds of their trade with the EC, so that economically they are more within the EC than some actual members!

The Single European Market

The important issue connected with 1992 is the Single European Act, which is leading to a more integrated legislation and policy in the EC. On many decisions a unanimous vote is no longer required but rather a majority vote, which makes it easier to get things done. In the decision making on the EC level four different elements form the decision system:

- the Commission, consisting of 17 commissioners (one from each country and a second one from the five bigger countries)
- the Council of Ministers (the foreign ministers of each country for general decisions and the resource ministers for detailed decisions)
- the European Parliament, elected directly all over the EC and with powers to approve the Council's position
- the Economic and Social Committee (ECOSOC) consisting of 196 representatives of employers, trade unions and independent groups, which gives advice to the Council.

The Commission is the executive arm which develops most decisions and which is the driving force of European integration. The Council is the highest authority, and the Parliament and the ECOSOC are places of discussion and information.

The issue of the Single Market in 1992 has been discussed widely and research has been conducted by numerous institutions and individuals. The following reviews some key themes to emerge from this work concerning:

- opportunities
- threats or risks

- consumer behaviour
- marketing strategies
- organisational strategies

Opportunities
The opportunities of 1992 are seen to lie in two areas: the effect on the market itself, and the logistical implication – savings of cost and time; a few minor aspects are also cited now and then in the sources we have reviewed. Regarding the market three developments are discussed (Vandermerwe, 1989; Directorate-General, 1988, p.132): growth, differentiation and increased competition. The question of logistics is seen both as an opportunity and a threat. On the production side there is the reduction of costs and the saving of time and energy through the elimination of border bureaucracy (Vandermerwe, 1989; Directorate-General, 1988, pp.44f).

The market growth likely to result from the Single Market is estimated very thoroughly in the EC Commission paper (Directorate-General, 1988). By ending direct costs at the frontiers, by reducing technological barriers, by better supply and distribution systems in the food and beverage industries and in the car industry, by better access to financial services, and by economies of scale and the reduction of inefficiency, the growth should be between 4.5 and 7 percent of GDP; the higher rate will only be reached if accompanied by a specific EC competition policy. In absolute numbers that will be an additional purchasing volume of 200 to 300 billion ECU, equivalent to the GDP of Spain.

Market differentiation will manifest itself in different ways (Vandermerwe, 1989; Tietz, 1990). According to some, the Single Market will be more receptive to standardised goods and services (Magee, 1989); there will be rapid diffusion and shorter life cycles (Ohmae, 1989; Stone, 1989; Directorate-General, 1988). The markets themselves will be more homogeneous (Magee, 1989) and there will be a switch over from national to regional markets (Giersch, 1990; Directorate-General, 1988, pp.132f). There will be more sources of supply, and a greater variety of customer groups in the Single Market. One of these emerging customer groups is the 'senior market', that is elderly people with special demands and buying power. This group may have been too small on a national scale to create a market, but it will constitute one on the European scale.

The increased competition in the Single Market is seen as an opportunity for firms possessing a competitive edge and it will induce growth or development of the markets (Vandermerwe, 1989; Friberg, 1989; Dudley, 1989). But this increased competition has to be regulated by the competition policy of the Community (Directorate-

General, 1988, p.139) because this increase is a threat to smaller firms, and those lacking a competitive edge.

Particularly emphasised are the various opportunities to reduce costs, including the saving of time and energy (all the following issues are mentioned by Vandermerwe, 1989, and Directorate-General, 1988). The barrier to be reduced which is mentioned most often is the technical one, where a harmonisation of technical specifications will take place (Ohmae, 1989; Magee, 1989; Stone, 1989; Giersch, 1990; Dudley, 1989, p.22). These technical barriers are very important, for example in the car sector, and they are highly important in the food and beverage sector, while in the paper and printing industry they are of little importance (Directorate-General, 1988); in the latter segment the language barrier is seen as more important. Other cost saving opportunities discussed are:

- less paperwork (most mentioned)
- cheaper physical distribution and inventory (all over Europe. It must be remembered that for a national market-oriented firm going abroad distribution channels will get longer and much more time-consuming, when the distances grow from 800 km to 4000 km.)
- rationalised product ranges
- better sourcing opportunities
- reduced costs of research and development
- time saved due to common procedures (single document)
- streamlining of organisation and administrative functions
- easier logistics, faster transportation (fewest mentions).

To give an impression of the amounts involved in the administrative costs of customs these range from 26 to 205 ECU per consignment, and are relatively higher for smaller firms and smaller consignments. The opportunities of the Single Market are not seen as one big issue, but as a multitude of interrelated marketing and production (including sourcing and distribution) conditions that can be exploited by business strategies, which will give another impetus to the market development (Directorate-General, 1988, p.132).

Threats
The threats or risks seen to evolve from the Single Market may be grouped into three major issues, and a group of minor ones. The three major issues are:

- intensified competition, with a number of sub-issues
- clumsy transition to the Single Market and non-compliance of member nations in different ways
- protection and reciprocity

The minor issues include fiscal barriers (if not subsumed under clumsy transition), more people having to change their jobs more frequently (Directorate-General, 1988, p.136) and the development of new regulations and legislation (Dudley, 1989, p.23).

Within the intensified competition the threat most feared is that of unfair competition from monopolist companies crossing the border (Vandermerwe, 1989; Magee, 1989; Stone, 1989; Directorate-General, 1988, pp.126, 137; Tietz, 1990). This applies to the national monopolies in the telecommunication and supply services, and to some other near-monopolistic industries as well. The other risks of intensified competition lie in the possible entry of companies from non-EC countries (Vandermerwe, 1989; Directorate-General, 1988, p.137; Dudley, 1989, p.117), and especially from third party high added-value niche players (Larréché et al., 1989; Magee, 1989), and with the problem accentuated by higher social costs within the Community compared with those prevailing in outside countries (Friberg, 1989; Stone, 1989). Other forms of competition that are feared are those from low-wage countries, from outsiders applying lower technical standards, and from new groupings and alliances resulting in the emergence of supra-nations and supra-corporations (Vandermerwe, 1989; Tietz, 1990). One anticipated consequence of this increased competition is the increase in marketing costs (Larréché et al., 1989; Tietz, 1990); on the other hand there is expected to be a simultaneous pressure on prices (Vandermerwe, 1989; Directorate-General, 1988, pp.80f). This is important (for example in the car industry) where the pincer movement of sinking prices and higher marketing costs endangers the profitability which is necessary for investment and growth, which in turn are needed to exploit the opportunities of economies of scale and scope which are of paramount importance in this industry (Directorate-General, 1988).

The threats stemming from a possibly clumsy transition to the Single European Market and from non-compliance have two major sources. One is the growing bureaucracy in Brussels and elsewhere in the Community, and the other, more important, is national self-interest and local orientation. An excessive bureaucracy is itself an obstacle to change, even when it is functioning as a change agent (Vandermerwe, 1989; Giersch, 1990; Dudley, 1989; Tietz, 1990). There is the possibility of a piecemeal approach to important issues due to a lack of knowledge, so that decisions are delayed; another possibility is the existence of double standards in the process of harmonisation, which will impede the quick elimination of technical barriers (Vandermerwe, 1989). But most of the impediments mentioned are based on national egoism or egocentrism (Vandermerwe, 1989; Tietz, 1990). There may be a lack of commitment to the harmonisation programme (Ohmae, 1989); there may be non-compliance of national legislative bodies with regard to new Community legislation (Giersch, 1990); there are still many examples of informal protection and blockages (Giersch, 1990; Directorate-General, 1988, p.136), and there are differences in languages and cultures discussed already which have to be considered (Ohmae, 1989; Friberg, 1989), all these being accompanied by insufficient education and preparation of the managers to meet the challenges of the new situation (Larréché et al., 1989).

Furthermore, there may be delays in the dismantling of barriers, for instance in the transport industry, where Germany is trying to prolong the quotas; in the brewing industry, where Germany wants to keep its purity law on beer; in the car industry, where Italy and France want to maintain the barriers against Japanese imports, and so on. These impediments resulting from national self-interest may not be of great importance if viewed singly but taken together they may threaten the gains to be expected from the opportunities.

This leads directly to the third major issue: protectionism and reciprocity (Vandermerwe, 1989; Magee, 1989; Stone, 1989; Giersch, 1990; Directorate-General, 1988, p.139; Tietz, 1990). Protection of the home industry from foreign competition – which is often called unfair just because the foreign product is cheaper or the foreign manufacturer more efficient – is a widely used precept of economic policy. Nonetheless, it is the wrong answer to trade problems. It is often combined with the concept of reciprocity, i.e. the other country should give the same conditions to our exporters which we give to theirs. Sometimes this concept is misinterpreted – voluntarily or involuntarily – to mean that the export volume of each country into each other country should be the same. But this, of course, depends on the production and marketing efficiency of the companies concerned and cannot be governed by economic policy. This (dubious) interpretation of reciprocity is likely to be used as an instrument of retaliation, rather than as a means of creating better trading relations.

The conclusion here is that most problems and threats come from the difficulty of establishing fair competition and of overcoming national egotism.

Consumer Behaviour
Any discussion of consumer behaviour has to be divided into a consideration of private customers and institutional (business) cus-

tomers, where different issues are important. With regard to private customers, members of the general public, the following emerge as particularly significant in the literature:

1 More demanding customers
   - wanting more information
   - more aware of the range of choices, making more compari-
     sons between products
   - more quality conscious
   - feeling that they constitute a niche market and wanting more
     added value, which of course leads to higher costs.
2 Sensitivity to price in a context where customers expect competition to push prices down.
3 More and better service, e.g. the demand of the new 'senior
   market'.
4 Pan-European purchasing
   - more similar tastes and demands
   - increased interest in global brands
   - greater confidence in pan-European goods
   - less demand for culture-bound products
   - decreased preference for local products
   - less loyalty to national products.
5 More 'mobile' customers, and fragmented market niches.

This scenario of the behaviour of private customers shows a development towards well-informed, price-sensitive, active consumers who know what they want and are trying hard to get the best value for their money. This will only apply to products or services with a certain sales volume, because the intensity of information processing and choice must be equivalent to the value of the product. But there is in this scenario the notion of shopping as a cultural event, going beyond the acquisition of the merely necessary.

With business customers the basic issues are similar, but with other implications. Here the pressure on prices has greater importance. Besides that there are the expectation and use of new Euro-standards, an increased demand for service and just-in-time delivery, a heightened search for alternatives, and the growing importance of public procurement. Price sensitivity, more and better service, and a widening of the supply base is common with both customer groups, whereas the other issues are group-specific.

Marketing Strategies
Whereas the assessment of opportunities and threats as identified in the literature has been relatively homogeneous, the recommended marketing strategies vary according to the particular firm and

industry context. The following group of issues are to be found in the literature:

1 The reshaping of marketing instruments
   - Europe-wide positioning of brands or products
   - Europe-wide pricing structures
   - strengthening the sales/distribution networks
   - advertising and promoting image.
2 New relations in the market
   - market presence through acquisitions and alliances
   - flexibility in relationships
   - clusters of cross-country segments.
3 Technology and innovation
   - interface between marketing and technological resources
   - assessing the impact of information technology on strategic marketing activities
   - product innovation
   - lead-country product design (in the sense of no global product, but a global selling of leading products).
4 Reshaping corporate structure to marketing strategies
   - centralisation of strategic marketing activities, decentralisation of marketing operations
   - adapting company structure to changes in marketing strategies
   - sending staff to Europe (or to work outside home market country)
   - co-ordination between countries (firms in different countries).

This overview of possible strategic choices, reflected in research on marketing opportunities and alternative ways of action (Dudley, 1989, pp.132–55; Tietz, 1990, pp.226–356), shows that most experts tend to favour global answers to the challenges of the Single Market, and to relatively classical ones. The main strategies are: going into acquisitions and alliances, and into the three classical marketing instruments – product positioning, pricing and the sales/distribution network. The really new strategies lie in the diversity of the sub-issues, mentioned only occasionally. This follows from a distinction in the impact of the Single Market on different kinds of markets (Directorate-General, 1988, p.135). The impact is held to be low on fragmented markets, whereas differentiated markets (niche markets) are expected to grow substantially due to the Single Market, and in mass production markets much depends on the development in public contracting. Most of these special strategies imply differential markets and how to gain position there, except for the last group of issues, where the strategic point is not in the market but in the organisational structure.

Organisational Strategies

In addition to the reshaping of corporate structure in relation to marketing strategy, a number of other organisational aspects are addressed in the literature. As organisational strategies these include:

1 Globalisation
   - as a general issue (mentioned most frequently)
   - general strategy for the Single Market, with country-oriented operations
   - the emergence of so-called European companies.
2 Staffing
   - having a board of directors that is more international in composition
   - global marketing, staff and training for marketing position
   - international rather than domestic.
3 Autonomy of subsidiaries
   - giving autonomy and support to foreign plants
   - 'insiderisation' in foreign markets
   - new locations for corporate subsidiaries.
4 Internal strengthening of companies
   - rationalisation and divestiture (mentioned most often)
   - organisational change without disruptions
   - necessity for a transformational leader
   - improved productivity
   - lines of communication and decision-making structure arranged according to strategic requirements.

In this discussion of organisational strategies the *leitmotiv* has been 'think global', sometimes accompanied by the afterthought, 'and act local'.

Throughout the literature there is the impression that the strategies must be global in concept, but that a special local, or national, application is necessary for an efficient realisation of these strategies. The marketing aspects indicated by headings such as 'seeing the customer equidistant' (Ohmae, 1989), 'flexibility in relationships' (Vandermerwe, 1989; Friberg, 1989; Giersch, 1990) and 'decentralization of marketing operations' (Vandermerwe, 1989) have to be combined with the idea of 'insiderization in foreign markets' (Ohmae, 1989) and international recruitment (Giersch, 1990). These strategies are aimed at market growth and differentiation, while mere technology and innovation are oriented to defensive cost reduction.

The message throughout the literature is loud and clear: look for the opportunities, they are yours. If you don't use them, they are those of your competitors. And don't forget the risks.

Eastern Europe

The 'event' of the Single Market 1992 has recently been overshadowed in West Germany by developments in East Germany, and more generally in Eastern Europe including Russia. The implications of these developments depend on the time-scale one has in view. The short-run consequences can be grasped clearly and in detail from the information flowing in almost daily and they relate mostly to East Germany. In the medium term the opportunities and risks of the economic inclusion, if not of integration, of some or all of the East European countries will have to be assessed. Here there are more uncertainties and speculative aspects. In the long term a more visionary scenario may be drawn, wherein all of Europe could form a single European Community, with a host of positive consequences for all its members and for their partners worldwide.

The Swish of the Curtain!
The opening of the Berlin Wall and the Iron Curtain on 9 November 1989 was the necessary consequence of the liberalisation policy in the USSR and in Poland and Hungary. It was accompanied by an enormous increase in the numbers of immigrants or, in German, of *Übersiedler* (people moving over). At the same time the numbers of people immigrating from other East European countries increased at a similar rate. In 1989 more than 700,000 people of German nationality migrated to West Germany. These numbers did not decrease until it was clear that East Germany would get the Deutschmark as its currency and that people could largely fulfil their demand for West German goods while 'staying at home'. That monetary union took place on 1 July 1990.

The number of inhabitants in the Single Market grew by 5 percent as a result of German unification. The impact of that does not sound significant but the addition of 15 million inhabitants to the West German population also adds 7 million workers to its workforce of 30 million; the former East German workers are able and well educated. What has been missing in the East German economy has been management and the regulating price mechanism of the free market. This latter issue makes all official economic data and calculations of the former East German administration obsolete; they have no (or at least quite a different) meaning in terms of profitability or efficiency.

The other important economic problem of East Germany is the infrastructure: the railway system was reduced after the war to a single track on most routes; the roads are narrow and often poorly surfaced; the telephone system cumbersome and too small – only 9 percent of the population have a telephone as against 98 percent in the Federal Republic. The industrial equipment in the formerly flourishing industrial region of Saxony and Thuringia tends to be obsolete and rundown, apart from some prestige projects. One of these, the EDP factory Robotron was the industry leader in COMECON, yet for the world market it is uncompetitive.

There is a market for a variety of goods: people want cars instead of their 'tin-can' Trabants and Wartburgs of 1950 design and a delivery time of 15 years; the used car market in West Germany is booming! There is a craving for books and journals after a 40-year diet of socialistic realism. Textiles, household goods, hi-fis and foods and beverages are all wanted. Most East German beers are considered scarcely drinkable by West German 'purists' and most breweries operate under the technical conditions of the 1940s. So there will be a market of 15 million people with an average consumption of 150 litres per year. Consumers and most of the new small entrepreneurs and free professions need the financial services of a free society.

All this needs investment and a restructuring of market conditions, which has already started. Some West German firms, like Volkswagen, started as early as 1984, when re-unification was not expected. They are reconstructing car production on a scale of a 250,000 capacity, i.e. a quarter of a million cars per year (IHK Lüneburg, 1990). The West German banks have set up networks of branches all over; former East German citizens are becoming entrepreneurs and West German firms are trading and investing.

There are some problems, too: the socialist government of the former DDR (East Germany) subsidised basic food and housing and guaranteed everyone their job. So there was no official unemployment and people had a secure but frugal life. The unemployment was hidden in the firms and administration, which were over-staffed, and where people not able or willing to work were carried by the others. The change in prices needs a change in income, which gives rise to problems because of the insufficiencies of the distribution and production system. There will for some time be a difference in living standards between the two parts of Germany, but that is no real problem as long as this difference is not too big. Even in West Germany there have been differences of more than 30 percent in wages over distances of less than 80 kilometres; but people did not emigrate, they commuted to the better-paying areas. Or again there have been differences in wages, labour costs of more than 600 percent as between Portugal and West Germany, though this has given rise to only small-scale migration.

The conclusion is that unification will give an additional growth to the German economy; and the financial strain will be borne by the reserves laid in the previous years of increasing economic development.

Other Parts of Eastern Europe

The inclusion of East Germany in the EC raises the question of the GDR's former European partners in COMECON. Hungary, Czechoslovakia and Poland, and to a far lesser degree Romania and Bulgaria, have shifted from socialism to capitalism and to an opening of their economies. One point of entry to these new markets could be the 40-year connections within COMECON, but there are other old ties between, for instance, France and Poland, Romania and Czechoslovakia, on both cultural and economic issues.

While the integration of East Germany into the EC was done quite easily – the mass of minor problems arising are reduced by the national bonds and common culture within Germany – the problems of association or integration of the other East European countries are greater. One consideration is that East Germany was the richest and most highly developed of the COMECON countries (Kraljic, 1990, p.74), so the difference in standards of producing and living was not as high as will be the case with the other countries, in ascending order, starting with Hungary and Czechoslovakia, then comes Poland, and at the extreme lie Bulgaria and Romania. The USSR is not included here, because its opportunities and problems would fill a chapter of their own, and Russia was never so exclusively European as Hungary, Poland or Czechoslovakia. Perhaps the Baltic states, if properly independent, could be added. The five European COMECON member countries looked at here have altogether a population of 80 million; if we add Yugoslavia and Albania it makes a clear 100 million. This is a market with great demands, with a relatively skilled, low-cost labour force, and various natural resources and the corresponding heavy industries (Kraljic, 1990, p.64). But they have the same problems as cited above for East Germany only in a higher degree: bad infrastructure, no managerial skills, no functioning market structure, and the political seclusion of the 'cold war' period, plus a technology gap.

The gross domestic product per head, estimated with much variation by different authorities, is very low. Taking the average from ten different sources it is for Czechoslovakia $8000, for Hungary $7000, for Bulgaria $5000, for Poland $4500 and Romania $4000; the lowest income estimates go down to a third of these values. With this level of GDP these countries are in line with the Iberian members of the EC and with Greece, or just below. The change into developing market economies will take more time than in East Germany, because the distance is greater and there will be no common taxpayer to carry the burden as is happening in Germany. But the market and the demand is there, especially in some focal issues like cars and household electrical goods. The number of cars per head in these countries, which corresponds with the low GDP per head, demonstrates not a low demand for cars, but the limited production capacity of the East European car industry. They could have sold many more cars, but they were not allowed to produce them, because other products were politically more important. The same applies to publishing, where West European literature will be in great demand, either in translation or in German or French, which are spoken and read widely in East Europe. In spite of being countries that rely more on agriculture than is the case in Western Europe there is a scarcity in foods and beverages which opens a market in these products too. Besides these consumer goods markets there is a big demand for machinery and equipment to replace the obsolete equipment that exists now. This will need a big EC investment programme, which will be amortised within a few years.

This assessment of the possible development of Eastern Europe leads to a long-term view of the development of Europe as a whole. If we assume that East–West hostility has begun to cease with these developments, and that the East European countries will associate (or associate more) with the EC, and that Russia will be just another big partner and competitor on the political and economic scene rather than the head of a threatening political grouping, then the situation of the neutral countries in Europe will require a new scenario. Under former political conditions, the countries sworn to political neutrality either by their own volition or by treaties were Austria, Finland, Sweden and Switzerland. These countries either could not or would not enter the EC, because EC membership was seen as implying NATO membership. Thus for these countries joining the EC would, in the past, have infringed their political neutrality.

This will change, if the process of détente continues. Without the political inhibitions, Austria and Switzerland and the Scandinavian countries no longer have a reason to stay outside the European Community with which they have much of their trade, as was shown in Table 1.4. In this scenario all European countries might then be in one united economic area. Other countries on the borders of Europe might also be willing to join this union, countries such as Turkey, Morocco, Algeria, Cyprus and perhaps even Israel.

No one knows today if this union of Europe and some of its neighbouring countries will be in the strong form of the EC with its legislative and administrative powers, or if simple associations and free trade agreements will arise. A really united Europe of 26 or more countries and 450 million or more people would be difficult to steer, because the differences within the community would increase compared with those of the present EC of the Twelve. On the other hand, such a development would provide a better chance to close the various gaps between the East European and other countries, and the richer West European countries, than would a seclusion of the Twelve in their Community of today. The instruments to achieve this are laid down in the Helsinki agreements and in the OECD programmes, so that there are more opportunities than those suggested by the EC legislation and administration.

Such a European market, whose development beyond 1992 is quite conceivable, highlights the need to prepare for this market, not only for the Twelve, but for others.

References

Directorate-General for Economic and Financial Affairs (1988) *The Economics of 1992. An assessment of the potential economic effects of completing the internal market of the European Community*. Brussels, March 1988.

Dudley, J. (1989) *1992 – Strategies for the Single Market*. London: Kogan Page.

Friberg, E.G. (1989) '1992: Moves Europeans are making', *Harvard Business Review*, 5/6: 85–9.

Giersch, H. (1990) 'Mehr Wettbewerb im freien EG-Binnenmarkt', *Die Betriebswirtschaft*, 3: 297–308.

Kraljic, P. (1990) 'The Economic gap separating East and West', *The McKinsey Quarterly*, Spring: 62–74.

Larréché, J.C., Powell, W.W. and Ebeling, H.D. (1989) 'Europe's Key Marketing Issues for the 90s', *PED*: 73–82.

Magee, J.F. (1989) '1992: Moves Americans must make', *Harvard Business Review*, 5/6: 78–84.

OECD-Wirtschaftsberichte-Deutschland (1990).

Ohmae, K. (1989) 'Managing in a borderless world', *Harvard Business Review*, 5/6: 152–61.

Stone, N. (1989) 'The globalization of Europe: An interview with Wisse Dekker', *Harvard Business Review*, 5/6: 90–5.

Tietz, B. (1990) *Euro-Marketing*, Second edition, Verlag moderne industrie: Landsberg Lech.

Vandermerwe, S. (1989) 'Strategies for a pan-European market', *Long Range Planning*, 22: 45–53.

Aus unseren Unternehmen, in: Mitteilungen der Industrie- und Handelskammer Lüneburg-Wolfsburg (1990), 8: 18.

Die Zeit (1988) (unsigned article) Düsseldorf, 11 November: 40.

2

The European Brewing Industry

Murray Steele

In many respects, the European brewing industry epitomises the paradox of European business. A principal component of this paradox is the degree of diversity which exists across the major European brewing countries.

A typical example of this diversity is the level of industry concentration in each national market. This varies significantly from country to country. In some a near-monopoly situation exists while in others the market is highly fragmented.

Again, in some countries the consumption of beer is a primary social activity; in others it is peripheral to the drinking of wine and other beverages. Where beer is purchased also varies considerably. In some countries, a significant proportion of beer is consumed where it is purchased, that is to say in pubs and cafés; in others it is mainly purchased in a retail outlet for consumption in the home. The relationship between the brewers and the channels of distribution is also diverse; for example, in Denmark brewers are not allowed to own bars or cafés directly; in the UK, however, the brewers own a majority of them.

An observer of the European brewing industry might think that because Europe displays similar economic and social characteristics to other large markets, for instance the United States, it will have the same level of market homogeneity. But this would be an unwise assumption in the case of the European brewing industry.

This chapter will highlight the diversities which exist, and is in three sections. The first describes the industry as it was at the end of the 1980s; the second discusses the views of the managers and their understanding of the strategic issues which will influence development in the 1990s. The third section offers scenarios for the industry.

Description of the European Brewing Industry in 1989

European Industry Structure
Figure 2.1 groups the European brewing companies in a convenient

classification. The horizontal axis represents the relative scale of the companies, with brewing output in millions of hectolitres of beer as the measure. The vertical axis indicates the geographic focus of their activities ranging from those who operate on a global basis to those who serve the market local to their brewery.

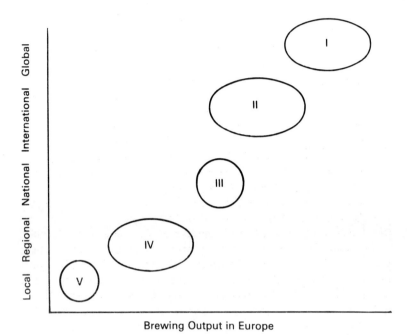

Figure 2.1   *Map of European Brewers*

Five general groupings can be derived from Figure 2.1. These are:

Category I   Global players, who have significant brewing and selling operations both across Europe and the rest of the world – Carlsberg and Heineken.

Category II   Euro-international competitors, those that restrict their activities principally to mainland Europe and that own breweries in a variety of different countries – Stella-Interbrew and BSN (Kronenbourg).

Category III National competitors, those companies that operate mainly in their market of origin, for example, the top six British brewers, or Peroni in Italy.

Category IV Regional brewers, that cover a particular region of their national market, for instance many of the medium-sized West German brewers, approximately a dozen British brewers and the smaller Italian breweries.

Category V   Local brewers, that serve a market in close proximity to the brewery, principally small British and West German brewers.

This is summarised in Figure 2.2.

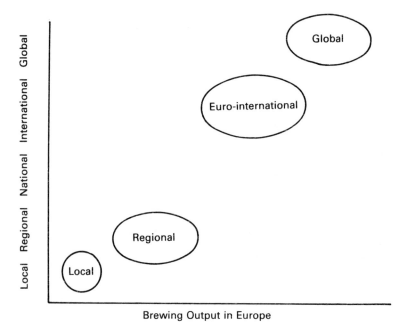

Brewing Output in Europe

Figure 2.2   *Map of European Brewers*

The several different groupings exemplify the high degree of diversity which exists in the structure of the European brewing industry. This is further reinforced by the fact that although the axes in Figure 2.1 were chosen to give as comprehensive a picture as possible, there are some companies which do not fit easily into any of the categories. Grolsch of Holland, for example, is a relatively small European competitor but operates internationally with a niche product.

Table 2.1 is a table of the top 15 major European brewers by their output. It can be seen that the European market is not very concentrated, the top five brewers having a combined market share of 31.5 percent. The European brewers are relatively insular. Only five of the top fifteen have sales of any significance, i.e. over one million hectolitres per annum, outside Europe. Similarly, for the majority of them, the bulk of their output is produced in their country of origin. On a global comparison, only six of the breweries listed in Table 2.1 are in the top twenty breweries of the world. Heineken is third,

Table 2.1   *The 15 largest brewers in Europe* (millions of hectolitres)

	Estimated sales within Europe	European market share %	Estimated sales in rest of world	Estimated total sales	Estimated total output from 'home country' breweries
1 Heineken BV (Holland)	25.2	10.0	17.8	43.0	11.0
2 Groupe BSN (France)	16.9	6.7	2.9	19.8	11.2
3 Carlsberg AS (Denmark)	13.7	5.5	2.3	16.0	8.6
4 Bass PLC (United Kingdom)	13.5	5.4	0.3	13.8	13.5
5 Stella-Interbrew (Belgium)	9.8	3.9	3.2	13.0	8.0
6 Guinness PLC (Ireland)	7.0	2.8	4.4	11.4	5.0
7 Allied-Lyons (United Kingdom)	8.5	3.4	0.5	9.0	8.5
8 Whitbread (United Kingdom)	7.9	3.1	0.1	8.0	6.5
9 Erste Kulmecher Actienbräu AG (West Germany)	8.0	3.2	1.0	8.0	8.0
10 Grand Metropolitan (United Kingdom)	7.5	3.0	1	7.5	7.5
11 Oetker (West Germany)	6.8	2.7	0.1	6.9	6.8
12 S & N Breweries (United Kingdom)	6.7	2.7	1	6.7	6.7
13 Dortmunder Union Schulteis (West Germany)	6.0	2.4	1	6.0	6.0
14 Paulaner Salvator Thomasbräu AG (West Germany)	6.0	2.4	1	6.0	6.0
15 Courage (United Kingdom)	6.0	2.4	1	6.0	6.0

^{1} = negligible
Sources: Annual reports, trade sources and ERC database.

BSN eighth, Carlsberg thirteenth, and Bass, Stella-Interbrew and Guinness eighteenth, nineteenth and twentieth respectively. To put this further in context, Anheuser-Busch of the USA, the largest brewing company in the world, has an annual output of the order of 90 million hectolitres compared to 43 million worldwide for Heineken, Europe's largest brewing group.

During the 1970s and 1980s there were significant cross-border acquisitions which consolidated the positions of the four principal European brewers – Heineken, BSN, Carlsberg and Stella-Interbrew.Table 2.2 shows the countries in which these four have significant stakes.

Table 2.2

	Heineken	BSN	Carlsberg	Stella-Interbrew
France	1	2		1
West Germany				
Belgium		1		2
Holland	2			
Denmark			2	
Spain	1	1	1	
Italy	1	1	1	
United Kingdom				
Ireland	1			

1 denotes an ownership presence.
2 denotes country of origin.

There is much diversity in ownership patterns across Europe. There is no ownership of breweries by other European companies in West Germany, Denmark and the United Kingdom. On the other hand significant proportions of the Italian and Spanish industries are in the hands of foreign brewers.

Similarly there is little ownership in Europe by non-European brewers. The largest example is Courage of the United Kingdom which is owned by Elders IXL of Australia. The only other examples are Labatts of Canada which owns two small breweries in Italy, and Stroh of the USA which has a minority stake in a Spanish brewery.

Additionally there are licensing arrangements whereby brewers in one country brew a particular brand from another country. This takes place principally in the United Kingdom. A good example is Whitbreads which brews and sells both Stella and Heineken under licence, giving them an expanded portfolio of brands.

European Market Trends
During the 1980s there have been some clear trends developing in the

Table 2.3   *Beer and soft drinks, including low-alcohol beers*

	1980	1985	1987	1988
West Germany	146	146	144	143
East Germany[1]	139	142	143	143
Czechoslovakia[1]	138	133	130	130
Denmark	122	121	118	120
Belgium	131	121	121	119
Austria	102	119	118	118
UK	117	108	110	111
Hungary[1]	86	99	100	101
Ireland	122	105	94	97
Holland	86	85	84	83
Spain	53	61	67	69
Portugal	38	38	47	53
Greece	26	34	36	40
France	44	40	39	39
Italy	17	22	26	24

[1] Eastern European country.
Source: The UK Brewers' Society.

different national markets. Northern countries, the UK, West Germany, Denmark, Belgium and Ireland have experienced stagnating or falling beer sales due to switching by the consumer to drinking low-alcohol beers, wine and in particular soft drinks. In the southern European countries the trend is in the opposite direction. Beer and soft drinks are substituting for wine, principally as drinks to quench thirst in the summer. Table 2.3 shows the consumption per capita in litres per annum for the major European and East European markets over the decade of the 1980s.

The trend to beer in the southern countries can be clearly seen in Spain, Portugal, Greece and Italy, but not in France, thus highlighting again the diversity of national markets. The northern countries exhibit either no growth situations or small declines. Ireland and Belgium have both experienced a significant drop in consumption in the 1980s.

Table 2.3 also highlights the different emphasis each society places on the consumption of beer. In West Germany, Denmark, Belgium, Austria and the United Kingdom, beer is the national drink. The consumption of beer is a major social pastime with each member of the population consuming the equivalent of over 100 litres of beer per annum in 1988. The West Germans have the highest consumption of beer per capita in the world and they take great national pride in this statistic. However in Greece, Italy, France and Spain, beer is only an occasional drink and the consumption of beer can only be classed as a peripheral social activity. Their consumptions per head are a fraction of those in the northern countries, e.g. in 1988 the average Italian consumed one-sixth of the beer consumed by the average West German.

Production

Table 2.4 shows the production outputs of the major European and East European beer producing countries during the 1980s in millions of hec⸱olitres. These statistics broadly match those for per capita consumption in Table 2.3. The countries showing significant increases in production tend to be those in the 'sunbelt' – Spain, Portugal, Greece and Italy, which from 1980 to 1988 show increases of 33, 53, 64 and 33 percent respectively. Also showing gains are Holland, Austria and Hungary. Holland's increase of 11 percent is against the trend of no growth or marginal decline of the other northern European brewing countries. This is due to increased production for export by Heineken and by Grolsch which has had international success through its niche product with novel packaging.

What is also clear from Table 2.4 is the strength of the two Germanys and the related countries. The combined output of East and West Germany in 1988 represents 33 percent of the total output of the countries listed in Table 2.4. When the output of the associated

Table 2.4

	1980	1985	1987	1988
West Germany	92.3	93.3	92.8	92.6
East Germany[1]	23.6	24.3	25.0	24.4
Czechoslovakia[1]	23.4	22.3	22.2	22.7
Denmark	8.2	7.9	8.2	8.7
Belgium	14.2	13.9	14.0	13.8
Austria	7.5	8.7	8.9	9.0
UK	64.8	59.7	59.9	60.2
Hungary[1]	7.9	8.7	9.1	9.5
Ireland	6.1	5.5	5.4	5.0
Holland	15.7	17.5	17.5	17.5
Spain	20.0	23.4	25.8	26.6
Portugal	3.6	3.7	5.0	5.5
Greece	2.5	3.0	3.8	4.1
France	21.6	20.3	19.9	20.1
Italy	8.5	10.3	11.1	11.3
Total	319.9	322.5	328.6	331.0

[1] Eastern European country.
Source: The UK Brewers' Society.

countries, i.e. Austria, Czechoslovakia and Hungary, are added to the output of the two Germanys the proportion rises to 48 percent, i.e. almost half of the total.

Distribution

European consumers purchase their beer in two principal ways. The difference between the two is the place of consumption. They either purchase beer in supermarkets to take home and drink there, or they purchase and consume it simultaneously in a bar, pub, café, restaurant or hotel. Table 2.5 shows estimates of the percentage of beer consumed in the home during the 1980s in the major European markets.

Table 2.5

	1980	1985	1987	1988
West Germany	60	60	60	60
Denmark	77	74	74	74
Belgium	52	57	32	32
UK	12	16	18	18
Ireland	6	6	6	6
Holland	60	60	60	61
Spain		Not available		
Portugal	24	38	35	37
Greece		Not available		
France	59	63	64	65
Italy		Not available		

Source: CBMC

The UK, Belgium, Ireland and Portugal are countries where beer is principally drunk in bars, although it is interesting to note a strong trend in the UK towards home consumption. The proportion of beer consumed in the average British home is predicted to rise from 18 percent in 1988 to 25 percent in the year 2000. In Denmark, beer is principally drunk at home, while in West Germany, Holland and France the balance is only marginally in favour of drinking at home.

The type of container in which beer is purchased also varies significantly from country to country. The four principal types are draught beer, where the beer is served from a container to a glass and drunk immediately, normally in a bar; returnable bottles, where the bottle is returned to the point of sale or some other point after the beer has been drunk; non-returnable bottles, where the bottle can be discarded after consumption of the beer; and cans which are also

Table 2.6

	Draught beer	Returnable bottles	Non-returnable bottles	Cans
West Germany	24	76	0	0
Denmark	4	96	0	0
Belgium	45	48	5	2
UK	73	7	3	17
Ireland	88	7	3	2
Holland	30	67	0	3
Spain		Not available		
Portugal	25	68	5	2
Greece		Not available		
France	25	27	44	4
Italy	16	25	54	5

Source: CBMC

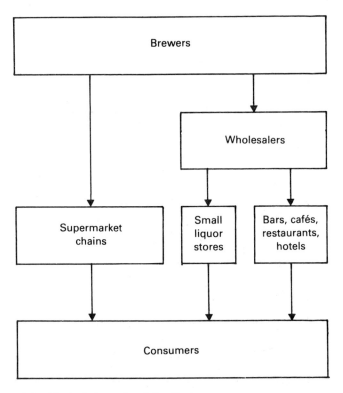

Figure 2.3   *Typical channels of distribution*

normally discarded after consumption of their contents. Table 2.6 shows the percentages of consumption by the different types of containers for the major European countries in 1988.

Table 2.6 is the epitome of the differences which exist across Europe. Consumers in France and Italy are happy to buy a majority of their beer in non-returnable bottles, whereas in Holland, West Germany and Denmark, consumers do not use them at all. With the exception of the United Kingdom, beer sold in cans is not a significant feature of the European market. The West Germans and the Danes must buy a significant amount of bottled beer in bars given the above statistics. The range of beer sold in draught is extensive, from only 4 percent in Denmark to 88 percent in Ireland.

Channels of distribution also vary, which is to be expected given the different consumption characteristics of each market. Figure 2.3 describes the channels of distribution which exist in most mainland European countries, i.e. France, Holland, Spain, Italy, Belgium and

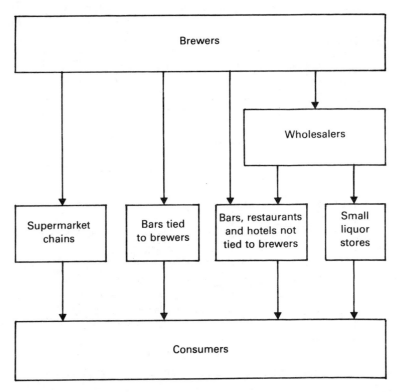

Figure 2.4 *UK and West German channels of distribution*

Denmark. What does vary from country to country is the proportion of beer sales which flows through each channel.

Since the brewing companies own a very small percentage of the retail outlets in these countries, they do not distribute directly to them. Distribution takes place through wholesalers, which may or may not be owned by the brewers. It would be uneconomic for the brewers to distribute beer direct to thousands of small bars, restaurants and hotels. The supermarket chains have substantial power in the distribution channels. They offer the brewing companies attractive economies of scale. Brewers can deliver large volumes to a central point in the supermarket chain distribution system. This power is growing across Europe as greater proportions of beer are sold through supermarkets.

Figure 2.4 depicts channels of distribution with a different structure. This is the situation in the United Kingdom and to a lesser extent in West Germany. In both these countries, the brewing companies own a significant proportion of the retail outlets – 59 percent in the United Kingdom and 22 percent in West Germany. Hence the brewers distribute direct to the pubs and bars in these two countries.

Characteristics of the Individual Brewing Countries
The competitive situation in each of the major countries is indicated in Table 2.7.

Table 2.7

Country	Industry situation	Number of competitors	Degree of concentration (%)[1]
Denmark	Monopoly	1	80
Holland	Monopoly	1	70
Italy	Monopoly	2	70
Belgium	Monopoly	2	85
France	Monopoly	2	75
United Kingdom	Concentrated	6	80
Spain	Concentrated	6	88
West Germany	Fragmented	5	12

[1] The degree of concentration relates to the combined market share held by the number of principal competitors designated in the middle column.

Some of the characteristics not already given will now be discussed for each of the major markets by country.

Denmark
Beer in Denmark is dominated by Carlsberg, which has 80 percent of

the market and is a major global competitor, being the thirteenth largest brewing company in the world. Its brand, Carlsberg, is the second most popular beer brand in Europe selling almost seven million hectolitres annually. Carlsberg is owned by a charitable trust.

There are 20 breweries in Denmark, almost all of which are controlled by the three major competitors in Denmark – Carlsberg, Albani and Faxe-Jyske. Danish brewers are also the largest producers of soft drinks in Denmark. This has been useful in gaining access, for beer, to supermarket channels of distribution.

Danish beer drinkers are by nature conservative. Most of the beer sold in Denmark is brewed domestically. There have been some attempts to introduce foreign beer, but they have not been very successful. Even foreign beer brewed under licence by a Danish brewery has been unsuccessful. In the mid-1980s Carlsberg brewed Budweiser under licence in Denmark, but it was not a success. A particular feature of the Danish beer market is the border trade on the German–Danish border. Many Danes drive across the border into West Germany, fill their petrol tank with cheap German petrol and buy cheap beer. What is interesting is that they buy Danish beer, supplied by Danish breweries to German retailers. The Danish brewers do not lose any production, but the Danish government loses tax revenue and Danish retailers lose sales income. It is estimated that the border trade accounts for 10–20 percent of all beer 'sold in Denmark'.

The beer market is dominated by the brewers' individual brands. However the big supermarket chains have introduced their own brands, which have been sold as cheap discount beers. These beers are also brewed by Danish brewers and are estimated to have 10–22 percent of the market. Approximately 70 percent of beer is sold through retailers, while the rest is sold through restaurants, bars, hotels, etc. The big supermarket chains are therefore extremely important customers of the brewing companies.

An interesting feature of the Danish beer market is the bottle re-use system. It is not legal to sell beer or soft drinks in Denmark in one-way packaging such as cans. Beer must be sold in re-usable bottles for which there exist standard sizes determined by the Danish Association of Brewers. It has been claimed that this bottle re-use system is a major entry barrier preventing foreign brewers from entering the Danish market. However there has been a ruling by the European Court allowing Denmark to keep its bottle re-use system for environmental reasons.

Until 1987 the Danish beer industry was regulated by the members of the Danish Association of Brewers. The regulations fixed minimum prices for beer, prohibited discounts, limited the form of advertising and regulated the distribution system. Post-1987 the market and industry are basically unregulated.

Holland

Like Denmark, Holland is dominated by one brewery, Heineken, which is the largest in Europe and the third largest in the world. Although Heineken only produces 6.6 million hectolitres of beer in Holland, it produces 43 million on a worldwide basis. Heineken also has ownership stakes in brewing companies in Spain, France, Italy and Ireland. The only major European countries it does not have ownership stakes in are the UK and West Germany, although it has a licensing agreement with Whitbread in the UK to brew Heineken for sale in the British market. Heineken is the largest imported beer brand in the USA, with 1.5–2 percent of the total market. The company has been exporting its beer to the USA since 1933, when prohibition ended. The Heineken brand can be purchased in 145 countries worldwide.

There are three other Dutch brewing companies with outputs of approximately 2 million hectolitres of beer per annum. One of these, Verenigde BV, is owned by Allied-Lyons of the UK, the only brewery to be owned by a British company outside the UK. Another is Grolsch BV, which is an interesting company.

Grolsch, despite its relatively small output of only 1.8 million hectolitres of beer per annum, has been able to carve out for itself a strong market position in many of the world's major beer markets. The company has only one brand, but it has a strong brand image, promoted by its unusual shape of bottle and swing top which allows the bottle to be resealed. It currently exports to 35 different countries and from 1985 to 1989 has grown its export sales as a proportion of total revenues from 14 to 31 percent, with a future target of 50 percent. Grolsch's main export markets are the USA and the UK, and its next marketing thrust will be into West Germany and to develop further its market penetration in southern Europe.

Holland is a major exporter of beer, probably the largest exporting country in the world. Its proportion of production exported has grown from 23.7 percent in 1980 to a third in 1988. Imports have doubled from 2.8 to 5.6 percent since 1980, and 90 percent of these imports come from Belgium.

Beer is mainly purchased in supermarkets in Holland for consumption at home. This accounts for 70 percent of all beer sales. The remaining 30 percent is sold through bars, cafés, hotels and restaurants.

Belgium

A feature of the Belgian brewing industry is the large number of beers produced: 420 different brands of 18 different types. It is claimed by the Belgians that no other country can offer such a wide choice. The trend in recent years has been towards more expensive beers in a market which is in overall gentle decline. These more expensive beers tend to be drunk in bars, which accounts for the decline of drinking of beer in the home.

Belgium is also a large exporter of beer. It exports approximately 20 percent of total production, whereas imports amount to less than 5 percent of consumption. Exports have remained relatively static over the last few years, while imports have fallen steadily. Over 95 percent of Belgian beer exports are to other EC countries. This is a function of Belgium's central geographical location in Europe and the problems of transporting beer over long distances while still maintaining quality. The biggest export market by far is France, which takes 63 percent of Belgian exports. Other major export markets are Italy, the Netherlands and the UK.

The Belgian beer industry is dominated by two competitors, Stella-Interbrew and Alken-Maes, who between them have 85 percent of the Belgian market.

Beer is distributed in Belgium through various channels. Principal among these is the specialist dealer or *negociant* who provides the following services: home delivery of beverages, operating a beverages discount outlet, delivering to the hotels, restaurants, cafés and bars sector, and dealing as a wholesaler.

The home delivery of beverages is a typically Belgian approach to distribution and highlights the importance of drinking to the Belgian consumer. For many years the role of the *negociant* was to deliver beer to the home and other beverages were subsequently added. Home delivery however has been declining slowly over the last 20 years, due to the growth of supermarkets which can offer a wider range of beers at lower prices, and to changes in lifestyle, e.g. increase in car ownership leading to greater consumer mobility, increase in real disposable income and more working women who are unable to take deliveries during the day. Home delivery is expected to decrease further in the future but at a slower rate than over the last two decades.

Discount outlets for beverages are a recent development. The first was opened in 1974 and there are now around 1000 in Belgium. This type of outlet combines the advantages of home delivery and supermarkets. These include a large choice of products offered, fast service and lower than average prices.

The hotels, restaurants, cafés and bars sector represents a large part of the market. In this sector the *negociant* plays a key role, offering a large choice of products and adding a certain number of services to the delivery of products, such as taking care of refrigerators. The *negociants* have had to adapt to changing market conditions and have kept their important role in the distribution of beer in the Belgian market. It is estimated that 49 percent of beer sales are distributed through *negociants*, 27 percent through supermarkets and 6 percent through direct sales in cafés and bars.

Italy

As a product, beer has not enjoyed a tradition in Italy as a popular, widely consumed drink. Italy has the lowest consumption per capita of all European countries. Production of beer in Italy only began on an industrial scale in the nineteenth century and today consumption is not as well developed as in the rest of Europe, being concentrated primarily in the north of the country. After 1960, beer began to gain popularity among all the social classes of Italy, whereas previously it had been a drink of the rich. Beer is popular with the younger sections of the population, with only limited sales to those over sixty.

Beer, in Italy, is drunk primarily as a refreshing drink with low alcohol content and at times other than meal times. However there is now an increase in the consumption of beer as an accompaniment for a meal. In the rest of Europe beer is regularly drunk as part of a meal. Italian beer drinking is frequently as an accompaniment to snacks, sandwiches, pizzas and fast food meals. The growth of snack meals has consequently stimulated the growth of beer consumption.

As beer is taken mainly as a refreshing drink, it is drunk above all in the warm summer months. Over half the total beer sales are made in the period June to September. The most popular type of beer in Italy is the light, low-alcohol product. This type of beer accounts for over two-thirds of total sales. However its share of the market is declining as Italian brewers are now making products of a higher alcoholic strength, which are considered as 'special' beers. Foreign beers are almost all classified as 'special' beers. It is expected that the market share of 'special' beers will steadily rise.

Imports, which were very small 15 to 20 years ago, doubled from 1980 to 1985 and have continued to grow since. Imports account for 16 percent of total consumption and this rises to 22 percent when foreign beer brands brewed under licence in Italy are included. The countries from which the imports are made are West Germany, the Netherlands, Belgium and Denmark, whose products are considered to be of higher quality. Exports are negligible.

Since 1970 there has been much concentration in the Italian beer industry. In that year there were 34 beer producers, but now their number has been reduced to 9. The market is dominated by Peroni and Dreher, which between them control 70 percent of the market. A feature of the Italian industry is the relatively high degree of foreign ownership. The main competitors and their annual domestic outputs, in millions of hectolitres, are:

Peroni	4.8
Dreher	3.9
Moretti and Prinz	1.1
Poretti	0.9
Wunster	0.8

Peroni was a family enterprise established in 1846 and is still 80 percent owned by the family. In 1989 it merged with Wuhrer, which was owned by the BSN group of France. BSN became a 20 percent shareholder in Peroni. The company has six breweries located in different parts of the country, giving it national coverage. Peroni produces a wide range of beers, including special and non-alcoholic beers, and also brews the Dutch beer Amstel (owned by Heineken) under licence. It has a strong sales network of over 3000 distributors and is well established in all categories of retail outlets and the catering trade. Dreher, the second largest brewer in Italy, is 85 percent owned by the Heineken group of Holland. It has five breweries and 1200 distributors. Moretti and Prinz were formed from two small brewing companies which were bought in 1989 and merged by Labatt of Canada. Poretti is half owned by the Italian group, Bassetti, and Carlsberg of Denmark. It has two breweries, brews Tuborg under licence and imports Carlsberg. Wunster has only one brewery and was bought from the von Wunster family in 1987 by Stella-Interbrew. The company had been making losses and this was one of the reasons for its sale.

Distribution is similar to that in most European countries. Hotels, restaurants, cafés and bars account for 46 percent of sales, supermarkets and hypermarkets a further 30 percent and traditional grocery outlets 12 percent. The traditional independent grocers are losing market share to the supermarkets. Door-to-door distribution is growing in importance in Italy. Traditionally this system has been used by wholesalers of soft drinks and, since beer is associated with soft drinks in the consumer's mind, it can be readily included in this distribution system. There are about 10,000 of these wholesale drinks distributors in Italy. They work on a very localised basis and in some cases only cover a limited area of a town or city. They are ideally suited for supplying small restaurants, cafés and bars, offering frequent deliveries and enabling small businesses to avoid tying up capital in stock. Only some of the large supermarket chains buy directly from the brewers. For supermarkets located far from a brewery or for smaller self-service operations, the wholesale distributor is often a preferable source of supply.

France

Beer is not a mainstream consumption product in France. Only Italy of the major European countries has a lower annual consumption per capita. Wine has a firm grip as the French national drink and consumption of beer has been declining slowly but steadily during the 1980s. This trend is opposite to that of southern European countries where consumption of beer per capita has been steadily growing in the same period. Despite this, the French industry leader, BSN-Kronenbourg, is the second largest brewing company in Europe and the eighth largest in the world.

At the end of the Second World War, there were 1000 breweries in France. Since then much concentration has taken place. Now there are three main brewing companies, which have 85 percent of the market. The remaining 15 percent is held by approximately 30 small specialist brewing companies. The principal companies with their domestic outputs in millions of hectolitres are:

BSN	10.3
Française de Brasserie	6.0
Artois-Interbrew	1.4

Française de Brasserie is wholly owned by Heineken of Holland, and Artois-Interbrew by Stella-Interbrew of Belgium.

France is not a major exporter of beer. It only exports 3.6 percent of its output, principally to its neighbours Italy and Spain. Eleven and a quarter percent of its consumption is imported, again principally from its neighbour, Belgium.

Brewing and the drinking of beer in France are essentially northern activities. BSN's main brewery is in Strasbourg. Consumption patterns vary substantially across the country. In the north, average consumption is 80 litres per capita versus the European average of 60 litres and the French national average of 39 litres. In the south average consumption is only 20–25 litres.

Distribution patterns have remained static throughout the 1980s with supermarkets and hypermarkets selling 60 percent of all beer and bars, cafés, hotels and restaurants the remaining 40 percent. Breweries do not own bars or cafés, but they will provide them with finance at preferential rates of interest in return for selling their beers under contract for five to ten years. The market is segmented in the same way as that of other European countries, with light or low-alcohol beers, ordinary beers and strong or speciality beers. The low-alcohol and strong/speciality beers are the fastest growing segments. The five countries already discussed – Denmark, Holland, Belgium, Italy and France – have much in common in their brewing industries. They have similar degrees of industry concentration and distribution systems. The countries still to be discussed, Spain, the United Kingdom and West Germany exhibit considerably different characteristics from the first five.

West Germany and the UK, in particular, can be considered the exceptions among the European brewing community. This point will be amplified by the use of a few quotations from the managers.

Spain
The brewing industry in Spain is not dominated by any one company. The major brewing companies with their domestic outputs in millions of hectolitres per annum are as follows:

Cruz del Campo	5.1
El Aguila	4.6
Mahou	4.2
Damm	4.1
San Miguel	3.5
Union Cervecera	1.9

There are three other small brewers with a local focus and small production outputs. The Spanish market is regionally oriented with three very strong regional groups that have been able to develop strong production economies of scale and distribution power. These three are Cruz del Campo, Mahou and Damm. Only San Miguel successfully markets its brand nationally at the moment, although this is expected to change as the international brewers take more interest in the Spanish market.

An interesting feature of the Spanish industry is the high degree of foreign ownership compared to other European countries (except Italy). Cruz del Campo, the largest beer producer, is a southern-based company which is 25 percent owned by the Stroh company of the USA, the seventh largest brewing company in the world. Mahou, the third largest producer, focuses its efforts on Madrid and is 61 percent owned by the BSN group of France. The fourth largest brewer, Damm, is based in Barcelona and is 18 percent owned by Oetker of West Germany. El Aguila is 51 percent owned by Heineken of Holland, San Miguel is affiliated to the San Miguel Corporation of the Philippines, the sixteenth largest brewing group in the world and Union Cervecera is 60 percent owned by Carlsberg.

The Spanish market is not as well developed as other European markets. It is almost entirely satisfied by domestic production. It only exports 0.5 percent of its output and imports 2.8 percent of its consumption. Importation from any country other than France is difficult due to the distances involved with Spain being on the edge of Europe.

It is only in recent years that the market segments well-established in other European countries have begun to develop in Spain. There are three basic market segments – those of ordinary, special and strong beers. However, the consumer's perception of these segments can vary from region to region, so strong are the three regional brewers. The market is developing rapidly, forced mainly by the foreign brewers such as Carlsberg and Heineken through strong advertising and brand development campaigns. The 'new' market segments, i.e. special, strong and a small non-alcoholic segment are the fastest growing.

Distribution in Spain is currently split 25 percent through supermarkets and 75 percent in cafés, bars, hotels and restaurants. However there is a definite move towards increased sales through supermarket grocery chains, as in the rest of Europe. This development has to do with the changing lifestyles of the Spanish. More of them are now buying beer in supermarkets to take home to drink while watching television. The quality of Spanish television has been improving during the 1980s, encouraging this trend. Packaging trends are also changing, from returnable bottles to non-returnable bottles and cans.

United Kingdom

The UK brewing industry is very different from that of the rest of Europe. The first major difference is the type of beer consumed. In Europe, virtually all beers drunk are of a light texture and colour, and consumed after chilling – the type of beer generally defined as lager. In the UK, three principal types of beer are drunk – lagers, ales and stouts. Ales are dark, brown beers which are generally drunk warm, or at room temperature. Stouts are heavy, dark coloured beers, which can be drunk chilled or warm – principal among these is Guinness.

In 1970, ales dominated the beer market, being 85 percent of the total market. Stouts and lagers each had 7.5 percent of market share. Since 1970, the market has changed dramatically. Lager now has 55 percent of the market, ales 40 percent and stouts the remaining 5 percent. This trend has been caused by changing consumer tastes, caused by increased foreign travel and large brand and advertising campaigns to promote lager by the major brewers. Lagers tend to be brands with national coverage, whereas ales are sold more on region loyalty. The trend towards lager is expected to continue.

The UK brewing industry is not as concentrated as that of other European countries. As we have seen there are six large brewing companies which have 80 percent of the market, eleven regional brewers who have 13 percent of the market and over 50 local brewers who have the remaining 7 percent.

British brewing companies are marked by high vertical integration. They own not only the breweries themselves, but also many of the outlets through which beer is sold to the consumer and even in some cases the sources of raw materials – hops, barley and yeast. In outlets not owned by breweries, a supply agreement known as a 'tie' may exist. This means that the outlet can only sell the beer products of the brewing company to which it is 'tied'. In return for this arrangement the owner of the outlet will receive a preferential loan from the brewing company. This situation has arisen because of the historic development of the UK brewing industry. In the nineteenth century breweries only supplied pubs which they owned in a small geographic locality. Gradually they expanded to cover wider areas, some establishing breweries away from their place of origin in an attempt to gain national coverage for their products and take advantage of economies of scale in distribution and production. In the 1960s there was a wave of mergers which led to the current structure. This is described in Table 2.8.

Table 2.8

Brewer	Market share (%)	No. of pubs owned	% of total pubs
Bass	22	7200	9.2
Allied-Lyons	13	6700	8.5
Grand Met.	13	6400	8.1
Whitbread	12	6500	8.3
Scottish & Newcastle	11	2300	2.9
Courage	9	5000	6.4

There are 78,600 pubs in Great Britain and a further 61,400 clubs, hotels and restaurants. The brewers directly control 46,000 pubs, equivalent to 59 percent of the total. The six largest breweries control 43 percent of the pubs. However the UK government takes a keen interest in the brewing industry. Over the last 20 years there have been two major government investigations into the industry, and five relating to specific business transactions. This may not seem a lot given the time-scale involved, but it is substantially more investigation than any other British industry has been subjected to. Nor has any other European government subjected its brewing industry to the same degree of scrutiny. The latest report was published in March 1989, and took over two years to prepare. Simultaneously another report barred Courage, a subsidiary of the Australian brewers, Elders IXL, from acquiring Scottish & Newcastle, despite the fact that the newly merged business would not have had a market share in excess of that of Bass, the market leader.

The findings of the March 1989 report were damning about the industry. The principal conclusion was that a complex monopoly existed, which restricted competition at all levels of the industry. The investigation concluded that the results of this had been:

● the price of a pint of beer in a public house has risen too fast in the last few years;
● the high price of lager was not justified by the cost of producing it;
● the variation in wholesale prices between regions of the country was excessive;
● consumer choice was restricted because one brewer does not usually allow another brewer's beer to be sold in the outlets which they own: this restriction often happens in loan-tied outlets as well;
● consumer choice was further restricted because of brewers' efforts to ensure that their own brand of cider and soft drinks are sold in their outlets;
● tenants of pubs were unable to play a full part in meeting consumer preferences, both because of the tie and because the tenants' bargaining position is so much weaker than the land-lords' (the brewers); and
● independent manufacturers and wholesalers of beer and other drinks were allowed only limited access to the on-licensed market (pubs).

The investigating commission recommended some strong measures to increase competition. Principal among them were:

1 No brewer should own more than 2000 pubs. This was later scaled down to 2000 pubs plus 50 percent of their original holding after substantial lobbying of the British government by the brewers. This means that the six largest brewers have to divest themselves of 11,000 pubs by the deadline of 1992.
2 The loan tie to be eliminated.
3 Tenants of pubs to be allowed to buy at least one brand of beer from a brewery other than the tenant's landlord.
4 The tie for non-alcoholic or low-alcohol beers, wines, spirits, ciders, soft drinks and mineral waters to be abolished.

The report concludes with the following statement: 'If no changes are made we believe it is inevitable that a very small number of brewers will increasingly dominate the supply of beer in the United Kingdom.' What this statement by the government means is that it will closely scrutinise any takeover or merger in Britain. The UK is not a significant exporter of beer, only 2 percent of output being exported. Imports are 7 percent of consumption, having grown from 4 percent since 1980.

A trend in the UK brewing industry which is similar to the trend in Europe is the increased sale of beer from grocery supermarket chains. This grew from 12 to 18 percent during the 1980s and is predicted to be 25 percent of all beer sales by the year 2000.

West Germany

West Germany has the highest per capita consumption of beer in the world, is the second largest market in the world after the USA, and is the largest beer-producing nation in Europe. However the structure of its beer industry is very different from the rest of Europe. The industry has not experienced industrial concentration on the same scale as the rest of Europe. There are approximately 1200 breweries in West Germany, producing an average of less than 80,000 hectolitres per annum. In Bavaria, there are 800 breweries, equivalent to one brewery for every 14,000 people. The Bavarians drink an average of 225 litres of beer each year compared to the national average of 143 litres. The West German brewing industry produces 5000 different brands of beer. This accounts for nearly half the world's total. Some signs of concentration are beginning to appear. Over the last 20 years, the five largest West German brewers have doubled their combined market share from 6 to 12 percent and the number of breweries has fallen from 3000 to the current 1200.

West German drinkers are very conservative and loyal to their favourite beer, normally a beer brewed locally. Ninety percent of breweries sell their products within a 30-mile radius. This conservatism and loyalty is encouraged by a unique feature of the German market, the *Reinheitsgebot* or 'purity law', dating from 1516 and requiring beer to be brewed only from four pure ingredients. The strength of this loyalty and the prospects of its changing in the future can be seen in quotations from two German brewery managers: 'The consciousness of the consumer of the *Reinheitsgebot* is very high. Ninety to ninety-five percent of consumers say they will only buy beer which has been brewed in accordance with the *Reinheitsgebot*.' And again: 'The Germans will still cling to the *Reinheitsgebot* in ten years time. It is a matter of marketing. Even if the Federal Government were to allow additives as in other European countries, the German brewers would not do it and the customers would not accept it.'

The purity laws were first introduced in the south in 1516 and ultimately became law all over Germany in 1919. The law states that only malted cereals, hops, yeast and water can be used in the brewing process. Artificial additives are not allowed to improve quality or extend shelf life, thus clearly inhibiting imports or the transportation of local products over any significant distances.

In 1987, following complaints by the French government and European brewers, the European Court of Justice ruled that the *Reinheitsgebot* could not be used to prevent the sale of imported beers in West Germany, provided that they met the laws of their country of origin. West Germany adopted a compromise law, allowing beers with additives to be sold, but they had to be clearly labelled and could not be called beers. This is clearly prejudicial to importers of beer and may be in contravention of the 1987 ruling by the European Court of Justice. Despite this ruling, only a few foreign companies have entered the German market. These are Carlsberg, Heineken and Guinness. Grolsch as well as Fosters, the Australian beer, are planning to enter the German market during 1990. It is claimed that Fosters will be brewed in accordance with the *Reinheitsgebot*.

As a result of the purity laws imports are not a major feature of the West German market. During the 1980s the proportion of beer consumption that was imported doubled to 1.5 percent. The proportion of beer production exported has grown during the 1980s from 3.2 to 5.7 percent. The principal countries exported to are the UK, France, Italy, Spain, Austria and Switzerland. The UK is West Germany's largest export market by far, where many of the successful lager brands are of West German origin.

Another feature of the West German brewing industry is the low profitability of the brewing companies. The manager of one brewing company summarised the situation thus: 'There are very large breweries in the Federal Republic of Germany which earn less than the hot-dog stand at the corner. They have not paid dividends for ten years and they say there will be no dividends for the next five years.'

Many of the German brewers are privately or family owned and enjoy significant support from the banking institutions. They do not have, and do not need to have, the same commercial thrust or ambition as publicly owned companies in other countries. The profit margins of German brewing companies are very much lower than elsewhere in Europe. One German brewing company manager highlighted the position: 'The margin in Germany amounts to about 1 percent. In the United Kingdom it amounts to 10 percent. The difference is that the British want to earn 10 percent and the Germans are very pleased with 2 percent.' This low profitability is another factor contributing to the low importation of beer brands. Distribution channels have some similarities to the rest of Europe, but also some differences. The major similarity is that 60 percent of beer sales are made through supermarkets for consumption in the home. It is estimated that 60 percent of all beer sales across Europe are now made through supermarkets. The German brewers sell and deliver direct to the supermarket chains. The remaining 40 percent of German beer sales is sold through cafés, bars, hotels and restaurants. Where Germany differs from the rest of Europe, with the exception of the UK, is that about 22 percent of cafés and bars are owned by the breweries. In addition many cafés and bars, not owned directly by the breweries, have 'arrangements' with breweries to sell only their products. This supply arrangement can be for as long as 25 years and usually involves the brewery making cheap loans to the café or bar. It is a strategy for breweries to maintain a strong hold in their local marketplace.

In summary, Europe is the major centre of beer consumption and production in the world. As a production entity European output is more than 50 percent greater than that of the USA, the world's largest single beer-producing country.

However significant diversities exist and Europe cannot be viewed as a homogeneous beer market. It is a collection of highly individual markets each with their own particular, and peculiar, nuances and characteristics. As a Dutch brewer put it:

> The Americans or the Japanese, they see the unification of Europe as an imminent thing, Europe is a new market of 320 million consumers. They do not realise, like we do, that it is a multi-local market. In Italy there has to be a different approach from Spain.

Managers' Perceptions of the Issues Facing the European Brewing Industry in the 1990s

The managers interviewed generally shared common views as to what the issues are that will affect the development of the European brewing industry in the 1990s, despite being from quite different national brewing backgrounds. There are, however, significant differences in the managers' perceptions of the effects that these issues will have.

Definition of Business Activity

A diversity of opinion exists between the UK and mainland European brewers as to the business they believe themselves to be in.

The mainland European position is summed up in the following quotations:

> We shouldn't limit ourselves to beer, we feel that we are operating in the beverage industry. This goes for most breweries. We notice that they are starting to diversify in the direction of hard liquors or in the direction of soft drinks and mineral waters, more usually the latter. There is hardly any European brewer which has not gone into the soft drink sector – waters, lemonades, colas, etc. (Dutch brewing manager).

Or again:

> Generally, I would define it that we are in the beverage industry. We do not only have beer production but we belong to a larger group which also produces refresher beverages. In the broadest meaning I would say we are a beverage manufacturer (West German brewing manager).

But the British position was stated thus: 'The problem with the British industry is that it has spent 200 years trying to work out whether it's a property company, a retail company or a brewing company' (British brewing manager). This difference in emphasis with the British having a much broader view of their business and sometimes describing themselves as in 'leisure' or 'entertainment' has implications for the future strategies of the UK companies: 'Soft drinks, like coca-cola, sell increasingly every year. Young people favour them because they tend to drink non-alcoholic drinks, because they are sensitive to publicity. So this trend will continue' (French brewing manager).

Related to this different perception of business activity is the fact that the UK brewers are not considered European by the continental brewing companies. This perception of the managers in the study is encapsulated in the following quotation: 'Nowadays there are four "European" brewers: Heineken, Carlsberg, BSN-Kronenbourg and Stella-Interbrew' (French brewing manager). Not one single interviewee considered a UK brewer as being European. There are some clear implications here for the UK brewing companies. Some will have to choose between being brewers and retailers. This process has already begun with two regional brewers, Boddingtons and Greenall Whitley, the UK's largest regional brewing companies, announcing in 1990 that they were to close their brewing operations and focus on retailing.

If the UK brewers wish to become Euro-competitive they will have to come to see themselves as in the beverage industry and not in the variety of interests in which they currently operate.

The Future Structure of the Industry
An issue around which managers showed a high degree of agreement

was the shape of the future structure of the industry. The managers' almost unanimous view is that the current structure of the European brewing industry as depicted in Figure 2.1 will continue to polarise. If the industry in Europe develops in accordance with the beliefs of the managers interviewed then middle-sized brewing companies, which tend to be those which focus on a single national market, will disappear.

The managers' argument is nicely caught by the following quotations:

> The first phenomenon is the phenomenon of size. I think that for breweries the intermediate size will not exist any more. Either you are a small brewer, not in direct competition with the big ones, and you install yourself in market niches which are too small to interest the big ones or you have to be big. This logic leads to two poles, on the one hand very large companies, and opposite small focused dynamic companies. I do not believe in middle-sized companies between these two extremes (French brewing manager).

And the same theme is echoed in another country: 'Intermediate breweries must make choices, either they must become big, or they must aim at a number of specific branches of the industry' (Dutch brewing manager).

The managers see these developments as a natural and logical progression from previous trends in the industry. Most of them believed that further concentration will take place in Europe. A driving force for this concentration is the growing power of retail outlet chains which are increasingly taking a bigger share of brewers' outputs across Europe. This trend is being driven by legislation in all European countries against drinking and driving, hence more people are drinking in their homes. One manager interviewed estimated that sales of beer in Europe through supermarket chains could be as high as 60 percent of the total! A French brewing manager believed that: 'Concentration will certainly continue, to improve industrial efficiency, to face the growing power of retail chains and to achieve the conquest of European markets in the 1990s.'

The management of the European supermarket chains have no desire to increase management costs by purchasing from a large number of different breweries. They will welcome further concentration in the European brewing industry until it reaches a point where the brewing companies have equivalent power to themselves.

The managers believe that the likeliest countries for concentration are the UK and West Germany, and to a lesser extent Spain. This is hardly surprising given the high degrees of concentration which exist in the other countries.

There is some divergence of opinion about West Germany, which should, in theory, offer the most scope for further concentration. In the main, the West German brewers interviewed did not anticipate this. Concentration, if it takes place at all, will be a slow process in their view. Some credence must be given to this view, given the previously slow rate of change in the West German industry, compared to the changes which have taken place during the same period in the other major brewing countries.

A few of the Germans, however, do anticipate a retailer-driven concentration in the drinks industry:

> I want to give you another example from the wine industry. Until two years ago, the Metro supermarket chain bought its wine regionally and had almost 400 kinds of wines in its range, because each Metrostore was responsible for purchasing its own wine range. That was abolished in the last year. The entire purchasing department has been transfered to the company's headquarters. Four hundred suppliers have been reduced to 40. The same will happen in the beer market. That is, a lot of regional brands will be thrown out of the supermarket ranges because they cannot produce the essential sales per space for a particular area (German brewing manager).

A characteristic, highlighted in the above quotation, of supplier–retailer relationships is that over the long term, the bulk of the available profit margin, and hence the power in the distribution channel, invariably shifts closer to the retailer. This trend is clear in European countries other than Germany and is an evolving force even there. It may well be the primary mover to reshape the structure of the West German brewing industry, given that 60 percent of beer is purchased in supermarkets.

From some of the evidence cited it is clear that there is a strong belief among German brewing managers that the basic structure of their industry will not change other than marginally, even in the long term. This view is perhaps fostered by the purity laws which have been in existence for over 450 years. One German manager put it thus:

> I cannot think of any other product which has an emotional touch which is as strong as the one that our product has. If we were to buy a brewery at a different location, then the people there would be really mad at us for taking over the poor, old, traditional brewery.

However the validity of this view must be questioned. There are few industries which have not concentrated significantly over time. Concentration is a natural evolutionary process of business, usually driven by the ambitions of some of the managers in the industry. It is hard to accept that quick-witted managers in the German industry could not take advantage of the conditions that currently exist.

Some contradiction also exists in the views on concentration. The managers interviewed said that there would be continuing concentration during the 1990s and that the obvious choices were West Germany, Spain and the UK. However when questioned about these markets individually, few believed there will be further concentration in them!

A major factor in restructuring any industry is the likelihood of new entrants. The managers interviewed who discussed potential entrants saw little likelihood of the US brewers entering European industry, but felt the Australians would develop further into mainland Europe from the UK springboard and were unclear as to the intentions of the Japanese as the following quotes indicate: 'I don't think the Americans will come in. I don't think Anheuser-Busch will, at least not in the next five years. I think if anything they will export product brewed in the United States in can form. Anheuser-Busch don't understand the European brewing business' (British brewing manager). And a variation on the theme:

> When Courage was available for sale in 1986 from Hanson Trust and again in 1989 when Scottish & Newcastle were effectively for sale, neither Budweiser nor the Japanese chose to make a bid. I think what's interesting to my mind is that the aggressive players on the world stage are the European and Australian brewers. The Americans are locked into their own market. Anheuser-Busch, in reality, are the largest regional brewer in the world (British brewing manager).

Nor is this only a British view: 'The Japanese are not present in Europe, until now they are not at all implanted in Europe. I don't think we ought to fear them in this business' (French brewing manager). Plus respect for Australian initiative:

> Elders is one of the most aggressive beer companies, in the positive meaning of the word, in the world. They approach Europe from the UK. They hardly ship any beer from Australia to Holland. Elders are one of those that might do some acquisitions in Europe. They are aware of the multi-local aspect and know that Europe can't be conquered from the UK. (Dutch brewing manager).

Most of the managers agreed that the process of entry would have to be by acquisition. They felt that creating a brewery in a greenfield site was not a feasible option, due to the problem of gaining access to the distribution channels: 'To enter the market by establishing a small brewery would be uneconomic, and if you set up a large brewery you will have problems distributing your products, because the only channel of distribution open to you will be through supermarkets, which are only 25 percent of beer sales' (Spanish brewing manager).

Interestingly a significant proportion of the managers did not mention entry by foreign brewers during the course of their interview. The factors influencing these negative views about potential entrants have already been mentioned – existing high degrees of concentration, UK government policy, German purity laws, low levels of German profitability, and existing cross-border ownership arrangements.

In summarising this section on the future structure of the beer industry, the author has the advantage of seeing the views of all the interviewees, a facility which was obviously not available to them. A significant number of managers believed that the industry will further polarise and concentrate. However, contradicting this was a strong perception that their own national market would not change substantially from how it was in 1989.

Critical Success Factors
There was a strong agreement among the managers that the two most important success factors that a European brewing company needed to possess for the 1990s were strong brands, powerfully marketed; and appropriate economies of scale, in production and distribution. Getting the balance right between these two factors will lead to sustained success. The following is indicative of the managers' views: 'To be successful in Europe in the 1990s you must have strong lager brands and the right economies of scale in production and distribution' (British brewing manager). There were numerous other quotations to support this argument. The following is only a minimal sample: 'The ability to create a brand with a high profile is important' (Danish brewing manager). 'The key success factor is brands, and brands marked by quality and image' (German brewing manager). And 'At present the first competitive factor is the brand or brands at our disposal. We need strong high image brands' (Italian brewing manager). Consumers are seen as identifying with the image of a product, and strong branding is essential to take advantage of this.

There is also structural evidence to support the managers' point of view. Figure 2.5 shows the top ten selling beer in brands in Europe. Not surprisingly the top three brands are marketed by the three largest companies which have the most extensive operations across Europe. Heineken has two of the top five brands, Heineken and Amstel, and Carlsberg has two of the top ten brands, Carlsberg and Tuborg.

A strong emphasis was also placed on the absolute importance of the quality of the product. In answer to a question about key success factors in the brewing industry a German manager responded:

> Quality, good quality and the attempts to achieve a clear market profile. If you do not have that, then you cannot sustain sales at your desired price level. If you cannot do that, then eventually you will get into trouble.

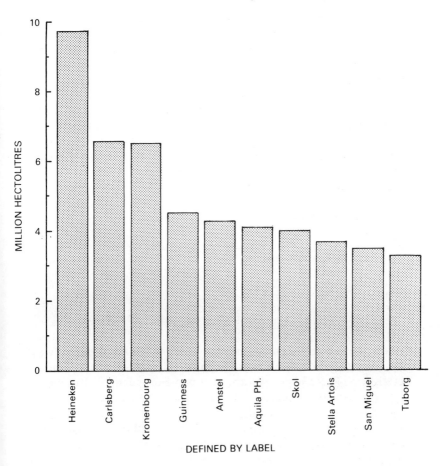

Figure 2.5   *Top ten European brands*

Views about economies of scale are typified as follows:

It costs as much to distribute beer as it does to make it, if you remove duty from the equation. Too many deliveries are made to too many pubs. Brewing in the UK is not a very efficient industry. So we need to be able to put together economies of scale. We have too many small breweries. We need economies of scale in brewing and production (British brewing manager).

We believe it is difficult to sustain a brewery with an output of less than one million hectolitres. In order to be viable a brewery must have an output of two million hectolitres (French brewing manager).

The relationship between economies of scale in production and distribution is also important: 'Thanks to lower production costs, larger breweries may cover a larger area, up to distances of 1000 kilometres, whereas small breweries may be limited to 30 kilometres' (French brewing manager).

It is hard to argue with the views expressed by the managers. Establishing the appropriate balance between marketing and operations in relation to an organisation's environment has been a perennial strategic issue. It is well summarised as follows: 'The name of the game has always been to focus on product and production. Watch your product [in the marketing sense], brew an excellent beer, don't do any concessions [to quality], and it will surely sell' (Dutch brewing manager).

Where there was a clear difference of opinion was whether it is possible to create a beer brand which will be applicable and successful across Europe. Some felt that it was possible and had indeed happened:

> I think Heineken have got it [a global beer brand]. You can go to an awful lot of countries in the world and go into a supermarket and buy Heineken and similarly Carlsberg. So they have got that franchise around the world (British brewing manager).

> The thing that will be changing is the policy of European brands. We will be thinking increasingly European (French brewing manager).

Others, however, disagreed, and felt that a portfolio of brands was necessary to make allowances for different national market characteristics: 'There is not yet any real pan-European [all-European countries] brand' (French brewing manager). And 'I'm not sure that it is a global individual brand, I think it is more a global portfolio of beer brands' (British brewing manager). This difference in view, from company to company, will be an influence on their marketing strategies.

The managers also agreed that creating new brands was difficult: 'I don't believe that it is possible to create new brands. It costs a lot of money and takes a very long time' (French brewing manager). A British brewing manager claimed that: 'We can create the liquid very well, but can we create the heritage of the product?' Clearly the art of brand management and the balance of economies of scale between production and distribution are going to be managerial factors demanding a lot of attention in Europe during the 1990s.

Market Segmentation

Related to the future polarised structure of the market and the importance of brands as a critical success factor is how the managers saw the European beer market developing. Clear segments of the market, with different characteristics, are beginning to develop. 'We notice that in a saturated market there is segmentation. In a growing market beer is beer, in a segmented market this is not the case' (Dutch brewing manager). A good example of a growing segment in a mature market is the increase in lager sales in the United Kingdom. During the last 20 years, the total volume of beer sold in the UK has not fluctuated substantially, but in that period lager's share of the market has increased from 7.5 to 55 percent. Four distinct segments of the European market appear to be developing. These are:

1   Low-alcohol or non-alcoholic beers.
2   Ordinary beers – the major volume sector, including supermarket chain low price own-label beers.
3   Premium or strong beers.
4   Speciality beers – such as aperitif beers, or beers for special occasions.

As with every attempt to classify a market the above segmentation analysis is not perfectly comprehensive. There are some other small categories of beer not mentioned above, for instance, light beers.

Aggregating the views of the managers, the various European market shares that each segment has can be estimated. Speciality beers have 5 percent, premium beers 25 percent, and low-alcohol or alcohol-free beers have 7 percent. The biggest market share is held by the ordinary segment which accounts for 63 percent. This is split 50 percent branded products and 13 percent supermarket chain own-label brands. What is interesting is that the segments seem to be developing consistently across Europe and the managers agree on this, even in West Germany: 'There will be stronger polarisation between very exclusive and expensive beers on the one hand and the discounters [supermarket chains] on the other hand' (German brewing manager).

Several interviewees drew comparisons with other industries and their product ranges:

> Take Ford as an example. They have segmented models across Europe, i.e. Fiesta, Escort, Sierra and Granada. Beer is heading in the same direction. It is classical consumer goods marketing. You will have product range extensions, which are already happening, and then you will have brand portfolios dealing with different parts of the market (British brewing manager).

The segments which have been growing and are expected to continue to grow are the low- and non-alcohol beers and particularly the premium and speciality beers. Also seen as growing are the supermarket chain own-label beers. This is a function of their low price and the distribution power of the supermarket chains: 'The beers selling increasingly are the premium beers, specialities and non-alcoholic beers which have doubled their sales. This has been the tendency for several years now' (French brewing manager). A British brewing manager said: 'Because of the anti-alcohol lobby and drink-driving, people will drink less but demand better products. Hence premium products will grow, they are growing all over the world. The growth in premium beer sales is even higher than the growth in supermarket own labels'.

Typical of the diversity of the European brewing industry is how different brands in their segments are viewed from country to country. Brands which do not have their origin in a country, which are 'foreign', are invariably viewed as premium segment products. A good example of this is BSN's Kronenbourg 1664, which is sold in France as an ordinary segment beer, but is viewed in almost all other markets as a premium product. As an Italian brewer put it: 'Foreign brands command a premium price for their image of higher quality.' However, potential hazards exist for brewers in pursuing this policy:

> In Great Britain, Stella Artois is a premium beer, one of the most expensive beers you can get there, and people buy it because it is expensive. It is marketed and promoted that way. The British are travelling people, so now when they come to Belgium, they discover that Stella Artois is a cheap beer. So they ask themselves if it is justified to pay so much for it in Great Britain (French brewing manager).

Another diversity exists in price relationships between premium and ordinary beers and by European geographic region, as a French manager pointed out: 'There is another interesting difference between countries. In southern Europe the price differential is high between the premium/speciality segment and the ordinary segment – of the order of 40 percent. In northern Europe the difference is much lower, only 15 percent.'

A possible source of explanation for this wide discrepancy could be the widely differing duty and taxation rates on beer across Europe. However, duty rates on beer tend to be much lower in the southern than northern European countries. Therefore these pricing policies must be part of the brewing companies' marketing strategies.

The whole question of future market segmentation is nicely summed up by a German manager: 'Specialisation will be much more important. That does not mean only the trend towards premium beers. We are concerned about the specialisation on particular groups of consumers – on elderly people, on successful people, on outsiders, on a lot of single groups.' The emphasis on specialisation is likely to continue under pressure from the demographic changes taking place in Europe. The typical European beer drinker is aged from 18 to 25, but this age category is declining in every European country. In 1990, every European country is experiencing a net population decline, that is, the number of deaths exceed the number of births each year. With this effect in place, there is unlikely to be overall growth in the European beer market, hence segmentation activity must intensify.

The Single European Market of 1992
The mainland European brewers were united in their agreement that they did not perceive the unification of the European market in 1992 as an event which was going to make any impact on the structure of the industry. Typical among the views are: 'European brewers did not wait for 1992, "l'Acte Unique", before moving into different countries. Our international development strategy, including acquisitions, started in 1978' (French brewing manager). And a Dutch manager: 'I say that 1992 started ten years ago for us, because at the end of the 1970s we saw that the home market was too small, if we wanted to expand on a global scale. So the board of directors decided as a policy line to make Europe our home. Since then we have made a lot of acquisitions in other European countries.'

On the other hand the British brewers saw it as a possible threat:

I think there is a danger for the UK in 1992. After 1992 it will be easier to move product across borders. If you can buy a can of beer at a third of the price in a supermarket in northern France compared to the price in the south of England, why can't you buy it at the cheaper price in England?

The opening of the Channel Tunnel will also have an impact on this effect.

Another danger for the UK was highlighted as follows:

Carlsberg, Heineken, Löwenbräu, Stella Artois are all big brands in the UK and they all happen to be brewed under licence in one form or another. But those licences will probably not be renewed, because no sensible person is going to licence products in the EC in individual countries, the way they used to do, because [after 1992] they can't control the territories any more that the licence applies to. So you are going to think twice if you are Heineken, before licensing in the UK, given that the UK licensee will be free to sell all over Europe, and there will be no ability to control them. So I think we may see a lot of licences turned into brewing subcontracts with the brand name taken firmly back to the mother-company.

There was a concern among the British managers about the preparedness of the UK brewing industry to face the challenges and opportunities of 1992:

The British industry, generally most British industry is introspective. The British beer industry is enormously introspective, because of the tie and tradition. I don't think many boardrooms in the UK brewing industry are talking about Europe that much. If they were, they should have made their moves by now as time is getting a bit tight. So I think from a management point of view they have a difficulty looking at themselves as European companies (British brewing manager).

One area which all managers agreed they were unclear about is the impact of the Single Market on the different duty structures which exist across Europe. In theory, some day they should all be harmonised. Not only do the rates of duty vary, but also the method of calculating them. There are two methods of calculating duty across Europe: the wort system and at the brewery gate (BG). The latter, as its name implies, means tax is levied at the 'brewery gate' on point of shipment to the next stage in the distribution channel. The wort system is more complex and dates from the last century. Duty is calculated during the brewing process, at the point of fermentation. Table 2.9 shows the different methods of duty calculation, the duty rates and also sales tax rates across Europe.

From Table 2.9, it can be seen that, in general terms, beer has high rates of duty in the north of Europe and low in the south. This has some clear impacts on the economics of brewing. In the UK, for example, raw materials, salaries, packaging materials, etc, make up one-third of total manufacturing costs, the other two-thirds is duty.

One British manager summed the duty situation up thus: 'The harmonisation of duty is a mess in Europe, frankly. There are very wide duty differences across Europe. You have the situation where

Table 2.9

	Duty system	Duty	Sales tax (%)
West Germany	BG	6.87	14
Denmark	BG	60.82	22
Belgium	Wort	11.39	19
United Kingdom	Wort	51.80	15
Ireland	Wort	85.37	25
Holland	Wort	20.38	20
Spain	BG	3.31	12
France	BG	2.78	18.6
Italy	Wort	20.17	9

A standard measure was used to ensure consistent comparison.
Duty is measured in ECU per hectolitre.
Belgium has a lower rate of sales tax of 17% on beer consumed in cafés and bars.
Source: Various national Trade Associations

there is a potential price difference between France and the UK of 25 percent in a very saleable commodity.'

It is difficult to envisage a scenario acceptable to all parties concerned, where duty rates, and systems of duty collection, are harmonised overnight across Europe. However, certain likely directions can be postulated. It must be reasonable to assume that there is going to be a move towards harmonisation of duty rates, and consequently duty rates will fall in the northern European countries, where per capita consumptions are high but static or declining: and rise in the southern European 'sunbelt' countries, where per capita consumptions are low but rising. This must have some effect on prices, probably falls in the north and rises in the south. What effect will this have on beer consumption? In effect, is the market price-sensitive? Managers' views differed on these questions. A French manager felt the market was price-sensitive: 'In 1992, with progressive harmonisation of the excise taxes in European countries, prices may fluctuate quickly with consequences on the demand in each country.' A British manager saw the situation differently: 'Beer consumption across Europe is basically a mature market and I'm not sure that even if you could get a price reduction to the consumer, that it would create market growth, because of other factors like health, drink-driving, advertising bans, etc.' These differing views on the relationship between price and demand will have an impact on individual company strategies.

The last quotation raises the issue of advertising. Brewers spend large sums of money on brand advertising, and across Europe, currently, there are a diversity of advertising regulations. One French brewer described the situation thus:

> What may possibly change with 1992 is what could be called 'open' advertising. At present all European countries do not have the same advertising regulations. For instance, TV advertising is forbidden in France, Denmark and Belgium. In 1992 the homogenisation of the regulations could open the market for European TV advertising for beer. It might accelerate the French market for instance and raise the economics of scale on advertising.

> On the other hand, if the anti-alcohol lobbies are effective the more restrictive regulations on advertising might dominate! Nobody can really predict what will happen.

The large European-scale brewers believe they are strong enough not to fear any impacts of the effects of 1992. They organised themselves for European integration ten years earlier. They feel there may be some increased opportunities in higher demand, due to duty harmonisation, the ability to move product more easily, and the possibility of

Europe-wide brand advertising. British brewers, on the other hand, seem ill-prepared for the effects of 1992 and have some significant competitive concerns.

The Importance of the Development of Human Resources
There was a clear identification, by the mainland European brewers to develop managers with at least a European, and preferably a broader international orientation. 'We are moving towards the internationalisation of management and an international cross-cultural organisation. I think that really is the mission in the years to come' (Dutch brewing manager). A Spanish manager commented:

> We have searched for 'European Spaniards' for our company. Managers who work for this company today are rather more European than those who worked here ten years ago.
>
> What we are looking for are people who 'think' European, the ones who have worked in multinationals, speak English, are accustomed to computers, and consider computerisation to be a strategic factor for success.

Training and recruitment were seen as important strategic areas: 'We have a number of international management programmes, where we put people together from all over the world, different operating companies, different cultural backgrounds and put them in our management training programmes for some weeks' (Dutch brewing manager).

The concept of cross-fertilisation was important to the managers, as was language ability, particularly in English: 'The entire rising generation must speak English relatively well. And this does not only affect the marketing and sales people, but also everybody else' (German brewing manager). A French manager stated: 'We should not recruit any manager who is not, at least, bilingual and mobile. When we have an international meeting, for instance, we cannot afford any language problem. Interpreters are not a solution . . . Recently we had a meeting where eight different languages were represented, and English speaking was the only way to conduct the meeting.' Given the French national chauvinism about their language, the above quotation is a remarkable measure of their commitment to internationalisation!

The six issues which have been discussed were the principal ones in the view of the managers interviewed. The next three were not as important, but still deserve some mention.

Technological and Packaging Developments
Few managers foresaw any major technological developments in the near future. Their general view was that there will be incremental

improvement developments through the entire brewing chain, from raw materials to distribution and packaging. Two French brewing managers summed up the range of possible technology developments in the following quotations:

> There are a few technological innovations foreseen, though they should not upset the market in the next few years:
> - the brewing process will become more and more automated, even in the medium-sized German breweries;
> - on-line control [of the brewing process] will be much more developed.
>
> Two new technological avenues are more uncertain:
> - at present beer is produced in a batch process, but it could be produced using a continuous process some day: this would be a revolution, but it is uncertain that this will happen;
> - genetic mutations [biotechnology] in the brewers' yeast are more likely; they would improve the process and maybe the product.
>
> The consequences of these technological changes would be higher barriers for some of the small competitors.

And locating the present in terms of the past:

> I think there have been a lot of technological innovations in the last ten years. At the moment, brewing is entirely automated.
>
> Whereas we formerly had master brewers, professions which were passed on from fathers to sons, now we have computers which have replaced them. We depend less and less on human beings, especially in packaging.

The basic brewing process of fermentation has not changed in over two centuries, and the managers interviewed felt that this situation will be maintained. One or two of the managers, however, thought that the Japanese may have made a breakthrough, and a British manager said: 'In the beer business, you are shipping water around and the Japanese, as I understand it, have two approaches – one is they have found a more effective method of brewing, and they have also perfected dry beer. You just add water to it.' At the moment, these innovations are only at the development stage.

A particular area of concern, strongly stated by many of the managers under the topic of technology developments, was packaging. The strength of this concern can be measured by the fact that the first response of a majority of them to the question about future technological developments concerned packaging rather than production. Their concerns, particularly in mainland Europe, were driven by the environmental pressure lobby. Indicative of their feelings is the following quote:

> The beer industry has to do with environmental issues, non-returnable bottles. You do not only sell beer, but the bottle as well. You don't want to get the bottle, because logistically this takes time and money, but perhaps

there is no alternative in the future. Perhaps there will be a standard bottle, a Euro-bottle (Dutch brewing manager).

Overall, although concerned about technological developments, the managers did not appear to have them as high on their agenda of strategic issues as the future structure of the industry, market segmentation, human resource development and so on.

Eastern Europe

Surpri ingly, the issue of Eastern Europe was only mentioned by a few of the managers. Opportunities would appear to exist, in particular for West German brewers, in the Eastern European countries. The manager of a small German brewing company put it thus:

> Naturally the German brewers will try to sell beer in Holland or Belgium as they do now. But I see greater possibilities in East Germany. Either in cooperation with the breweries over there, by supplying them with new equipment and they function as a wholesaler and sell our products with their own. Or you build your own brewery. There is a much bigger market in Eastern Europe for us than there is in the other European countries.

As Table 2.3 showed, East Germany and Czechoslovakia have the second and third highest per capita consumptions after West Germany in an enlarged European market. These 'adjacent' markets must offer opportunities to European brewers. Perhaps the lack of emphasis on Eastern Europe by the interviewees is explained by the following quotation from a French manager: 'I think there surely will be opportunities for European brewers in those countries [Eastern Europe], but their economies must be restored and the people must obtain a purchasing power which allows them to buy these types of products.'

Perhaps it is the fragmentation of the West German brewing industry which is at the root of the apparent lack of interest in, or awareness of, the possibilities in Eastern Europe. If the West German industry had an industrial structure similar to say, France or the UK, then these 'adjacent' markets would probably be receiving more attention.

Conclusions and Future Scenarios for the European Brewing Industry

To conclude, the major findings of the brewing study can be summarised in three categories: those where there is consensus, areas of difference or uncertainty, and topics which the author feels are worthy of comment. This summary will form the basic assumptions which are the foundation of the proposed scenarios.

Consensus was high among the managers on the following topics:

1 Concentration will continue in the industry, and the structure will polarise into niche players and large general brewing companies.

2 National markets for beer will not exhibit any significant growth trends during the 1990s.

3 Because of this lack of growth, market segmentation and specialisation activities by European brewers will increase. The four segments already outlined will become firmly established.

4 The critical success factors are strong brands and economies of scale in production and distribution.

5 The power of grocery supermarket retail chains will continue to increase across Europe.

6 Those brewers considered as Euro-competitive, such as Heineken, Carlsberg, Stella-Interbrew and BSN organised themselves for 1992 ten years ago and will continue to be strong and effective competitors.

7 The quality of human resources is a key strategic weapon.

8 There are unlikely to be any major technological breakthroughs in the 1990s.

9 Eastern Europe is unlikely to offer substantial market opportunities in the near future.

10 There are unlikely to be many new entrants to the industry in the foreseeable future.

Those issues upon which the managers disagreed or were uncertain about are:

1 Where further industrial concentration is going to take place.

2 The effect of some of the detailed proposals about 1992, for instance concerning television advertising.

3 Whether beer brands could be created which would be successful across Europe.

4 How the harmonisation of beer duty across the different national markets would be handled post-1992.

The final category are those topics which the author feels he should comment on, as a result of the knowledge gained in undertaking this piece of research.

The first is the managers' view that there are unlikely to be any major new entrants to the European industry in the near future. This view is surprising and potentially dangerous. Brewing is a global business which is highly capital-intensive. Consumption of beer in almost every developed country is static or falling. To maintain utilisation of capital assets, the major brewers must seek ultimately to develop their sales on as widespread a basis as possible.

The second is the rather disinterested approach to Eastern Europe. This may be an opportunity missed. Although the economies of these countries are in poor shape after years of neglect in terms of investment, the pace of change has been so great that it would take a brave person to predict what is likely to happen in these countries. As late as October 1989, most pundits believed that Communism would still be the basis of the political system in the Eastern Bloc countries into the 1990s. People in the Eastern European countries can now see, at first hand, the wealth their western neighbours enjoy. It is likely that they will wish to emulate them as rapidly as possible. With economic aid from the West that may happen sooner than anticipated.

Finally, the strongly held conviction among German managers that the structure of their industry will not change significantly during the 1990s must be challenged. There are several forces conspiring to change the German industry. Germany is Europe's most fragmented market, and is thus tempting to outside would-be 'restructurers'. Then again the power of the German supermarket chains is continually increasing. Reunification has conferred opportunities to expand. The market segments seen in the rest of Europe also exist in Germany, hence consumer tastes must be becoming more European. The author believes these factors may well have a telling impact on the structure of the German brewing industry by the end of the century.

The scenarios created will be described as singular entities, but inevitably there will be some overlap among them. The three proposed scenarios for the European brewing industry for the 1990s, which have been developed from the findings of this study, are:

The Industry Changes Gradually   The title of this scenario suggests that there will be no great changes to the industry, more a series of slow, incremental developments.

The structure of the industry will move slowly to that described in Figure 2.4, i.e. small to medium sized niche competitors and international players. There will be no major entry by a brewing company from outside Europe. There will be some small increase in concentration in West Germany, driven primarily by the increasing power of the retail chains, but the German brewers will remain essentially focused, as before, on their regional priorities. The West German brewers will slowly take advantage of the opportunities in East Germany, but this will make them less interested in further developing in the EC.

The UK industry will not change substantially. Some of the regional brewers will continue the trend to retailing and exit from larger brewers. The large brewers will reduce the number of pubs they own, in line with government orders, but will still retain a strong grip on the market. One, or perhaps two, of the large brewers will split their operations into brewing businesses and retailing businesses. The number of pubs in the UK will reduce. The volume of European business done by the UK brewers will increase only slightly, in single figure percentages. The volume of lager sales will continue to increase, although under a different administrative set-up which will make little difference to the consumer. After 1992, the mainland European brewers will, when they come up for renewal, convert the licensing agreements which currently exist with UK brewers into brewing subcontracts. This will give them greater control over the volumes brewed and where they are sold. Consequently only those UK brewers that own their lager brands will be able to compete in Europe, currently only Bass and Courage.

Spain will concentrate further, with more foreign involvement and another European-scale size brewer will be created, but its principal focus will be on Spain as that market develops in lifestyle towards its EC counterparts. The other European national industries will change very little. There will be increased segmentation activity, with possibly some exciting new lifestyle beer products being developed. There is already an aphrodisiac beer being marketed in France. The major brands will still continue to dominate beer sales, but around them, niche brands will be introduced which may only have short life-cycles. Beer, in effect, will become like many other consumer goods.

The creation of the Single European Market in 1992 will create a period of confusion for approximately two years, till brewers calculate the impacts on them. For a few years, 1994–7, brewers will enjoy a halcyon period. They will have the benefit of supply agreements arranged before 1992, product will be easier to move across national boundaries, the gradual harmonisation of duties and sales taxes will lead to some small increase in beer consumption in countries which had previously been mature, European advertising through satellite communication will be possible and the strong brands will be further promoted.

However simultaneous with this halcyon period, there will be a growth in the effectiveness of anti-alcohol lobbies in influencing national governments and the European Commission, as they also formulate their reaction to 1992. This influence will grow until, in the last three years of the decade, advertising bans for alcohol will become prevalent across Europe, beer will only be saleable in returnable containers, drink-driving legislation will harmonise across

Europe at the strictest level, and supply agreements of the form which existed in the 1980s will be outlawed. In effect there will be a free market for the distribution and sale of beer across Europe. The power in the distribution chain will pass from the brewer to the retailer and the wholesaler.

An Explosion of German Euro-competitiveness   As the title of this scenario suggests, its main focus is on likely events in the 'new' Germany. The essence of the scenario is that one or more of the current larger West German brewing companies forces, at a rapid pace by West German brewing industry standards, a process of concentration. These larger brewing businesses would be able to overcome the inherent low profitability of the industry by lower costs, through higher economies of scale. They would need beer brands which are acceptable nationally in West Germany, but this trend is already developing. One German manager described it as follows: 'Today the first national products in Germany are beginning to appear, that will accelerate and then these products will for sure be European.' This process of concentration will be encouraged by the increasing power of the grocery retail chains. These chains are now beginning to develop international strategies, whereas previously they were mainly focused on their domestic market. A good example of this is Aldi, the West German supermarket group. Aldi has 2000 stores in West Germany; it also operates in Belgium, Holland and Austria; it is expanding its chain into France, Italy and the USA and has recently opened its first stores in the UK. They may well drag along with them the development of the German brewing industry.

Simultaneously, with the process of concentration, these growing West German companies will come to dominate the old East Germany. The combined output of the beer industries of the two Germanies will be 117 million hectolitres, almost twice the size of the second largest producing European country, the UK. Consumer tastes have not differed substantially since 1945, and much loyalty still exists in East Germany to the 'purity laws', facilitating the coming together of the two markets. This process of market 'annexation' can also be extended to other adjacent similar markets, such as Czechoslovakia, with the third highest rate of consumption in a 'new' Europe, and Austria and Hungary, which are both high consumption countries at over 100 hectolitres per capita per annum. It is not inconceivable that, as economies develop in Eastern Europe and disposable incomes rise, beer sales will increase. A restructured German brewing industry with increased economies of scale, and hence lower costs both in production and distribution due to their proximity to these 'new' markets, will be well placed to take advantage of these opportunities.

Whilst these events are taking place the German brewers could also further develop their activities in the EC. They have certain advantages which they could develop. There is a strong movement in Western Europe towards all things 'green'. This is particularly noticeable in foodstuffs, where the demand for organically produced food, i.e. those without any artificial additives, is growing rapidly. The German brewing process, adhering strictly as it does to the purity laws, could become a significant marketing advantage. The concept of having a totally 'green' meal, including the alcoholic beverage, bearing in mind that beer is a drink to accompany meals in many European countries, will have certain attractions.

Their other advantage, principally in the UK, is that many of the best-known lager brands are German. Post-1992, this position may be strengthened, if the German brewers change their licence agreements to brewing subcontracts. Lager will continue to grow in the UK and the Germans will possibly gain a significant proportion of the benefit.

The author believes that this scenario is feasible in the time-scale of the decade of the 1990s. West German managers, in other industries, have shown themselves to be more than adept as European and, indeed, global competitors. A trigger for the changes envisaged in this scenario could be the hiring, by a major brewery, of a chief executive from outside the brewing industry who has a track record of managing on a European or global basis and is not limited by the beliefs of the brewing industry.

This scenario could have far-reaching consequences for European brewers. If the Germans become as competitive as described in the above scenario then the landscape of the European brewing industry will be changed fundamentally with the emergence of some very powerful new competitors.

UK Brewers Get Their Act Together   At the time of writing (October 1990), the trigger for this scenario was in the hands of the British Secretary of State for Trade and Industry. On 21 August, he received from the Monopolies and Mergers Commission a report about the proposed swap of pubs for breweries between Courage, a subsidiary of Elders of Australia, and Grand Metropolitan. The length of time from receipt of the report to the announcement of the decision (long by normal standards) is a measure of the significance of the impact the proposed arrangement may have, not only on the UK brewing industry, but also on the European industry.

The essence of the proposed arrangement is that Courage would place its pubs in a joint venture with Grand Metropolitan pubs in return for their breweries and beer brands. The pub estate will be managed by Grand Metropolitan. The proposed swap will allow Courage to focus on brewing, and the marketing and development of strong beer brands. Grand Metropolitan will concentrate on retailing. A supply agreement will exist for Courage to provide beer to the pubs. The two companies had made commitments on the details of the proposed arrangement to comply with the requirements of the Monopolies and Mergers Commission Report into the UK brewing industry, published in March 1989. This included selling off a number of pubs and one brewery. If the UK government allows this deal to take place then a feasible scenario is that the UK brewing industry will be galvanised into a higher level of competitive activity, both in the UK and Europe.

Traditionally UK brewers have not needed to be very competitive. The tie, between breweries and pubs, and high degrees of vertical integration, have obviated the need for increased competition. Brewers have enjoyed more than respectable profits, and changes in competitors' market shares have happened only slowly. Consequently UK brewers have been very insular. The UK brewing industry only exports 2 percent of its output. There has been no need to develop overseas activities with high degrees of risk, which were unlikely to provide rates of return as good as were available from domestic operations. A significant proportion of lager sales, the growth sector of the British market, is of continental European origin, mainly brewed under licence in Britain. After 1992, when these licences come up for renewal, they are unlikely to be renewed in their present form. The European brewers may decide to supply Britain from their own breweries or convert the licences to production subcontracts. In either case, greater control of the distribution of popular lager brands will pass to the European brewers. The British brewers will have no alternative but to become more competitive. The only British brewers that own significant lager brands are Bass and Courage. Thus the push to become more competitive will fall mainly on them.

The 'new' Courage would operate on the same basis as the major European brewers. They would have an output equivalent to that of Carlsberg, although concentrated in the UK, and be one of the five largest brewing companies in Europe. In Fosters, they have one of the few potentially global beer brands. Elders top management have frequently talked, in public, about 'Fosterising' the world. It is inconceivable that if this swap is allowed Elders will not use Courage in the UK as the springboard for an assault on Europe. The 'new' Courage will have two of the critical success factors identified by the managers in the study, i.e. brewing economies of scale and strong brands. The only ingredient missing is access to distribution channels. These will be more easily obtainable post-1992, when the European market will be more open. Another potential route into mainland Europe could be by strategic alliances whereby, for example, a Spanish or Italian beer is distributed in the UK by Courage, in return for distribution of Fosters in Spain or Italy. Elders also has a reputation for developing by acquisition and this is also a possibility in Europe.

The new, more competitive, company would also have an impact on the UK market. Bass have been the market leader for many years with no real challenger to their supremacy. Although they are of a size to be Euro-competitive, they have chosen to focus their efforts mainly in the UK. Their current UK market share is 22 percent. The next largest market shares are Allied and Whitbreads with 13 percent each. If the proposed swap is allowed, Courage will have a market share of 18 percent. They will also have a very strong portfolio of beer brands. Without pubs they will be free to concentrate their competitive efforts on penetrating as many outlets as possible.

If the British government allow the creation of the 'new' Courage, the decision will have significant implications. It will create another British brewing company, capable of being Euro-competitive and with clear intentions of being that by competing more strongly and effectively in the UK and mainland Europe. This must have an impact on Bass. Can they afford not to compete more strenuously in the UK? Will they sit back and watch the 'new' Courage develop its activities in mainland Europe without following them? The result could be new levels of competition, previously unseen in the UK, and a twin attack on mainland Europe.

This chapter epitomises the paradox that exists in Europe at the start of the 1990s. On the one hand there is substantial and significant diversity in the structure and activities of the brewing industry, and in the managers' perception of the developments likely to occur during the 1990s. Europe, in 1990, has to be viewed as a series of multi-local beer markets, each with their own characteristics and idiosyncrasies, and not as one large and consistent market entity. On the other hand, there is much agreement about the future directions in which major strategic influences will shape the industry. Pan-European brands exist and are being further developed, and consistent market segments are developing across Europe.

In short, the landscape of the European brewing industry is likely to undergo many interesting changes and developments in the next ten years.

3

Retail Banking

Jenny Piesse

During the last few years, the financial services sector worldwide has focused a lot of attention and resources on their corporate business as opposed to their personal banking. In particular, the banks which have expanded internationally have done so by increasing their concentration on the wholesale money markets and taking advantage of the rapid growth of Eurocurrency instruments. Recently, however, these activities have lost their appeal, due to a new, more prudent attitude to risk on the part of investors, accompanied by an increasing awareness on behalf of the banks of the extremely small margins which can be earned in this way.

Thus the corporate business, which once appeared so glamorous, is now being overshadowed by the retail sector, which is seen to offer higher profitability and a more solid trading base on which to face the deregulated, and increasingly competitive, future.

We will begin by looking briefly at the present European banking sector, trying to put this into a global perspective, and identifying the key players, and then outline the legislative changes which will be implemented during the 1990s. The main part of the chapter then discusses the opinions of senior managers from a number of retail banks in several community countries about the future of their industry, including what changes they anticipate in the coming decade and how they expect their individual institutions will respond to these changes. Finally, we offer some personal thoughts about the pattern of retail banking in Europe, and highlight the important issues for the future of the industry.

The Structure of the European Retail Banking Sector

The problems of European retail banking in a deregulated environment were beautifully summed up by one of the French bankers in our interview sample:

> The average Frenchman perceives his banker to be a thief, like his insurance agent. This is possibly true. He also thinks that German and

English banks are best. This is not necessarily true. The danger is that our customers will put their savings in German or UK banks and we are left to mind the store, providing basic services for which the customer does not pay.

Retail banking systems exist in all countries for similar reasons. First, they provide a payments mechanism, which facilitates the transfer of wealth between individuals, and is essentially the bookkeeping role of banks.

Secondly, they supply a variety of financial services to their customers to support their deposit facilities and advanced credit operations. These include portfolio management products, maybe in the form of a unit trust or mutual fund, financial advice and mortgages.

Finally, banks are financial intermediaries. This function in its simplest form merely brings together borrowers and lenders but in addition absorbs the risk inherent in providing credit. They then allocate the returns on that risk to the deposit holders, in the form of fixed payments, with the residual being distributed to the shareholders of the bank. This intermediary function of banks has led to the development of huge information systems, both to enable careful screening and monitoring of potential borrowers, and to identify sources of available funds.

However, although these objectives are common to the vast majority of retail banks throughout the world, there are many differences in the way they approach their business, due to the specific traits of the individual institutions and contrasting national environments.

The development of the retail banking sector in Europe reflects the cultural variations and specific needs of the markets which it was established to serve. Most of the diversity is centred around two main characteristics: the type of institution (which includes to some degree its size) and the extent to which it is constrained by state regulation and supervision. We shall see that these same variables can account for many of the differences in opinion which exist between the contributing practitioners.

It may be helpful to look at these structural distinctions more closely, in order to put the comments of the managers in our study into perspective.

The Type of Institution
As suggested already, all countries have a payment system of some kind, which ensures a means of cheque verification and payment, usually built around a network of branches and administered by universal or multi-purpose banks. Every member of the European

Community has one or more national banks, but in addition there is a miscellany of banks aimed at a specific region, banks serving individual industry sectors (such as agriculture), savings banks and co-operative banks, mutuals and the so-called 'near-banks' (such as UK building societies). Some European banks are in the public sector, in particular in Germany, Denmark and Italy, where a large percentage is owned by government or local authorities. Efforts at privatisation are being made in these countries, but will take time to be completed.

State Regulation and Supervision
It is important here to differentiate between regulation and supervision, since while a large degree of deregulation will take effect with the implementation of EC legislation during the 1990s supervision will remain the responsibility of the national central banks (at least at present). Some countries, in particular the Netherlands and the UK, have functioned as liberal, open markets for some time, while others, including Spain and Italy, will remain highly regulated until they are forced to conform to the 1992 directives.

A related issue is the extent of state intervention in the banking sector. At one extreme there is direct state ownership such as in West Germany where almost half the banks are in the public sector, or in Italy where 80 percent of the banking system is owned by government or local authorities. At the other end of the spectrum are Holland and the UK. In the latter case, although all the banks are public limited companies, the government actively encouraged the merger movement of the 1960s and 1970s, which resulted in an oligopolistic, non-competitive structure.

So there is considerable variation in the structure of the industry and although some authors compare European banks as a sector with those in the United States or in Japan, it is a mistake to lump all the financial institutions in continental Europe together. It is exploring these differences between the countries of the European Community which is the essence of this chapter.

Key Players in the Industry
Identifying the key players in any industry is often done by ranking by asset value, and historically the asset base (deposits from customers) has been the most frequently used measure of bank size. However capitalisation (shareholders' funds) is now the established criterion and is the result of a change in the capital adequacy ruling set by the Bank of International Settlements in 1988. This is an attempt to reflect the underlying strength and stability of the institutions rather than simply the volume of deposits, and it represents a shift of emphasis in many banks from asset building for its own sake towards

Table 3.1   *Top ten European banks*

New Capital (shareholders' funds) $ billion		Old Size (assets) $ billion	
1 National Westminster UK	10.9	Credit Agricole, Paris	214.4
2 Barclays, London	10.5	Banque Nationale de Paris	197.0
3 Credit Agricole, Paris	8.7	Barclays, London	189.4
4 Union Bank of Switzerland	6.7	Credit Lyonnais	178.9
5 Deutsche Bank, Frankfurt	6.5	National Westminster	178.5
6 Swiss Bank Corp	6.1	Deutsche Bank, Frankfurt	170.8
7 Lloyds Bank, London	5.9	Group Ecureuil, Paris	150.3
8 Banque Nationale de Paris	5.6	Société Général, Paris	145.7
9 Midland Bank, London	5.5	Dresdner, Frankfurt	129.7
10 Credit Lyonnais, Paris	5.4	Paribas, Paris	121.6

Source: The Banker, July 1989.

Table 3.2   *Top ten world banks*

Capital (shareholders' funds) $ billion		Size (assets) $ billion	
1 National Westminster	10.9	Dai-Ichi Kangyo, Tokyo	352.5
2 Barclays, London	10.5	Sumitomo Bank, Osaka	334.7
3 Citicorp, New York	9.9	Fuji Bank, Tokyo	327.8
4 Fuji Bank, Tokyo	9.0	Mitsubishi Bank, Tokyo	317.8
5 Credit Agricole, Paris	8.7	Sanwa Bank, Tokyo	307.4
6 Sumotomo Bank, Osaka	8.6	Industrial Bank of Japan	261.5
7 Dai-Ichi Kangyo, Tokyo	8.5	Norinchukin Bank, Tokyo	231.7
8 Industrial Bank of Japan	8.2	Credit Agricole, Paris	214.4
9 Sanwa Bank, Tokyo	7.6	Tokai Bank, Nagoya	213.5
10 Mitsubishi Bank, Tokyo	6.3	Mitsubishi Trust, Toyko	206.0

Source: The Banker, July 1989.

off-balance sheet (things other than loans and deposits) fee-earning business. These new rules have been applied in respect to UK banks since 1989 and will be extended to all community countries by 1992. Table 3.1 shows the top ten banks in Europe, ranked with respect to both the new and the old criteria. A similar ranking, by both capital and asset size, of the top ten banks in the world, shows the extent to which non-European (in particular Japanese) banks dominate the sector.

As can be seen from Table 3.2, the Japanese banks are very strong in terms of asset-based rankings. This may be explained by their high presence in the capital markets, whereas European banks take a greater intermediary role, raising funds for industry. This is especially pronounced in countries such as Germany, France, Italy and Spain and has led to speculation that Europe is 'over-banked', a view which is supported by some of the practitioners. Certainly there are more banks per capita in Europe than in either the United States or Japan. There has been some cross-border merger activity in anticipation of the completion of the Single Market. Predators have included the Deutsche Bank, Credit Lyonnais and Midland. Others such as Commerzbank, Banco de Santander, the Royal Bank of Scotland and some of the Scandinavian banks have completed equity swaps to make former ties more concrete, but there have been fewer outright acquisitions. Savings bank federations have been active in consolidating co-operative arrangements for their members, but several of these institutions are constrained by legislation which has been in place for many years. For example, co-operatives worldwide have an agreement which limits competition among others in the movement.

There has been some internal merger activity, prompted by a wish to create stronger national groupings within each country, and as a defence against other predators. Defensive mergers of this sort have taken place in Spain, Italy and Denmark, for example.

Finally in this introductory section, it may be helpful to give a brief outline of the recent legislation passed by the European Commission relating to the financial sector, since this will affect the managers' strategic planning both with respect to their own institutions and the future of the industry as a whole.

Directive on Capital Movements

Restriction on capital movements has been largely eliminated by many countries independently over the last few years, and will be imposed on the rest of the European Community by 1992. Thus there will be an end to any form of exchange controls. This should make it possible for anyone to open a bank account anywhere in the Community, to obtain a loan from any bank in any member state and to invest in the most competitive marketplace wherever that might be. In addition, there will be no restriction on the actual transfer of capital and discrimination in the taxation of investors is forbidden.

The Second Banking Directive

Far and away the most important externally ordained set of changes are those enjoined by the famous Second Banking Directive. This has been promulgated by the European Commission and will achieve the force of law in member states in 1992. There are two components to this Directive, both of which have particular relevance to providers of retail banking services:

Single Banking Licence This enables any bank validly established and licensed in one member state (that is, its home country) to provide financial services in any other member state, either directly from home or through an overseas branch, without a further licence. Thus once a licence is granted, equivalent services can be offered in any other Community country.

Home Country Control and Reciprocity Banks providing services outside their home country will remain subject principally to their home country rules and control. This means they will be able to continue to provide the same range of services in host countries as they do in their home country. Consequently, if the home country rules are more liberal than those of the host, banks validly authorised in their home country may be able to offer certain services in the host country which are prohibited to that country's domestic banks. Equally, a licensed bank whose home country rules are restrictive will only be able to offer the services authorised by the home country licence, even though the host country rules are more liberal.

The rules relating to non-Community banks enable those which are already established to continue, and to enjoy the benefits of the single banking licence granted by the Directive, but only if they are subsidiaries with their head office in a member country. If they are simply branches, they can continue their existing business, but will not be allowed to take advantage of additional expansion throughout the community.

Reflections on Retail Banking in the 1990s

Defining the Market
One aspect of retail banking which is common across all the countries represented in our study is the definition of their market: banking for the individual, for the family and the small business venture. However, within this definition, various markets are emerging, delineated by different income groups such as blue- and white-collar workers, and demographic changes such as the increasing number of older people in the Community.

This idea of the market for retail financial services being something which can be segmented has great appeal to the retail banks and in many cases forms the basis for their strategy on marketing, servicing and even pricing. The banks' response has been to identify specific groups and then either choose a subset to focus on – the niche market model – if they are a small or specialist bank, or divide the whole customer base into groups and treat each group as though it were an separate business if they are a national bank.

Examples of market segmentation are scattered throughout our sample. Some of the Danish and the French banks, for example, have divided their customers into categories; those receiving special treatment because of the volume of their business at the bank and the type of products they require (approximately, high net worth individuals); those who require regular service from the bank, although with a smaller volume of funds; and those who need no personal contact with their bank, and can do their banking business by machine. These banks identify another group which, if not actually discouraged, is known to make a negative contribution to the bank – that is to say, they are time-consuming, they demand many transactions, yet they have only small accounts. One Danish bank in our sample claims the size of these groups is 20, 40, 30, and 10 percent respectively. They are obviously concerned about the 30 and the 10 percent.

Banks in the Netherlands face a market which is already segmented, due to some extent to historical accident. During the 1960s salaries began to be paid into personal accounts, and since the state-owned Postbank had a national network of branches in the form of the post office network, customers who needed nothing more sophisticated than simple transactions opened an account there. Only those wishing other services would open a second account elsewhere. This has resulted in a market share for the private banks of only 65 percent, but which is made up of middle- and high-income customers. This positive bias towards higher potential margins is not lost on other Community institutions.

Market segmentation is possible because of better information systems, but they are still far from complete in some countries. The manager of one of our German banks explained:

> The difficulty arises when you have identified a customer as being in a particular age group and income category. You know they are interesting to you, since they are not constrained by the cost of buying a house or other debts, but have a high income which is at their disposal for the creation of assets.

> But we do not know about the personal circumstances of the client, since the information systems are not oriented towards that, and we, as a bank, have not taken the trouble to get to know the client, although they have had an account with us for many years. We must have a closer relationship with our customers, and anticipate their needs.

This illustrates a common attitude on the part of the bankers we talked to. Market segmentation is a tool, a method of learning more about the client so that an effective strategy can be developed to attract and keep the right customers. The German manager quoted above also argued that: 'We have to develop product strategies, product innovations with the individual customer segments in mind', and this point was reiterated by an Italian banker, who asserted: 'We must use this information to offer our customers an appropriate mix of banking services.'

Many banks use demographic information from the general population, rather than just their current customer data, to increase their client base. The big UK clearing banks for instance aim to get young account holders, offering financial incentives to students in the hope that they will be big earners in the future and aware of past evidence of British loyalty to their bank. Others (TSB in Britain, for example) acknowledge that historically their client base is biased towards lower income, working people and offer products and services which will appeal to that group. One of the Italian savings banks in our study tries to attract both young people, again hoping for customer loyalty, and married women, since they control the family budget. The French aim to use the market segmentation to improve their marketing, an area they consider one of their weak points: 'Our problem is less the nature of the product, rather the sales capacity. I think French banks are at a disadvantage in marketing and commerce' (executive, French bank).

Successfully identifying and exploiting a niche market is, for many banks, the preferred strategy with which to face the increasing competition at home and to provide a product with which to enter other Community countries. This may also provide the justification for developing a product for which there is an inadequate domestic market, but which may be viable internationally. For instance, in the Netherlands the banking sector is very liberal, there is a lot of competition, and margins are small. Entering new markets with a speciality product may be the solution for the Dutch banker:

> In my opinion, if you want to sell a specialist product which would appeal to high net worth individuals, you cannot do as Coutts does in England, the Dutch market is too small. But if you identify for yourself a nice market segment you could offer that product all over Europe, and that will achieve the scale you need to justify your investment.

A niche product that can be exported is attractive, but the information which highlighted the existence of a potentially receptive market can also be used to test foreign opportunities. Direct marketing is probably the least risky way to approach international markets, and is a current concern to, for example, one of the Danish banks:

> Direct marketing is a way that foreign banks can target the Danish market. If, say, a German bank picked the Copenhagen area and identified high

income individuals, they could offer them cheap loans, foreign investments or attractive savings arrangements. But they would have to have the right image, a suitable profile to attract people's money.

If used carefully this direct marketing, typically in the form of 'mail shots', can be beneficial. But it is possible for this technique to go wrong. For example, one of our French banks which undertook a direct marketing campaign did not define the target audience precisely enough. The response rate was 0.2 percent, whereas the breakeven point was a response rate of 1.5 percent – an expensive exercise. Or again, one of the British organisations sent piggy banks to encourage young savers to a customer set that included old age pensioners!

Segmenting the market to identify customer groups is often the most effective way for small or specialist banks to compete, but managers of the large institutions that already have a national network may have different ideas. They may prefer to concentrate on particular products, those which they know best, while still offering the full range of retail banking services. The deputy chief executive of one of the UK clearing banks assesses the strength of his bank: 'The clearing banks are about lending money, that's the skill they have. They make good credit decisions and that's a good market. It has better margins, because you are paying for knowledge.' But they also need to concentrate in the markets they know best, and he comments on less successful operations abroad: 'We did not know the business. We are not unimaginative, but in the 1990s we need to fundamentally change our service position, and deal with customers we really understand. I don't want to compete with Société Général in Lyon for the French market.'

Others, while being confident they have a competitive advantage in their home market, find this very restricting in an international context. The UK's Abbey National converted from a building society to a bank in 1989 for domestic reasons unconnected with the coming Single European Market (1992). But increasing their European presence will not be straightforward: 'Our skills and expertise lie in the mortgage market, which in Europe is rather idiosyncratic. Housing systems and housing finance is locally developed and tastes reflect social history, things which are not just economics.'

Defining the Business
A topic which generates more controversy than simply defining the market is a description of the business. As a consequence of this, the bankers in our study presented a variety of views not only on what products should be offered to the customer and the way these products should be delivered, but also on the nature of the competition.

Responding to the Customer

All participants agreed that the character of the retail bank has undergone considerable change. Banks in some countries such as the UK and the Netherlands are already facing liberalised financial markets, and have been exposed to increased competition, and thus lower margins, for some time. But others that have not yet been subject to deregulation to the same degree, for example those in Denmark and Spain, are only just beginning to find their traditional role challenged by an increasingly sophisticated consumer. One Italian banker described what he called an 'increasing financial culture', where customers are demanding automated services, and this in a society where the Central Bank must give permission for a new branch to be opened. Markets all over Europe are now seen to be customer led, rather than supply driven as they were in the past.

The common response to this new consumer demand has been twofold. First it has led to the development of an entirely new relationship between the retail bank and its customer, with the banks acknowledging themselves as being predominantly a service industry and where the quality of that service will give them a competitive edge. Secondly it has resulted in the creation of a vast range of innovative products which have not traditionally been provided by banks.

This new relationship between bank and customer has demanded new buildings in which to conduct business. Traditionally, the contact between bank and customer was through the branch. This was seen as the centre of bank activity, and the number of branches a bank had in a particular region was an indication of its importance in that region. But attitudes towards the bank branch are changing. In France, the branch network is still one of the perceived strengths of retail banking; in the UK it is a millstone around the bank's neck. For Italy there are marked regional differences within the country itself, with modular branches (small, and staffed by only three or four relative juniors) the solution in rural areas, whereas in the cities, customers will accept a high degree of technology in the branch, or a combination of the two, as one manager suggested, 'a fully automated "self-service" area on the ground floor and a "boutique" on the first floor' (Italian banker). However, being aware of the demographic mix of local business is crucial, as one cautious Italian manager notes: 'We must bear in mind how many elderly customers love the collection of their pension. They crowd outside the office every two months from early morning to tell each other stories – it is a social event.'

A consensus view is that proximity to the customer is paramount, although in some situations the network was so inefficient that it imposed a huge burden on the institutions in terms of cost. When this issue was explored it appeared that much of the rationalisation proposed by the banks was in this area. One Spanish bank had five branches in a rural community of 6000 people – evidence of over-branching in Spain, if not over-banking. Equally, a London clearing bank has 27 branches in the City of London – clearly a situation in need of urgent revision!

Some banks are more innovative in their attempts to keep in contact with their customers in quite straightforward ways, staying open in the evenings and weekends in communities where the population commute to town during the day, and going for locations in sites which are more accessible, such as shopping precincts, rather than the traditional centre of the business district. 'Put the banks where the people are, and open when they want them', says the Midland. Responding to community needs leads one French banker to say: 'Banking networks were conceived 30 years ago, but now country villages will reduce their economic activity and the banks will follow.'

More innovative attempts to offer a convenient service to customers are the various forms of home banking. An example of the simplest form is the Midland Bank's subsidiary, called First Direct, which is a telephone service. True home banking, where the customer has a terminal outlet connected to the bank's system, is being developed, primarily in France, although the investment costs are prohibitive.

The market segmentation and customer analysis already discussed has made it possible for banks to employ a tiered approach to customer service, offering a mixture of some fully automated, some personal and some home banking. However, not only the customer has to adapt to these changes, even if they are desirable ones, but these changes also have work, training and recruitment implications for staff.

Many managers discussed the changes in attitudes towards employees. The somewhat feudal relationship between banking officers in the branches and senior management is fast being eroded, and the value of the staff is now being recognised. Career structure and training are important to the majority of bankers in the study. Until recently, the 'dead man's shoes' model of career development was the norm, with few incentives for imagination or performance, although performance-related salary is still resisted by the unions in some countries. Some banks, however, still face problems, noted by an Italian manager: 'Senior executives move around, they expect this to advance their careers. More junior staff are reluctant to disrupt their families. Also women, they pass the exams, and are excellent at client liaison, but will not travel for long periods.' Again, staff with special knowledge of a particular region are important in some EC countries where cultural variations are very pronounced, such as France and Spain, where even language may be local to the area. Hiring and training have received considerable attention. While some countries, for example Italy, are constrained by legal requirements and by the unions in their hiring practices, higher educational standards are demanded throughout the Community. Many banks are increasing the proportion of graduates on their staff, and those that do not at least offer training programmes and staff development in-house. Hiring practices have become less rigid and senior staff are brought in from outside the bank. Some banks, such as those in Germany, have personnel strategies which involve training from entry to the bank, first in product knowledge and interactions with clients and then in sales, marketing and management techniques. The increased importance of client contact has led to a new professionalism in retail banking which some banks see as crucial to their success.

Two areas which are particularly important in the training programmes are information technology and languages. Furthermore, the huge investment in technology has produced a need for staff who are familiar with the systems. This is important both in a front office capacity to assist customers in the semi-automated branches to access account information and carry out transactions, and in the back office as systems specialists where operations are highly automated.

Banks with international operations, or those that aspire to them, recognise the need for foreign languages and experience for their staff. One German banker states: 'We attach great importance to the combination of languages and professional experience in a specific country in which an activity is planned or already undertaken. We prepare our workers well for their employment abroad.'

While determining how to respond to the present-day customer, retail banks have reviewed the concept of the branch, its location, the form it took, and the staff within it. They have also developed a range of new products, either led by client demand or by anticipating that demand. Two reasons for the existence of a bank are money transmission and the provision of deposit and credit facilities. The payments systems, although of no interest to customers until they go wrong, have nonetheless been the cause of enormous capital expenditure to the banks. A huge investment has been made in technology by financial institutions in all the Community countries in the last few years, and many managers speculate that the front office will be entirely dedicated to sales and advice while the back office contains an automated payments system.

One Italian co-operative bank has been able to expand its network by opening many small branches, with three to four employees, linked to head office by computer. Unlike the UK, where employees state which institution should receive their salary, Italian banks rely strongly on relationships with local employers to manage the wages and salaries, and will compete for a company account. Italian companies pay into a single bank, which forces all employees to have an account there. One particular bank found their automatic payments system very satisfactory: 'We have a system which receives all the employees' salaries and also pays all their bills, utilities, pensions, insurance, etc. This would burden the customer, but we can ensure all this is done automatically' (bank executive, Italy). But some managers think insufficient importance is attached to the technology employed by the banks relative to its cost, illustrated by a comment from Germany: 'Thirty years ago technology was new, and was viewed as electronic data processing, only used as an accounting tool. It has moved a long way since then, but still senior management does not think technologically. You will hardly find a systems expert on the board of any bank.'

The distinction between a money transfer system and the provision of other banking services to the public is now growing very thin. For example, the innovation in the accounting process which was developed to increase the efficiency of the payments system has become a product which is available to customers. Automatic teller machines which give account information and facilitate cash withdrawal are one of the services extended to customers. Most were enthusiastic about this sort of product, except one of the Dutch bankers who had reservations. He claimed his countrymen were by nature somewhat sceptical – 'what's that, new tricks from banks', although they soon discovered the convenience of a 24-hour service.

One barrier to the use of technology-based products is the fear of fraud or breaches of security. Many countries, Denmark and the Netherlands in particular, have powerful consumer organisations which promote high standards of safety and protection. Customers who are reluctant to conduct their financial business at a machine in public may speed the development and introduction of home banking. A note of caution is offered by one of the Spanish bankers who applaudes the innovations in the process of banking, but does not want to lose contact with the customer: 'Technological innovations suppressing the personal contact would be bad for our culture. Clients need a close relationship with their banker, not with a machine.'

Another product which is a direct result of technology in information systems and automatic payment is the credit card, which is, in the words of a French manager, 'an indispensable accessory nowadays'.

The type of credit cards varies across the sample countries. The UK issues debit and credit cards, with increasingly a charge for the latter. The Dutch banks issue a more sophisticated one which is a Eurocard on one side and a bank card on the other, with one bank claiming a competitive edge by allowing customers to change their identification numbers if they wish. The French produce smart cards, and claim they are superior to any other, while the Italians have issued cards jointly with other banks to share the risk and the cost.

But while credit cards exist in all the community countries, the cultural background and attitudes of nationals will dictate the extent of their use, and it is a form of credit which worries both the bankers and their clients. An Italian bank has found that the use of a credit card has worried their older customers, who will not use it even to withdraw their own money from the machine, whereas the card was used as a marketing tool to attract young customers. The British are very happy with credit, regardless of the cost, and can freely acquire what amounts to a negotiated loan in, say, Italy or Spain, simply by using their card up to its credit limit.

The acquisition of cash on deposit, and loans for consumer goods, cars and houses are traditional banking services, but insurance, pensions and especially non-financial products such as consultancy and tax advice are not. But these are increasingly being sold in institutions throughout the Community because customers demand them, and they are encouraged by the banks which need to make higher margins somehow. Fee-earning activities have been one of the most profitable parts of the business for some time in countries where increased competition has lowered spreads on loans and deposits. 'The role of the consultant will increase in the banking sector', claims one French banker, 'and it is one area which cannot be replaced with a robot'. This has implications for the selection and training of staff, and their skill in face-to-face dealing with customers.

Some of the products which are non-traditional to retail banks, such as insurance and pensions, are nevertheless suitable for distribution via a network, which is something the banks do have. But some bankers question whether customers want to buy insurance from a bank. The deputy chief executive of the Midland is one of the doubtful ones: 'Does the ideal of the "financial services institution" extend the boundaries of the product, since everyone is not going to buy everything from the same organisation, however much you, the banker, would like them to?'

A more congenial solution would be an alliance with an insurance company, or a joint venture such as that between Midland Bank and Commercial Union, or a state-owned Italian bank with Hambros in the UK, where the bank only distributes policies, and leaves the underwriting to the insurance company. But in Germany the idea of a single institution offering all services is attractive: 'Private clients will surely prefer to deal with one person, a personal banker, who will offer mortgages, insurance and banking services. Universal banks can meet this need, and the overall financing business will take the lead in the 1990s' (banking executive, Germany).

Finally, one group of products which banks are now offering is centred around the provision of information. Banks have always generated information for their own internal use, for example data on which to make credit decisions and evaluate risk, but with the public their dealings were primarily with money and money supply. Now they find they are required not just to provide money, but to provide information about money.

Responding to the Competition

Awareness and respect for the competition is crucial in any business, and banking is no exception, but the changing demands of customers, accompanied by new legislation and deregulation, have caused more apprehension in this industry than in most. Many of the products now offered by banks, such as mortgages, insurance and credit cards, are a direct response to their competitors. For instance, British banks, worried by the losses made by loans to the Third World, turned to lending in the domestic market and started to enter the lucrative mortgage business. Not surprisingly the building societies replied by offering banking services.

Competition from non-financial institutions such as retailers has existed in some countries for a while. In Britain, Marks and Spencer have operated a financial services division for many years, which is seen as a threat by some of the banks. As the European Development Manager of one British bank put it: 'They have a huge and loyal customer base, and no branch network to maintain since they have stores already in place, and a reputation for reliability. They are underestimated by the clearing banks.' In Italy there are also threats from retailers, and the banks are countering that by joint agreement with companies such as car distributors or furniture manufacturers to tie the consumer to that bank. This strategy of approaching the firm, both as supplier and employer, contributes to their success.

Other non-traditional competitors which are proving to be more of a concern to retail banks are the suppliers of information. This is due to their size and strength in the market in their own right, and also to the nature of their expertise. Their networks are already in place, and in most cases impossible to duplicate. One Dutch banker aware of the opposition said: 'The suppliers of networks, soft and hardware systems can arrange mutual linkages between companies to provide them with information directly. Those with these networks in place in the market are Wang, IBM and General Electric. Few can compete with them.' The same manager had concerns about companies such as Dun and Bradstreet 'supplying information about credit and credit risk'. This was previously the realm of the banks.

But the threat is not only from other domestic financial institutions. Retail banks in Europe are currently faced with competition from the financial and non-financial organisations in their home markets and will increasingly encounter international players too. Competition from foreign sources seems to be considered less of a threat for the small, regional banks than for the large national ones. The specific knowledge and expertise required to succeed on a local level is thought to be a sufficient barrier to entry, even though there will be no tangible legislation to prevent new entrants.

Direct entry by a foreign competitor, who sets up a branch network which duplicates their operations at home, is a very remote possibility in the view of all the bankers in the study. If competitors do aim for that kind of presence, they will do it by acquisition. One Danish banker states: 'If a foreign bank should be interested in the Danish market, they will simply buy a Danish bank. No foreign banks will establish themselves as retail banks in Denmark.' In Spain, it is also unlikely – 'there is not room in Spain for other networks' – and the French think the cost would be a deterrent.

But if there is general consensus about the non-appearance of foreign institutions starting from scratch on a national level, there is fear of predators. The smaller national banks, such as the TSB in Britain, know their branch networks are very attractive to large institutions which want to buy a retail banking operation outright. The greatest threat is from the large European banks, particularly French and German which are highly capitalised, and American and (especially) Japanese banks with their large asset base. This fear is compounded by the removal of the protection offered by many central banks which has been a shield to acquisition in the past. Protection from government has also meant that bank failures are very rare, although they are commonplace in the United States. In Germany regulation exists which prevents a bank from disappearing totally, and facilitates a takeover by another institution, so that it continues, maybe in a slightly changed form. One German banker speculated that many co-operative and savings banks may merge or operate in syndicates or networks, and thus consolidated, be large enough to be protected against predators.

It is of some comfort to the vulnerable that hostile acquisitions are rarely a success in what is essentially a service industry. In most organisations, the technology is the same and the products are the same. The value added is found in the quality of the staff, their specialised local knowledge and the management team, and if a hostile bid drives them away, the bank loses a large part of its value.

Along with the deregulation which will have to take place to comply with EC Directives, many governments may have to relax their own rules. For example, Danish legislation was strict in the past to discourage 'adventurous expansion' and puts many constraints on the activities open to banks. Other countries, such as Germany, allow banks to venture into more risky projects through subsidiaries, and also to have a decisive influence on industry via the companies in which they have equity holdings, although it was suggested that legislation may be introduced to change this. Conversely, the French view is that bank involvement with industry will increase in their country.

One way to defend against the threat of acquisition is to consolidate domestic market share. This is the route one of the British institutions is taking: 'We will protect our market position in the UK, and expand gradually in Europe, taking our specialist expertise to countries like Spain, Italy and France, but it is the risk to our UK base which is the major concern.' A Dutch bank has a similar strategy: 'Being big is important to keep down costs and maintain position in the market. Growing larger, maybe through merger, beats the competition.'

Another way is through alliances and agreements of various kinds, some with equity swaps, some much less formal. One French bank sees some value in alliances between banks which are similar: 'A regional bank like ours does not intend to join a bank based in an English, German or Italian city. We want bilateral relations with complementary banks, maybe sell their products and they sell ours. We understand each other's clients better, even though they are in different countries.' Some obvious partnerships may be formed among the co-operatives. If they can reconcile language difficulties they may make good partners, operationally they are similar, and a common corporate ethos exists between them.

Whereas alliances and agreements may be preferable to loss of control through a takeover, some doubts are expressed about the future of such agreements. One Italian bank feared that once the foreign partner had learned the product and the business, they would sever the relationship and take market share themselves.

Internal mergers are now more likely, and to some countries this has meant a radical change in attitude. While the UK government encouraged the mergers of the 1960s, a merger in Denmark even five years ago would have been blocked by political pressure. In order to retain national control of the financial sector, the Danish 'small is beautiful' attitude has been reversed.

Different organisational cultures may exist, and be a stumbling-block to the success of the merger, and the period after a merger is when the new organisation is most vulnerable – a lot of management attention is given to making it work, rather than keeping an eye on the competition. However, mergers between retail banks in different member countries are not likely, according to the manager of a large French bank: 'I think retail banking must be done at home, not in other countries. On the other hand associations between retail banks can be established, but not with the aim of doing retail banking in each other's country. The ones that have tried it have failed. Mergers within a country are very likely.'

On an optimistic note, opportunities are seen in the deregulation of Europe, and many banks had already made considerable investments in other countries. 'Providing a link for clients with business interests abroad' is a rationale put forward by some institutions, but the traditional correspondent banking relationships have proved adequate in the past. Most choose to use a preferred product or service in which they felt they had some comparative advantage, or pursue a niche market. A German bank which has interests in several member countries decided to enter via its specialisation:

> We already have market strength in two areas, investment management and mortgages. The ways we plan to expand will vary, some joint ventures, co-operations with partners who are already in the market or new businesses. In Great Britain we have a mortgage subsidiary and in Spain we have a partner. In this latter case, we provide the capital and the Spanish have knowledge of the construction industry.

One Dutch banker warns of the dangers of approaching Europe as though it was homogeneous:

> Cultural differences are underestimated. Everyone speaks of Europe, but there are different languages, different customs, which will not change very fast if at all. So enterprises and banks which think that in 1992 uniformity will be installed from one day to another will have a rude awakening. Government interference will disappear, but attitudes cannot change quickly.

Finally, in discussions about new business opportunities and areas of business expansion, none of the participants failed to mention the countries of Eastern Europe, which was described as a potentially profitable market but one which has considerable risk attached to it. Certain countries in this group are more attractive than others, for cultural and economic reasons. In some countries there has been a high propensity to save, since employment rates are high, and there have been shortages of goods to spend money on, and if this continued the demand for saving and investment products would be high. But this combination looks unlikely to last for very long.

Certainly the former East Germans have shown less enthusiasm for consumption than many westerners expected, but on the other hand employment levels have already fallen and will almost certainly continue to do so.

There is already a need for basic banking services, payments systems, deposit mechanisms and credit facilities, and at the corporate level this already exists. Most of the large European banks are represented in Eastern Europe, particularly in East Germany and Hungary, but the retail sector is still largely a cash economy and it takes a long time to establish a cheque-clearing mechanism. Many small banks are resigned to observe the national banks of Germany, France and maybe the UK positioning themselves to take on the risk and exploit the opportunities, although approving the concept of a stable personal banking system in these countries.

There is a social dimension too in this support of the new democracies. A Spanish banker showed his concern – 'we must help these countries to increase their standard of living' – although this is tinged with doubts about the effect these changes will have on the poorer countries of the community. A French manager was wary about too close an involvement although sympathetic to the situation, and wanting to look at each country individually: 'There are considerable risks for banks in the Eastern European countries, and I would be cautious. Some countries have structured economies like Czechoslovakia, but others like Poland and Romania have difficulties. I think we must help them, but we must be very careful in granting credit to them.'

Some countries of the old Eastern Bloc do not appear to offer much incentive for new entrants, although the brave predators may find some bargains when the state institutions are disposed of. The new entrepreneurial spirit may create a need for small business advisory services, but the lending, insurance and mortgage business may take a while to develop. The west may have to accept that people need time to become acquisitive!

Conclusion

Two topics which dominated the discussions with managers in all the countries in the study were the competitive advantage gained from offering superior service to the customer, and the importance of technology to the success of the organisation. It may be interesting to examine these issues from an overall European perspective.

Retail banking is an industry which offers a fairly well-defined set of products concerned either with money or information relating to it. As in many other sectors where the output is fairly homogeneous, competitive advantage has to be created by product differentiation either through price, packaging, delivery or service. But until relatively recently, the banking community appeared not to have recognised this.

A common theme throughout this study is the power of the client, who is described by some as sophisticated, by some as demanding, by some as discriminating and even by some as capricious. However, to an interested observer this represents the gratifying conclusion that the customer for banking services has now matured as a consumer. I would like to suggest, however, that this transformation has occurred not because of any change in the nature of the client, but as a result of deregulation and a trend towards liberalised financial markets which have given the customer the opportunity to be discerning, and have forced the banks to reconsider their business practices. Now that they are operating in a competitive economic environment, the suppliers of financial services have been forced to consider their market very carefully, in order to maintain their profitability. This has led them to think about the demographic and economic structure of the population, and to ask their customers what they really want from their bank.

The results have been interesting and may be a surprise to some. However, the Italian bankers who are concerned at the low uptake of credit cards probably have much in common with other sectors of Italian industry that find conservatism among their customers. Equally, British banks which found that their customers' response to charges on credit cards or zero interest on current accounts was to change to a competitor, would find that other industries face the same price sensitivity. Retail banking is now simply another service industry, one which requires specialist skills and professionalism, but one which must aim to serve customers well, or they will go away.

The new market information has highlighted the concept of the niche market and this appeals to many European banks. The problem is that they have almost universally identified their target segment to be high-wealth individuals! Certainly the demographics show us that the population is getting older, and there are changes in the income distribution in many countries. Germany increasingly has an older, wealthy population, with the obvious consequence being a number of youthful wealthy beneficiaries. The rapid inflation in property values in the UK over the last decade has resulted in a class of inheritors who would in previous generations not have had such a windfall gain. In Spain and Italy, an increase in the standard of living, and salary increases, has produced a wealthier population.

But is this niche sufficiently large for all the players in the industry to base their future profits in this segment? Historically the private banks have catered to very wealthy individuals, offering products which are more representative of a wholesale rather than a retail division, where they take advantage of off-shore investment facilities and tax shelters. But this is a very limited market and not one which is easily penetrated. The recently wealthy tend to be new consumers rather than new investors, and will not immediately embrace the investment products offered. The demand for advisory services may be there, particularly in the small business area, but the fee structure must be competitive.

Technology is the other issue of general concern. The widespread use of technology in the banking sector was motivated by a need to increase efficiency and reduce costs and to increase the level of service to the customer. Certainly it has achieved a higher level of efficiency throughout the industry, but whether it has resulted in a reduction in costs is open to debate. The difficulty in defining precisely the return on investment in technology has made managers increasingly uneasy, and there is some evidence that investment appraisal is less rigorous in these projects than in others. Technological investment can be justified if it is successfully managed and fully utilised. Economies of scale in terms of decreased unit costs, and economies of scope in terms of synergy in product distribution, can make a real contribution to profitability, but not if the systems are limited simply to storing accounting information.

Traditionally the development costs of a new product are passed on to the consumer, but this has proved very difficult in such a competitive industry as banking. An important industry difference is that new product innovation in banking does not allow for any long-term advantage, since all innovations can be copied and none patented, and this can be the case for technology-based products too. The solution has been joint development and thus shared costs. The major national banks with a large corporate customer base have been able to achieve an advantage in automated systems since profits from wholesale operations have funded the investment in technology for the bank as a whole. Smaller banks, or those wholly dedicated to retail, are less fortunate.

The need to spread the cost has led to several alliances being formed between Community banks based on delivery systems and networks, such as credit card operations, and this has provided an opportunity for international expansion which would not otherwise be possible. It could prove that for some banks the disastrously high costs of installing technology may in the long term be recovered by activity in new markets which they could not reach in any other way.

This study has shown that the dissimilarities identified by the managers interviewed are not a function of the sector itself, but of the cultural variations in the customers and communities they serve. Complementary management styles are essential. This implies that knowledge of the customer is crucial, and cultural differences across Europe have to be respected. These differences present intangible barriers which are less easy to remove than the legislative ones, which are fast disappearing. An awareness of the individual customer, and a careful and balanced approach to technology, will be beneficial to the consumer, the shareholder and those employed in the retail banking sector.

4

Book Publishing

Alessandro Sinatra and Paola Dubini

In this chapter we will examine the European book publishing sector. Until the last decade or so, the main business of the industry was restricted to a small number of activities. A publisher produced books and perhaps academic journals which were sold either through bookstores or to libraries, or magazines and newspapers which were sold in shops or at bookstands in the street. The only medium was the printed word, and the size of the market was constrained by literacy levels in any given country. The international perspective was limited with language an enormous barrier, both restricting exports and providing protection against the import of books. Thus any international trade which did take place was confined to markets in those countries sharing a common language.

But changes in the last few years have drastically altered the shape of the industry as a whole. The range of activities in the publishing sector has been extended in two separate ways. First, innovation has transformed publishing, largely due to technological change in both the products offered and the process itself. This can be illustrated by the move from purely printed matter to on-line text and computer readable material, which is now established as accepted practice both as input from authors and sold as output to the consumer. Secondly, publishing companies have moved into other areas of the communication industry. This can be seen by an expansion into media products such as cable television, and in the supply of information. This latter aspect of the business originated in the area of financial information, but has grown to include data of all kinds, both qualitative and quantitative. Databases of text are now common, as well as on-line search procedures and the retrieval of information from a number of sources and in a variety of forms.

So it in this climate of expansion and diversity that we have attempted to analyse the view of senior managers in the industry, trying to confine the discussion to that subset which is directly concerned with book publishing, although conscious that in some cases the other businesses impinge on the organisational, and certainly the financial, structure of the firm.

We start by identifying the main players in the sector, concentrating particularly on those which are European in origin. This inevitably leads us to stray from the narrow definition of book publishing, since the largest organisations are those which have interests in the other areas of global communication already outlined. There are also many examples of consolidation within the industry, and this has led to companies which are less known for their book publishing to feature at the top of an industry-wide list in terms of turnover/asset value.

The next section groups the companies into three categories. This enables us to identify the common features as well as the differences, since the responses within each group are quite similar.

We then go on to discuss the frequently occurring themes brought out in the interviews and to highlight the complementary features of book publishing which exist in many countries in the Community. Some divergence exists across the sector although these differences are few and generally arise from the perception of the threats and the attitude to the opportunities created by the increasingly global nature of the industry and the Single European Market.

Finally, we draw some conclusions about the overall structure of the book publishing industry, the growth trends within it and the nature of its response to the changing demands of an international market in the next decade.

Structure of the Industry

The large players in the areas are not easy to define, because of the overlap of interests into the fields of communication and media, as well as publishing in the narrow sense, but Table 4.1 will give some idea. The figures given attempt to exclude printing and represent only that part of the turnover arising from publishing.

Within the sector there is a growing trend of cross-border operations of international companies. In consumer books Bertelsmann in Germany has made several alliances, as has Murdoch with Harper & Row, and Hachette with Groiler. In education and professional books there is Maxwell with Macmillan, and Pearson with Addison-Wesley. A graphical illustration of the publishing sector of the industry looks something like Figure 4.1, although there are many overlaps.

The top two quadrants illustrate products of the publishing industry which are delivered in the traditional printed form, although they do include the extended range of speciality and business and professional literature. The lower two quadrants show the increase in the type of delivery mechanisms available, from on-line search to

Table 4.1   *Worldwide top 20 publishers*

	Total publishing sales £m	Publishing as % total sales
1 Bertelsmann (Germany)	3100	85
2 News Corporation (US)	2067	60
3 Times Mirror (US)	1816	86
4 Thomson (Canada)	1712	57
5 Time Inc (US)	1692	59
6 Gani ett (US)	1648	78
7 Dun and Bradstreet (US)	1465	54
8 Knight Rider (US)	1324	100
9 Hachette (France)	1311	57
10 Reed International (UK)	1251	80
11 New York Times (US)	1036	96
12 Dow Jones (US)	1019	100
13 Reuters (UK)	1003	100
14 MCC OAG Macmillan (UK)	924	54
15 Springer (Germany)	895	100
16 McGraw-Hill (US)	887	77
17 Washington Post (US)	870	100
18 Pearson (UK)	822	69
19 Paramount (US)	759	23
20 United Newspapers (UK)	740	98

Source: Financial Times

global satellite reception. On the other dimension, the left side of the diagram shows the traditional products of the sector, and on the right the move into entertainment and media activity.

Many of the companies in our study are not involved in more than

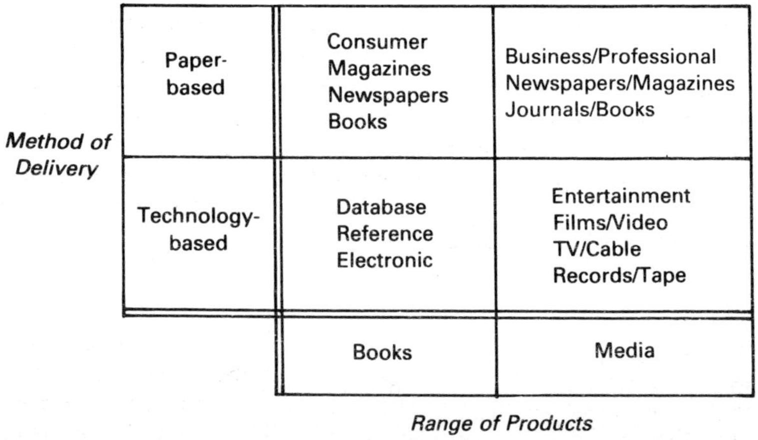

Method of Delivery		Consumer Magazines Newspapers Books	Business/Professional Newspapers/Magazines Journals/Books
	Paper-based		
	Technology-based	Database Reference Electronic	Entertainment Films/Video TV/Cable Records/Tape
		Books	Media

Range of Products

Figure 4.1   *Publishing sector*

one of these divisions. Some are involved in them all. The respondents therefore speak from very different viewpoints, and are inevitably influenced by their own company culture and trends in the industry as a whole.

Company Classifications

Since the publishing industry, and therefore our sample within it, is made up of many different types of firm, it is useful to divide them into groups. Of course, the characteristics common to the industry cross the boundaries of these groups, and it is the differences between them which emphasise their membership of one group rather than another. The companies fall into a pattern which can be summarised in the following way:

Specialist
These companies are those which are known for a particular type of publishing, by subject, or perhaps by market. They have focused their strategy on the selection of one or more specialised fields and are aiming at worldwide circulation in a particular subject. In these cases, the degree of diffusion of the subject defines the size of the market. One example is a Dutch firm, a representative of which observed: 'Our scale cannot be rapidly enlarged by big projects. We depend on many specialised products in several market niches.'

They are very dependent on location, and are often based in university towns. Their authors are professors who want to see their book published, and who have a captive market of students. Each book has a limited print run, illustrated by a British academic publisher: 'There is a limit to the expansion per book, we sell up to 2000 copies per title. Growth is through expansion of the product range, rather than an increase in the number of copies per book.' This group aims for global niches. Sometimes these publishers distribute via specialised bookshops, are often represented in campus bookstores, and sometimes by direct marketing. Their business is vulnerable to peaks and troughs in topic popularity although the academic market is fairly robust, since controversy generates more research and thus more publications.

Traditional
The companies in this group are involved in several different activities and appeal to many segments of the market, including popular literature, textbooks, dictionaries, magazines and newspapers. Historically, they are the mainstay of the industry. The prestige of a company within this group is measured by the authors on their

lists. This group can be divided into the established companies, and the emerging publishing houses. Some of these firms are rather unimaginative, relying on their existing products, showing little concern for innovation and development, and identify their role as 'culture operators': 'Literature is different from any other business. This is where people come in the door and say: "I have written a good book. Will you publish it?" ' (Denmark). Others may be long-established, but are moving with the market: 'The key success factor is the material. I am very organised around having the right editorial list and producing the right books and other products in relation to what we perceive as being the public's interest' (UK).

The emerging companies are led by professionals at senior management level and are business-oriented, pursuing profit-generating strategies while being determined to support their independence. They see growth as the means of survival.

> So I think, after a period in which the one important thing was talented authors, this is not sufficient any more. Of course without talent we cannot make books, but without strict management, without careful analysis of the markets, companies are doomed. The publishing industry has to move to a more entrepreneurial approach (France).

Book Division of Conglomerates
This group also has a professional management approach, but it is also protected from acquisition by the parent firm. Companies of this kind are sheltered from threats about their identity and continued existence. Financial security is probably the most important difference between this group and the others.

Firms within this group, however, often struggle to maintain their individuality, and not stifle the creative culture of the company. A German manager highlights the possible problems if a balance is not found: 'The worst is to come into a publishing house as a businessman without sensitivity and destroy the creative environment. It is important to manage the creativity.'

These broad groups were contrived from our sample, but can represent the industry as a whole. The next section looks at similarities and dissimilarities among the contributors to our study.

Issues in Book Publishing in the 1990s

Several common variables were identified by the managers interviewed which they considered contributed to, or exerted significant influence on, the successful performance of their company. The issues were raised regardless of the markets they operated in, that is whether they are small or large, a specialist company or a more general one. Further, there was a high degree of consensus, although a couple of topics did attract some controversy.

These variables can be considered from three viewpoints: those which are exogenous to the firm, that is factors over which they had no control but which are imposed by the marketplace; those which are endogenous, or the result of strategic decisions determined within the company; and those which have elements of both.

External Variables

Language Traditionally book publishing was considered a local business, and the linguistic differences between countries were viewed as powerful barriers against internationalisation. However nowadays, particularly in the scientific and technical segments, English is more and more considered to be the international language and is increasing its dominance as the world's commercial language too. A large UK publisher that produces reference books and textbooks states: 'All is published in English. In general publishing, anything significant is published in English, regardless of the mother language of the author. Higher level academic journals, they will all be in English.'

Therefore while historically within Europe the conventional wisdom was that language and cultural barriers made it difficult to take published material from one country to another, recent experience, particularly in the Europe Community, shows that it is not these barriers but the attitudes and aspirations of the readers that are more important. A Dutch manager confirms this view, predicting that English language skills will grow so that people can gain access to these publications:

> I don't think language will be a problem in the near future. I do not adhere to the idea of one common language for all countries of the Community, but I think that soon all European citizens will be able to read three or four different languages. People will be citizens of Europe in the next century.

If consumers are ready to accept books from other countries the result will be the transfer of the idea of literature rather than just the export of a product. Many people will enjoy reading a book in its original language rather than in translation. The language issue should be dealt with in a skilful way, not simply by sending out poor translations just to increase sales. A British publisher advises caution:

> Translations of foreign books need a separate infrastructure. A book appeals in one language more in one country than in another, it is not equal. The book might be a little bit successful in Italy, but very successful

in Germany and medium successful somewhere else and you cannot force things. You cannot force a book on people just because you own the rights.

However, it was agreed that, in some subject areas, demand would continue for material to be published in the native language of the reader: 'Law publishing, for example, unless it is EC law, needs to be in the native language, since national law is obviously only of interest in the national language. Civil law, needs to be published in Italy for Italian lawyers, and in the Italian language' (Italy).

Regulation   There are three areas of regulation which affect the publishing industry, those imposed by national governments, those imposed by the European community (or under the control of the community), and those imposed by the industry itself. The majority of managers in our study commented on all of them, although the individual effects varied considerably.

National Government Legislation.   Government plays an important role in setting and maintaining educational standards at primary and secondary level. In most countries in the Community, government education departments set the curriculum to be met for national examinations, which in turn determines which textbooks should be used. Also, and most importantly, they allocate the budget. For publishers involved with textbooks, this represents a valuable bulk purchase. However, being in what is essentially a monopsonist situation, publishers are at the mercy of the government. Recent changes in Britain, such as the introduction of a national curriculum and the new General Certificate of Secondary Education examinations, present authors and publishers alike with many new opportunities arising from a market for additional teaching materials and texts.

Another factor which affects demand is a shift in the demographic pattern which changes the number of schoolchildren requiring textbooks. The proportion of the population attending higher education varies considerably across the Community and in some cases the demand for textbooks will continue for several years after high school, whereas in others it does not. Regardless of the total number of years of education, there is rarely a smooth transition from the institutional purchasers to the private consumer as each cohort leaves school.

The allocation of funds also has an important impact, not only in the school system, but for libraries too, since they are an important institutional purchaser. The provision of libraries is well established in some countries and there is a tradition of borrowing books. Generally government-funded purchases play a key role in some publishers' strategies.

Another aspect of government influence is the imposition of censorship. In the UK the issue of censorship has been prominent recently when Salman Rushdie's *The Satanic Verses* was published although it caused offence to an ethnic minority in the country. However, any change of policy in this regard would have put the UK at odds with most countries in the world. Spain, for example, has been free from censorship for many years: 'There is no intervention whatsoever. That is, during the dictatorship we suffered from censorship, now at this point there is no intervention at all. I need not account for my publications to anyone.'

A final legislative issue is that of copyright, and the violation thereof. Copyright can be described as the intellectual ownership of a book, which is normally vested in the author, but sometimes in the publisher; it is never the right of the consumer. The law protecting copyright is universal among those countries that subscribe to the Berne Convention and European Community agreements. Piracy, that is the violation of copyright, is a big problem in many countries and there is often no means of protecting material. The following is a selection of views from the managers in our sample, representing several countries:

> The big problem is that of copying. This is really scandalous. The state, its institutions, universities, big enterprises, research centres, laboratories, schools and the public, in fact all readers are completely unaware, and do not care at all about the laws on copyright of 1957. Photocopying a protected work is part of everyday life for many people. There are five billion photocopies a year in France alone which cheat us, authors and publishers alike.

> The Danish book market has shrunk, in particular for scientific books, due to the use of the photocopier.

> Piracy is definitely a problem for British publishers. You can try to sue, but it does not work, because the books are already in the shops. You have to beat them by commercial rather than legal means.

Community Regulation. Although currently sales tax is set by national governments, some harmonisation will occur in preparation for European integration in 1992. The issue of value added tax is considered to be important by most of the managers interviewed. The debate centred on the principle of the tax itself, rather than on what rate was appropriate. Great Britain is one country which currently does have a zero rating for books, and the imposition of a tax is viewed with dismay.

> A tax on knowledge, education, literature, is appalling. An important point is that Europe does have a pacemaking role on cultural issues in the rest of the world. We need to show our enlightenment, in the knowledge that a great many other countries are watching us. If the taxation of books

is seen to be acceptable in the European Community, it will spread, and that is damaging, unprogressive and uncivilised.

In Denmark, where there is a high rate of value added tax, 22 percent, it has been reluctantly accepted, but in the hope that it will be lowered. Market research shows that consumers are price responsive, and if the total price is lower, demand will increase: 'If VAT is reduced, then people will to a large extent start buying literature in greater amounts than they do at the moment. I am convinced that in many cases, because of VAT, people do not buy a given book.'

One interesting development which has resulted at least in part from the diverse VAT regulation is the growth of book clubs. If a book is sent from Denmark it is subject to 22 percent tax but if that same book is sent from Germany it is subject to 14 percent tax. Thus the free movement of goods means that regulation such as VAT can be avoided through postal selling.

Industry Practice.   The net book agreement (NBA) is an entirely voluntary arrangement under which a book can be placed at a so-called net price, and no bookseller can sell it below that price. It is the trade's own system of resale price maintenance, and the majority of the industry, supported by the authors' and library organisations want it to continue, although there are some dissenters. The last time it was reviewed was in 1962 and at that time it received general approval, and at present only two countries in the European Community, Belgium and Greece, do not possess a legally sanctioned equivalent. The topic is again on the agenda of the European Commission, and there are indications that it will be allowed to continue.

Many managers suggested that if it were abolished it would cause considerable disruption in bookselling and publishing for at least a year or two, and there would be a permanent loss of quality in the business. Some larger booksellers would probably increase their revenue, while smaller firms would be at risk, and not only the inefficient ones. The range of books available to the consumer would be restricted. There is ample evidence for this from countries which have abandoned any kind of retail price maintenance for books.

The stance of the supporters of the NBA is expressed by a British publisher:

> Without the net book agreement the chances are that bestsellers, which contribute to everyone's business, would be sold only by the large chains. And if you take that business away from the quality bookshops they may find survival difficult, and the communities would be culturally and socially diminished.

The opposing view is that the NBA protects inefficient bookshops. It cossets the publisher from the full effect of market forces and is the principal means by which publishers have been able to maintain their tight control of the book trade. It means high prices in the shops, in an industry where book prices are already rising faster than the rate of inflation in most of the Community countries. If retail price maintenance were abolished there would be a transfer of power from the publisher to the retailer, and from the retailer to the consumer. Such a shift from these traditional relationships within the trade would increase the competitiveness of the industry.

Changes in the Market   One challenge to the publishing industry is the change in the structure of their market. Existing consumers are specific in their demands, and whole new markets are opening up, both in developing countries and in Eastern Europe.

The move towards increasing levels of globalisation is coinciding with a trend towards greater segmentation of the marketplace in terms of both consumers and authors. The demand for books on fairly narrow, specific topics is increasing. Customers do not just want a general cookbook, but one from a particular country or for a particular type of food, or do not just want a computer book, but one focusing on an individual machine. Publishers will have to recognise the changes in the market, and change from the traditional generalist approach to find new ways to appeal to the customer. There are many publishers who will not be able to continue with a more segmented approach to the market, and those who persist in having a list which is characterised by a wide spread of subject areas such as fiction, biography, travel, humour, children's books and so on, with no expertise or inclination to be a speciality player, will not survive. Unless there are clearly definable and accessible markets, sufficiently convincing products and the marketing clout to sell them, life is likely to be short for the unfocused publisher. A Spanish publisher commented:

> Probably our catalogue is the richest of those on the market. We are working on all segments, from infancy to senior citizens. We entered the academic segment, but our consultants advised us against this. We need to exercise strict management, because without reflection on the state of the markets we are doomed.

General publishing is viable, but it has to be conducted with great realism and precision of direction. Specialisation is being taken seriously by the large companies too. These are truly international and while their individual subsidiaries are generally rooted in individual countries their overall marketing capability is genuinely worldwide.

The new markets of Eastern Europe are being eagerly pursued by most of the European publishers, both in terms of authors who in the past have found it difficult, indeed dangerous, to have their work published, and the large population of potential customers who have been denied a great choice of material. In Czechoslovakia where there has been censorship, there is a huge demand for books which have been banned up to now. In Russia also, there is no longer any censorship, and publishers can print what they choose. People can now read the work of dissidents which was previously only available abroad. People are extremely hungry for these books which were forbidden, and everyone is very keen to read them. Several contributors from Spain, a country which itself has been subjected to censorship in the recent past, commented on this:

> The Europe community of 12 countries may become one of 20 in the course of the next few years. The events of the last months force us to readjust our frame of reference. Poland, Hungary, East Germany, Romania are not just potential markets, but potential suppliers of material as well.

> There is greater liberty in communication. Who could have foreseen the happenings of three months ago in the Eastern European countries? I am sure in all bookshops books by Polish or Russian authors will appear which until now were not known in the West.

> Authors from Eastern Europe will now appear. In all countries where there is a dictatorship there are authors in the shade who will appear when the dictator is gone. The impact will be very important for all publishers. We have been distanced from those countries, as opposed to English, French, German and Italian literature, which is plentiful. The readers will be very curious about the work of these hidden authors.

Publishers entering these markets will find a healthy level of consumer demand, a demand that may have to be met in the first instance by imports. Domestic production is difficult because of the outdated printing machines, and shortages of paper and other materials. Unlike some industries, the publishing sector has had a representative private sector, for example 20 percent of East German bookshops are already privately owned and so there is an entrepreneurial base, although their operations provide a sharp contrast to the state booksellers. Operationally, there is a great deal of new knowledge to be acquired. In a country so used to shortages and rationing, managers will have to reverse the habit of ordering 100 copies of a book to obtain the ten they actually want.

In terms of global markets, the United States is extremely large, very wealthy and open to all competition without restriction, and thus is always attractive. Australia and the Far East are also appealing, and while the latter does have some language and cultural barriers, the residents aspire to a proficiency in English. These combined markets provide a large demand for English language books, and many publishers aim for a presence there: 'An attractive model for us would be an acquisition or co-operative merger with a partner of approximately the same size as us, preferably with an international orientation and located in the English-speaking world' (the Netherlands).

However, while the market controls many aspects of the publishing sector, others which were considered important to the success of the business emanate from the internal structure and management culture of the firm. This is the next set of variables to be discussed.

Internal Variables
The managers in the sample characterised these endogenous variables to be the result of strategic decisions made within the company, and they include the following:

Relationships with Authors   This relationship is considered to be the most important determinant of the success of a publishing house, illustrated by a Danish publisher: 'I think a lot depends on having the right titles and those having some kind of lasting value. Then we can exploit that as much as possible. We have to market the name, and can only do that if the author believes we will do this with integrity.' In many respects this drives the need to grow internationally, since expansion on a global level is often a response to the demands of the authors who have an international reputation in their own right. Publishers must offer a vehicle which has a market position corresponding to their writers' own standing, or better still, a market position which enhances it. A German manager comments on the success of one bestseller: 'The most important thing for us is to develop relationships with authors, and then we can sell them all over the world. For example, Tom Wolfe's *Bonfire of the Vanities* was first published in New York, but then also sold very well in Germany.'

Relationships with Other Companies   A common characteristic of the larger publishing groups is their propensity to specialise, and achieve this by paying sometimes enormous sums to acquire specialist companies that have an established market share. Again the unique nature of book publishing is relevant. It is not possible to establish a commanding market presence in mature specialist markets very quickly. Thus the large groups often make the decision to be patient and thereby gain a dominant market share in a sector which has proved to be profitable.

But attractive targets are not cheap, and one reason for their high price is that such specialist companies are becoming an increasing rarity. This does mean that any small and specialist firms left will be vulnerable to predators in the 1990s. Particularly attractive seem to be English-language specialists who may have to adopt a defensive strategy.

Companies which fit into the specialist, global-niche group discussed above, have to be careful to choose their partners well:

> If you are little you have to build strategic alliances to keep going. You will not survive and someone will buy you. Especially in the science, technology and medical segments, you will have to be able to sell around the world. Your national market is not big enough. The specialist author in any field will want access to international readers, you have to be in a network of distributors. If you fail to do this, the big publishers will steal authors from you (UK).

The idea of a network rather than a full acquisition seems the most attractive option, where synergies can be achieved in distribution, but publishers can maintain their own lists and relationships with authors: 'Our firm has started to create a European network, with Swedish, German, English and perhaps Spanish publishers, in order to publish certain books in European countries simultaneously. When this is achieved, we can try to attack the American market' (France).

Distribution   Closely allied to interfirm relationships, distribution is the basis of many networks and the motivation for many alliances. One of the British publishers has no traditional distribution channels at all, and sell all their books through another company: 'We sell and do our own marketing, but they do the physical distribution, and do it very effectively. It is not a partnership, in fact we are competitors, but it works very well.' The cost of distribution leads many publishers to find such partners:

> Distribution is one of the key factors. In our country (Italy) publishers traditionally specialise in manufacturing the product and the distribution has become a separate industry. Distribution is very expensive and highly specific. If you want to give a high level of service you need either a large number of peripheral warehouses, or to centralise, which is costly.

It can also be the basis for acquisition: 'Companies try to buy distribution abroad. For example the French have been very active, and Hachette bought into the UK, not big firms, but small ones. Really buying market distribution rather than the product' (UK).

All contributors commented on the changing pattern of bookselling. In the UK, for example, non-specialist book retailers which include supermarkets, variety stores, garden centres, etc, account for 41 percent of book sales. In addition, book clubs command 14 percent. The small bookshop is considered a niche which it is important to retain, and one which is defended by a French manager: 'I think the small bookshops have a certain role, and they should not be abandoned. I fear some will disappear, and be replaced by larger shops, maybe chains as they have in Great Britain.'

New Product Development   There are opportunities for enhancing products by global expansion, exposing management to overseas competitors and their products, and thus tapping new ideas and techniques, which can be applied to domestic products. It is notoriously easy to copy techniques and ideas in publishing, and equally difficult to maintain differentiation. Publishers need a constant source of new ideas and features.

Some managers, however, warned against contriving a demand for specific books which does not seem to arise from a desire to satisfy an increasingly demanding consumer, but rather from a set of decisions which are made inside the firm. These are prompted by the wish to achieve a given level of profitability, to satisfy shareholders, or as retaliation against foreign entrants, the desire to purchase rights and the general bandwagon of the international trail: 'You cannot lead the readership by too much. If you do, you may be called a visionary, but you will not remain in business' (UK).

Costs of Production   Costs are, of course, crucial to the level of profitability, and publishers are searching out cheaper inputs: 'Publishers have discovered that printing in Spain is less expensive because labour is cheaper. This approach we want to apply in Asia, because they have good production knowledge and again labour is cheaper' (France).

Managers in all the countries in our sample agreed that economies of scale are a lot harder to realise in publishing than in many other industries, and inefficiencies of size are much easier to uncover. The blame is put on the creative element inherent in much of publishing which prevents the achievement of the real economic efficiency seen elsewhere. Sometimes after a successful merger or acquisition, the substantial savings that were predicted are realised. These are mostly mechanical in character, such as warehousing, distribution and administration, marketing and advertising. But the cultural differences in staff groups involved in one specialised segment of the market rather than another, may make many seemingly logical synergies unmanageable:

You have to develop opportunities, to consider how you can use the same material several times. This is the chain of multiple utilisation of material. When you have the entire chain you can divide up the costs. But if the links are not complementary, the chain does not work (Germany).

Economies of scale in publishing, as opposed to printing, are sought particularly in the areas of editorial, sales and distribution and promotion. It is hoped, for instance, that editorial skills in one country can be transferred to another, thus saving on staffing and research. However there are pitfalls in the search for strong synergy across frontiers. These are varying cultures, infrastructure and language which make such synergy difficult to achieve.

Scale of operation is now a significant factor in publishing performance. Huge investments are required to manufacture the necessarily big print-runs that, for example, the US consumer book market has to produce after a heavily promoted blockbuster, to the detriment of what is known as the mid-list, the bulk of general interest books. The smaller publisher with limited resources simply cannot play this game:

> We develop expensive art books, and the costs of production are extremely high. If you make books only for the French market the cost price will be too high in comparison with the amount of books printed, so the price will not be competitive. The only solution is to make international co-editions.

The producers of high price, high-profile art books may ˜nd that there are synergies. For books which contain a large number of photographs or much graphical material, inserting translations in a range of languages is cost-effective, since the text is not the expensive part. Incidentally these books are often gifts, and are thus bought by consumers who are not especially price-responsive.

Technology and Internationalisation
Not included so far in our discussion are two variables which influence the internal decisions of the firm, and affect the market in which they operate, namely, technology and internationalisation.

Technology   Some of the most profound changes in the publishing sector, as in many other industries, are the result of the introduction of technology. This has affected the internal decisions of the firm and also changes the external market conditions in which the company competes.

It is important to differentiate between technological innovation in publishing and in printing. Changes in the printing process have affected all the publishers in the sample, and in most cases have resulted in lower costs and faster production times. But in addition, technology is increasingly used in the preparation of the manuscript by the publisher. Authors frequently now deliver their work on disk and publishers have been forced to install a certain level of technology in order to maintain relationships with their authors. Thus the input, the completed work, is in machine readable form: 'Some years ago, when an author brought us his or her manuscript it was a real tome. Nowadays they send us their floppy disks in an envelope' (Spain).

But how do publishers approach the increasing levels of technology in their industry? One British publisher took a pragmatic approach:

> I think we define our business via the areas we are in, rather than the way we package the information. How it is delivered is rather a matter of whatever is appropriate to a particular market segment. Sometimes we give them looseleaf binders, or CD-ROM, or a book, or a video or audio cassette, or use satellite broadcasting if it is a multimedia-based product. It really is something that emerges from the needs of the marketplace.

The most successful users of technology will be those publishers who can judge which processes are appropriate and will use them selectively, as discussed by one of the French interviewees:

> There are two kinds of technology. There is that which is a tool for us; here we use everything which seems justifiable, for example computers to construct databases for dictionaries and encyclopaedias. But there are also computers in the area of linguistics. These are not perfect yet and we use them with discretion. Finally there is technology which changes the product, creating substitutes for books. This is an area of concern for the future.

So is there a chance that books will disappear? Thankfully, the managers we spoke to did not think so.

> I do not think the book is going to disappear; whatever the advantages of a computer, it is not very friendly to read from! I think there will be some technological developments, particularly in terms of teaching material. Often teachers come to us with a program they have developed and ask whether we would like to market it (Denmark).

> I am sure that books are irreplaceable, both as a tool for students, and for the pleasure they give to everyone (Spain).

The theoretical advantages to technology are plain, and the managers in our study were all aware of them. These include greater reliability, output of a high standard, and the ability to produce new products easily and efficiently, and at a low cost. But complementary to that is the need for the people with the skills to really make it work. This is required both in the production and, maybe more importantly, in the management area, since there may be implications for the business caused by the impact of the new technology.

International Expansion   There are many forms of internationalisation in the sector. In some cases, products are exported in their original form, for example the *Encyclopaedia Britannica*. Others can be international versions of a domestic product. This is often a magazine or reference manual where appropriate changes have been made to accommodate national differences. Finally global market penetration can take a more comprehensive shape, leading to ownership of publishing activities in foreign countries, often through acquisitions: 'We are building networks in Europe, for instance in the management area we have partners in UK, Spain, Italy, Germany and Sweden. We will create an educational centre with schools, bookshops abroad in towns and on campuses' (France).

The main reasons for internationalisation, or at least the main justification for foreign expansion, is simply one of geographical diversification. This may be because the home market is regarded as being too small, either in a physical sense or due to monopoly constraints. Geographical expansion may arise because prospects are judged to be more appealing in foreign markets.

Alternatively, foreign expansion may have its roots in the historical lessons learned in a particular country. An example of this is the UK presence in the old Commonwealth countries where the language is known and the educational system similar.

Finally, a motive for international diversification may be to achieve scale economies by becoming large, and at the same time decreasing the chance that another company will be big enough to acquire you. But for whatever reason, there is no doubt that global expansion is taking place.

> Our missing international scope is an important weakness, and we have to create some strategic alliances, because we have to be prepared, when the really big foreign publishers will enter (Denmark).

> Why an international approach? Because we are increasingly aware of the fact that there is an important stake to be made on certain products, like buying the rights of a book (France).

Any international expansion must be accompanied by a commitment to other languages. Many publishers who saw their growth limited domestically, observed the phenomenon of the English language infiltration of scientific and technical literature and set about participating in it. One result is that Elsevier is now the world's largest English language producer of scientific publications. Wolters Kluwer demonstrated their acceptance of English as the language of the future by deciding to use English as the standard language within the group. Hachette in France also made a dramatic conversion to a wholehearted acceptance of English.

Inter-company Differences
Some differences do occur across the industry, although these do not appear to arise from variation in the country of origin, but are rather the result of size and type of the company which influences their response to the increasing internationalisation of the sector.

The cultural barriers which exist in some industries do not seem to present obstacles to trade, rather they enrich the industry by creating a wider body of literature to present to the customer.

One disparity is between the trade and non-trade publisher, that is the consumer literature, compared with academic, professional and reference publishing. They both present different opportunities for the future and face different threats.

Those dependent on trade publishing expressed more concern at the increased level of competition, and the threat of acquisition. All small firms fear the loss of independence, and these were not only vulnerable to takeover, but to the loss of identity as a result. It is easy for them to become part of the multi-media publisher, and be lost in a large corporation. This fear is reinforced by the opinion that the industry will become more concentrated, and dominated by some huge organisations, such as Thomson International, Murdoch and Maxwell, all large because of non-book activities. Thus they are increasing their efforts to arrange alliances and partnerships for protection: 'The time of small publishers is finished. The economic forces have won over the cultural ones. Very powerful groups are being built. The next development will be the restructuring of book distribution which is still fragmented' (France).

In terms of the market for trade publishers, they are aware that some of their material is not easily exported. This is demonstrated by one of the few country differences, that is in the selection of entries to the bestseller lists, both in fiction – 'I think it extraordinary that more European novelists are not major novelists in the UK. There are some here at the moment, but it is a very narrow audience, up-market fiction' – but also non-fiction, where for example, the UK's fascination with DIY and gardening has not spread across the European Community!

Because of their more specialist expertise, the managers in the academic and reference side of the business expected either no change or an increase in their business as a result of the European Community integration. The lack of regulation made the new trading conditions similar to those existing currently, although the general increase in economic activity will benefit everyone, including the publishing sector. A British manager showed considerable enthusiasm:

> I can think of nothing we will be able to do in 1992 that we cannot do now. That is not to say that 1992 is not a fantastically important change for us, because of the increase in broad economic growth and changes in reskilling and internationalisation which makes Europe important to us. But those legal or financial barriers which some industries have been up against do not affect our industry.

Some subject areas will see bigger demand, in particular for professional material relating to shared Community activity. For example, Community taxation and the harmonisation of systems, comparative accounting and Community law, although those topics on a national basis will stay rooted in domesticity.

One of the few identifiable areas where the international nature of the market has actually declined is in the market for educational publishing at primary level. There was a time when Nigerian eight-year-olds had to puzzle their way through an imported English reader that described the discomforts of a northern winter. Those days are now long past. More positively, language books will also be demanded as people move between countries for education and employment.

One outstanding factor is the varying levels of government support given to the arts generally – for example, the French government gives the Department of Culture a high profile:

> Books are taken very seriously by the Community, the officials and politicians, but all the other countries take culture vastly more seriously than we do. This is a constant embarrassment to me that our own arts minister does not have the strength and standing nationally, as the ministers of culture in all the other countries have (UK).

This has implications for the degree of interest in literature and encourages the habit of book reading and purchasing among the population, illustrated for example by the high level of book consumption in Denmark, whereas the level for the UK is low.

Managers throughout the sample considered that the greatest threat to their markets from European competitors will come from the Germans, the Swedes and the British:

> Springer, Elsevier, Pergamon and others will enter the French market in the next years. Authors will turn to publishers who offer them the best markets. The Swedes are also very effective in book publishing and are willing to take a position in the EC (France).

> Sweden has eight million inhabitants, it is a very dynamic country. Frequently I am astonished by the advances they make in the industry.

They travel a lot to study the market, and they speak several languages. They are the Japanese of the publishing sector (Netherlands).

American and Canadian companies are obviously important, as can be seen by their presence in the 'top 20' list earlier in the chapter, although they publish predominantly in English and do not undertake extensive translation work. The Japanese obviously face a language barrier, but their success in other industries, and the financial strength of their organisations make them a threat at least in theory if not in practice at present.

Conclusions

Although the managers interviewed identified similar factors as being crucial to their industry, the emphasis put on each individually defines the direction of the future development of the firm, and at the same, confirms their membership within a group.

Overall implications for general strategy formulation in the next decade emerge as follows:

- The book publishing industry is undergoing dramatic changes in its structure; significant product and process innovations in technology have enabled some companies to broaden their scope and to redefine the industry.
- Regulation by national governments will be replaced by Community legislation. This is particularly pertinent in the area of taxation. Price setting will need careful consideration, whether this is controlled by the European Commission or the industry itself. The publishing industry is affected by the general pace of deregulation throughout the world, including the creation of free trade areas, the elimination of exchange controls and the phasing out of subventions. In the private sector, deregulation means the break-up of cartels, the exposure of companies to takeover, the curtailment or elimination of previously accepted restrictive practices, etc, leading to higher levels of competition.
- The role of language is changing. In the past the common assumption was that the spread of English would automatically favour publishers from countries where the mother tongue is English, and language was a barrier to non-English-speaking countries. This is no longer the case, and there is a rapid growth of English language publishing by the Dutch, German, Swedish and other publishers. Local culture is still important, however, and it is important not to confuse language with culture.
- The diffusion of technological innovation across the industry has increased the range of products. For those firms which are part of

large media organisations the influence of technology is enormous. These companies will have technological change imposed on them, unlike those in the group of specialised and independent firms that may choose to delay its impact, in the knowledge that the book as a physical product has no acceptable substitute, at least for existing consumers.

- New barriers are emerging to differentiate and protect existing publishers. Those companies in our sample that fit the 'traditional' definition of their own business consider book publishing as a mature industry. Corporate culture and attitudes will maintain the integrity of this group, as long as they can continue to be competitive according to their own rules.

- The industry is not homogeneous, and is becoming more varied still. Those that succeed develop a competitive strategy based on their own strengths rather than on competitors' weaknesses. It is important to appreciate that there is room in the industry for companies with different cultures and values, and competing with companies in an unfamiliar area is not the best policy.

- Concentration of the industry is taking place for market and economic reasons. The fact that the average size of companies has risen does not preclude the existence of small independent publishing houses. Big companies are not necessarily the leaders in opportunity identification. There is a desire to retain a mix of publishing houses. The urge to grow and become global should not be achieved at the expense of identity.

- Be aware of the nature of the market. In interpreting book trade statistics, it is vital to distinguish between reading books and purchasing books. The two are often confused and specious comparisons made about comparative book use between various countries. National patterns of how books are made available to the reader can also differ radically. For example, historically Britain has one of the most extensive public library systems in the world, far more woven into the fabric of society than in North America, although this may change. The latest and most extensive research into book use and book-buying habits shows that people read more than they buy. Book borrowing, from libraries, friends and relatives, and gifts, is an integral part of the culture. This may change when the power of the media divisions of the global institutions take effect.

- Finally, the effect of globalisation of the industry. In this climate of change, company culture and history can be crucial in determining its behaviour and need to be understood fully to make optimal decisions on the strategy. It may be important to question whether for any particular company global publishing is interesting or even necessary. To the extent that some books have widespread appeal and are sold throughout the world, then there is little that is new in the concept.

Global publishing, however, has come to have a more precise meaning indicating the retention by a particular publishing group of world rights to a particular book title and the exploitation of those rights through its own international network. As a rule of thumb, on a successful title the overseas profits can be three times as great as when the foreign rights are sold to other publishers. Knowing which role to play in the overseas market is the first stage in developing a European strategy at the business level.

5

The Car Industry

Gianluca Colombo and Giovanni Comboni

> In Madrid companies have been set up offering motorists who are stuck in traffic jams the possibility to phone, thanks to young people moving around the cars with portable telephones. These companies are very successful because they cannot meet demand (Car industry executive, Spain).

This little excerpt from our interview with the head of an automobile company in Spain is not just a celebration of entrepreneurial spirit in a country where consumer spending increased by 16 percent in 1989 as against the previous year. As a vignette of Madrid street life it highlights a paradox running through the car industry: it is a mature industry, old established, indeed for many people the car factory is a prototype of industrial society. At the same time there is change, there are interesting developments, the industry and the product may well be quite different by the start of the next century.

One of these developments is the idea of the automobile as 'the third accommodation' or *résidence troisième*. The simple fact is that many people spend more time in their cars than anywhere else after their houses and places of work; the car is the third place in which one resides. This has implications not just for safety, but for making the time spent in this third accommodation agreeable, productive and stress-free. The 1950s gave an in-car temperature and ventilation control, the 1980s added the cassette player to the car radio. The 1990s may give us much more: the car telephone may become a near-standard feature, fax facilities readily available, and while as one interviewee put it we will probably never reach the stage where drivers can sit there and read the newspaper while mobile, we may well have a situation where the newspaper or other reading matter of the drivers' choice can be read to them while driving. In short, the third accommodation needs to be properly furnished – the Madrid marketplace démarche simply anticipates this development.

Side by side with this development is the notion of putting more safety into driving, and taking some of the stress out of it, by what one interviewee called 'the de-responsibilitisation of the driver'. Mostly electronic aids will increasingly offer road-environment information, and take decisions on the basis of it, albeit with the possibility of a driver override. This will limit the scope of human error, make driving safer, and take some of the decisional anxiety out of driving. The idea is not as revolutionary as it sounds. Consider for instance that cars run on a mixture of air and petrol: no one has ever expected that the driver will do things to produce this mixture, a function that is safely left to the carburettor. So why should the driver decide at what speed the vehicle should enter a bend?

Some of our interviewees also see a change coming in market/model segmentation. Traditionally this has been by car size, especially engine size measured in cubic capacity, and we offer the standard typology later in the chapter. Against this background two developments are anticipated. One is pure demography. Europeans are getting older, while everyone else is getting younger! This has implications for both car design and for segmentation. The second perhaps more interesting development is that of segmentation by end-user category rather than by engine size, a possibility heralded at the 1989 Tokyo motor show with its cars for lovers of water sports, cars for sporty young men, cars for pretty girls, and so on.

A possible development that is feared, rather than confidently expected, is a change to the 'showroom' model of distribution. The essence of this model is that the distributor will fill the showroom with, say, lots of Fiat Pandas, not with the whole range of Fiat cars, and customers would make their choice in terms of the various versions of the Panda, colour and fittings. Taking the showroom model a stage further the showroom proprietor might specialise in, say, smaller cars, and pack the showroom not just with Pandas but with Golfs, Renault 5s and Peugeot 205s. All this would cut down the traditional manufacturer–distributor link, and have disruptive implications for the established notion of a *range* of models. It is one thing to ask where VW would be without the Golf, but another to suggest they discard the rest of the range!

Not only is there this paradox of a mature industry suffused by the excitement of innovation. There is also a paradox of industry self-understanding and reaction to 1992. The common cry is that this is a global industry, so 1992 will have little importance. This idea is captured in the Ford quip that for them 1992 happened in 1967 when they set up Ford of Europe. Yet 1992 makes Europe more attractive to the Japanese and intensifies their drive to establish European bridgeheads. The Japanese threat in turn has all sorts of implications, explored in this chapter, and is a major theme in the testimonies of our European car executives. Moreover, while these executives propound an international self-image they are often nationalistic

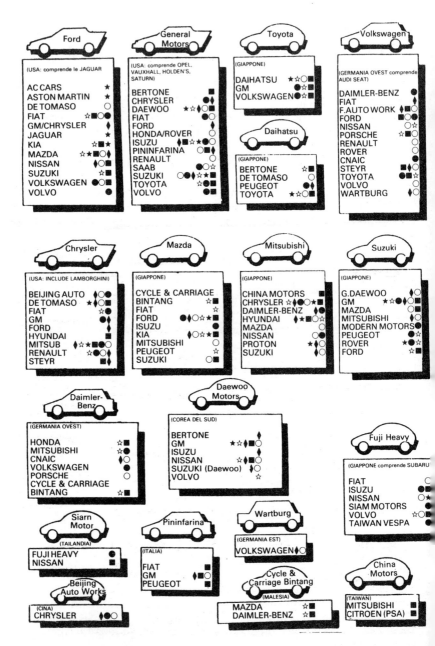

Figure 5.1 *Major alliances and acquisitions*

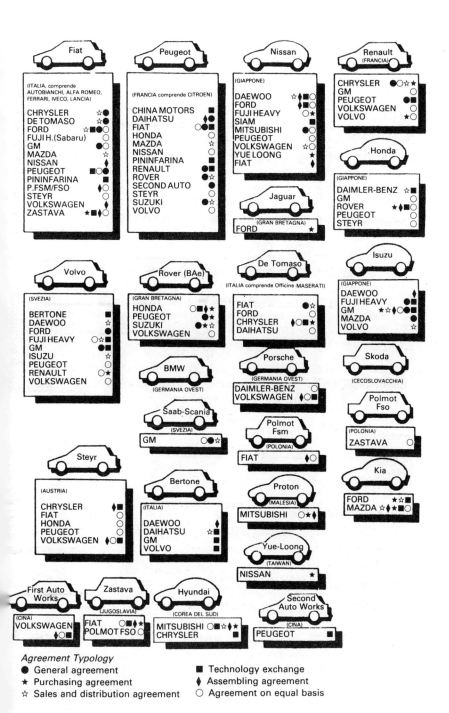

Agreement Typology
- ● General agreement
- ★ Purchasing agreement
- ☆ Sales and distribution agreement
- ■ Technology exchange
- ♦ Assembling agreement
- ○ Agreement on equal basis

when it comes to the Japanese, their domestic market, and the conquests they hope to make in *other* European countries.

Background

As we have suggested, despite its maturity there is much change in the car industry as a result of competition, especially Japanese, and pressure from society including concern for the environment.

Europe, the focus of our interest, is in fact the world's leading market. In 1989 Europe produced 13.5 million cars out of a world total of 35.2 million. European production was up 6 percent on the 1988 figures; the European share was bigger than the American share, and the latter was down 9 percent on 1988 figures. Europe is likely to continue to be the leading market, and be seen as increasingly attractive. There are several factors here:

- it is a collection of mostly healthy economies
- 1992 itself is expected to lead on average to lower car prices through tax harmonisation and thus to stimulate demand
- the redefinition of European borders in real terms, so that to the EC population of 323 million is added the 400 million of Eastern Europe.

Such considerations make the desire of non-Europeans to enter or prosper in this market entirely comprehensible. Europe's pre-eminence is clear from the world production figures as shown in Table 5.1.

Table 5.1   *World car production for 1989*

Europe	13,219,049
Asia	10,499,580
USA	6,146,745
Eastern Europe	2,145,760
South America	1,538,914

Of this over 13 million vehicles produced in Europe, over 60 percent are produced in France, Italy and West Germany, with the well-known impact on their national economies. The breakdown among the Western European countries in 1989 was as shown in Table 5.2.

All the European manufacturers think that capacity has to be increased so as to reach the critical mass necessary to stay in the market over the next five to ten years. The same period, it is felt, will see the irreversible penetration of the Japanese. The consensus is

Table 5.2   *Car production in Western Europe by country, 1989*

West Germany	4,451,557
France	2,868,227
Italy	2,053,214
Spain	1,740,130
UK	1,287,377
Sweden	382,398
Belgium	302,846
Netherlands	133,300
Total	13,219,049

that there will be no room for companies producing less than 400,000 units a year, and two million is likely to emerge as the operating norm during the 1990s, at least for the 'generalist' car manufacturers (those that make the full range of small, medium-sized and large cars).

The non-generalist manufacturers that are differentiating through quality-luxury-price, such as Mercedes, are not seen as subject to this dynamic of competitive scale. For those smaller companies alternative strategies exist including growth by acquisition, or a strengthening move via an alliance with one of the generalists. The six generalists in this connection are Ford, General Motors (Opel and Vauxhall), Fiat, Renault, PSA (Peugeot and Citroën) and VAG (Volkswagen, Audi and SEAT in Spain). The most recent of these alliances is that of Volvo with Renault, announced in the spring of 1990. Thinking in the industry about mass and viability has obviously been influenced by the various takeovers of smaller manufacturers including the part-acquisition of Saab by GM. The network of agreements has now reached epic, not to say intricate, proportions, as Figure 5.1 makes clear.

Both the need for alliances and the drive to increase scale to reach critical mass are related to the European perception of the Japanese threat. The force of this threat is captured in the sharp contrasts portrayed in Table 5.3.

Table 5.3   *Comparison of efficiency and quality*

Indicator	Japan	EC
Hours worked per vehicle	17	37
Years of model turnover	3.5	5
Productivity per hour (EC=100)	134	100
Average absenteeism	6%	13%
Faults per 100 vehicles	60	105

This contrast shows why some countries seek to restrict Japanese imports, a conviction voiced by Peugeot's Jacques Calvet in an interview published in *European Motor Business* in November 1989: 'We need to defend European technology and, at the same time, European employment!' A counter-opinion, however, is voiced by Martin Bangemann, Vice-president of the EC Commission for industrial policy: 'It is wrong to believe that Japanese cars can be kept off the European market through import quotas or ban of local production . . . The Japanese car is beaten only by manufacturing a better product. It is not a race between two commercial powers, but a competition to produce the best car for the consumer' (*La Repubblica*, special supplement, 20 May 1990). Bangemann's view finds a response in the battle for quality between Japanese, European and American manufacturers. Table 5.4 shows where the battle lines are drawn.

Table 5.4   *Comparison of productivity indicators*

	Japanese factories in Japan	Japanese factories in the US	US factories	Japanese factories in Europe	EC factories
Output Hours per car	19.1	19.6	26.6	30.9	35.9
Quality Faults per 100 parts	13.8	63.9	86.7	83.2	89.7
Net output Cars per hour	98.9	67.5	61.5	59.3	77.7
Robotisation Ratio	4.2	4.0	2.1	1.6	2.7

Source: MIT, 1989.

The European Competitors

Although united by certain developments the European car manufacturers, even the generalists, have distinctive profiles, and a note on these may be helpful before proceeding to a more direct discussion of the views of the interviewed managers.

At present the position of VAG (the Volkswagen group) seems to be very aggressive. In January 1990 it scored an increase in its order book by 14.2 percent vis-à-vis the same period of 1988, with a strong recovery in the domestic market (+22 percent), where the Japanese boast rather a substantial market share (14 percent). On the strategic level, VAG is trying to differentiate in a geographical sense: towards southern Europe with the SEAT (Fiat's former subsidiary in Spain) trademark and towards countries of Eastern Europe with the Volkswagen trademark, thanks to the preferential channels created by German reunification.

As suggested earlier, probably the most significant event of the alliance policies pursued by European carmakers was the 1990 Renault–Volvo agreement, which the experts view as a move necessary to both companies. Renault, in spite of the recovery of the 1988–90 period, still suffered from a substantial indebtedness. The legacy of negative results earlier in the last decade was aggravated on the competitive level by a recent erosion of domestic market share owing to the increase in the market shares of various foreign makes and to the rise of the PSA (Peugeot group). On the other hand, Volvo has solved by means of this alliance, at least partly, the problem of critical mass, by getting the support of a carmaker that is a generalist, and consequently, is in a position of competing in all the market segments A to F, defined by cubic capacity – see Table 5.5.

Table 5.5 *Segments based on cubic capacity*

A	–	Small cars, max. 900 cc.
B	–	Small cars, max. 1100 cc.
C	–	Medium cars, max. 1300 cc.
D	–	Medium cars, max. 1600 cc.
E	–	Medium-big cars, max. 2000 cc.
F	–	Big cars over 2000 cc.
G	–	Luxury cars
H	–	Sports cars from 1600 to 2000 cc.
I	–	Trucks, 4-wheel drive

PSA is in the process of widening the range produced on both its makes, Peugeot and Citroën, with the declared objective of reaching within two years the leadership of the European market, at present disputed between Fiat and VAG. Today PSA finds itself in the process of repositioning its trademarks in search of a greater differentiation, and of a business recovery in the most prestigious segment of the market through the launching of the new Peugeot 605 model.

The Fiat group is still growing. In Europe it has reached an aggregate market share of 14.8 percent (31 December 1989), with a very high concentration of the sales turnover in the domestic market (a share of 53.63 percent – of which 37.63 percent for Fiat Auto – data referring to 31 January 1990). This standing of Fiat in the domestic market is a strength as well as a weakness. Like PSA and Renault which also have a large market share in the home market, this strength tends to conceal the rather more limited penetration of these companies in the so called 'free' European markets; those, that is, where the Japanese are under little constraint.

In order to reduce such a dependence on the domestic market the Fiat group is in the process of targeting some emerging areas in which it can boast preferential relationships, such as in Turkey, North Africa, Poland and the Soviet Union. Fiat is careful about redefining the product range and in terms of technological innovation the company seems to pay more and more attention to segment D of the market (see Table 5.5), which appears to be more and more important as an area of competition in the continental market. In fact in 1989 this segment D accounted for 25.4 percent of the European market, against 24.8 percent in 1988 and 24.7 percent in 1987.

The two American car manufacturers, Ford and Opel–GM, also appear to be aggressive and well positioned. Clearly they are now to be considered for all practical purposes as continental manufacturers, with particularly significant market shares in northern Europe, and especially in the UK.

Strategy formulation is often conducted in conditions of total uncertainty, with only a few complex reference points. The only certain fact is that the 1990s will be decisive for defining the product and the market for the next century. The manufacturers that reach the end of this century are likely to enjoy lasting competitive advantages. Conversely, the market is likely to 'expel' those companies that cannot compete in the course of the present decade.

The whole reflection of the managers interviewed is tied to survival logic and we shall try to reconstruct some of this in the following sections.

Critical Issues in the Managers' Perceptions

There are interesting variations of opinion among the automobile executives that we interviewed, perhaps paradoxically so for such an international industry. A comprehensive but necessarily summarised overview is offered as Table 5.6.

Japanese Competition

There is a basic division between the Euro-Latin countries of France and Italy on the one side and the northern European countries of Britain and West Germany on the other. The Euro-Latin view is that the market will tend to stabilisation and saturation, and only eight or ten competitors will survive. Therefore any new entrants (Indonesia, Korea) and of course Japan must be opposed.

The 'northern' view is more *laissez-faire*, that the market lends itself to maximum liberalisation. Thus according to one British car executive it is necessary '. . . to enhance exchanges and reciprocal ties, that is to work on the reciprocal opportunities'. In other words, keep it open to exploit the openness ourselves.

The Euro-Latins are conspicuously impressed by the Japanese achievement, especially by the short time between the design of a vehicle and actually bringing it to the market, and also by the quality of the Japanese relationship with suppliers. On the whole, 'we can say we are at least five years behind them' (French executive). So the Euro-Latin view is that 1992 is an opportunity to define the border, that is to close it, and to get some balance in investment in Europe, including American investment as well as Japanese. For the Euro-Latins then 1992 represents a possible solution, via a common EC foreign policy, rather than the inauguration of a new phase of competition.

Evaluation of Eastern Europe

1992 is a step in the process of integration between east and west. The opening of Eastern Europe has consolidated the position of the centre of the globalised panorama. On the other hand the globally decentralised manufacturers now want to 'Europeanise' their trademark, make it familiar and marketable in the east as in the west.

There is a cleavage in the attitudes to Eastern Europe. The executives' valuation is divided between the intention to 'immediately aim at those countries' (West German manager) and the preservation of a 'more prudential attitude' (French executive). Side by side with this cleavage is the more selective response of, say, Fiat, indicated in Table 5.6 where the company aims at some selected countries in Eastern Europe rather than at all of them equally. It is a short step from here to focusing on other areas in Mediterranean countries like Turkey, or Northern African ones such as Algeria. So that the opening up of Eastern Europe may be a catalyst in the widening of territorial horizons.

Growing competition and increasing concentration in this industry have led manufacturers to set the objective: '. . . of strengthening of their strong points and, at the same time, of eliminating their weak points, in order to reduce the incidence of negative quality' (Italian executive).

Table 5.6

	Critical success factors	Industry dynamics	1992 impact	Attitude towards Japanese	Eastern Europe	Corporate strategy
Rover	1992 Overcapacity Free European Market Micro-segmentation	Competition Ecology	Cross-European distribution Price down	Liberal	No mention	Micro-segmentation Human resources
Jaguar	Confront Japanese in production quality & productivity	Japanese will be winners Others losers	Distribution opportunity for luxury cars	Liberal	No mention	Product quality Customer satisfaction
Ford	Cost reduction	Merger & acquisition	Less important	Liberal	Big opportunity	Cost leadership
Renault	Technology & production	Demography Japan Technology	Wants EC foreign policy on cars	Protectionist	Less important	Alliances Changes in plant location
Peugeot	1992	Japan Alliances	Wants EC foreign policy on cars	Protectionist	No mention	Lobbying for protectionism
Fiat	Quality Technology 1992		Wants EC foreign policy on cars	Protectionist	Concentrate on particular areas	Total quality
Lancia Alfa	Micro-segmentation			Liberal	No mention	Customer satisfaction Product quality

BMW	Different services	Demography Customer income Ecology	Less important	Liberal	No entry	Global 'nichisation'
Opel		Develop in Eastern Europe Concentration in distribution Merger & acquisition	Less important	?	Important	Globalisation
Porsche	Customer satisfaction	Penetration in Japan	Strong in F & I segments Low in segment G	Liberal	Irrelevant	Penetration in Japan Restructuring Market segmentation
VW	Quality Price Technical development		Less important	Liberal	Important	Globalisation
SEAT	Car safety Utility car Quality Ecology	Homologous production & emphasise B & C segments Micro-segmentation New distribution Merger & acquisition	No impact	Liberal	No mention	Human resources
Mercedes	Image High quality Services	Society getting richer; Move from C-D segments to D-E Distribution	Important	Liberal	No entry	Global 'nichisation'

Alliances

Alliance and acquisition strategies are seen by our car executives as being one way of achieving this end, and Figure 5.1 maps both the extent and intricacy of the alliances. These alliances are seen as very topical by the practitioners. As one of the British executives put it: 'Today everyone speaks with everyone', in a logic that may be either partial or global. There is a specific type of alliance typified by agreements about production, R&D, marketing and distribution. But there is also a more general type, of which the agreement between Renault and Volvo announced in 1990 is an example. This more general version envisaged a sharing or integration of strategy. Interestingly, given the strength of feeling about Japanese competition in some countries, none of our interviewees excluded *any* potential partner in principle; and Japanese manufacturers do figure in Figure 5.1. At the same time the majority go for the specific rather than the general alliance, both to preserve the individual trademark and because: 'The evaluation of the opportunities of agreement must stem from the analysis of the company's internal need' (Spain). In most cases this need is seen as specific rather than global.

Finally, alliance strategy is seen as an opportunity to overcome geographical barriers. There were a number of references in the interviews to the value of alliances as fundamental to an entry strategy for Eastern Europe. As an Italian executive put it '. . . here all the possible and necessary joint ventures must be privileged'.

Design Strategy

Product design strategy is another component, driven by an anticipation of customer satisfaction, the products being supported by 'innovative and aggressive marketing' (British executive). The emphasis on customer satisfaction is now emphasised more strongly than in the past but there are some specific, new elements.

First there is the demographic issue mentioned at the start of the chapter. As a Spanish executive put it: 'In Europe man is becoming older and older, in other countries he is becoming younger. You are young now, but one day you will find it difficult to turn your head back while parking your car.' Considerations of this kind have clear design implications, and responding to them may become a competitive weapon in an ageing market.

Secondly, design is meant to reduce costs, and to do so against a background of falling prices after 1992 (through tax and other harmonisation and as a result of enhanced competition) at the same time as R&D and distribution costs are receding. Design-led cost reduction is one means of salvation. It operates both via design change that facilitates greater productivity and the design of components that suppliers can be required to deliver more cheaply.

Thirdly, with regard to the design of the manufacturing system as opposed to that of the product and its component parts, design means planning the quality system, contributing to total quality, described by one of the European executives, perhaps with a touch of paranoia, as having 'become the bottomless container'. Furthermore, process design is critical for controlling (shortening) the time lapse between product conception and the product being offered on the market, again seen as a Japanese strength (Table 5.3).

Market Segmentation

Many of the interviewees believe that segmentation policies will be competition-driven, with the 'sort out' being among the smaller car brands, segments A-C as depicted in Table 5.5. The managers concerned see two reasons for this.

First it is anticipated that new entrants to the European market, Korea and Indonesia, will penetrate northern Europe first where resistance is less. This will lead northern European manufacturers to try to sell more in southern Europe to keep up volume, which in turn will mean concentration on the A-C segments where French and Italian manufacturers especially are at their strongest. The second reason is rather less convoluted. It is expected that the Eastern European market will become a new competitive battleground, and that the demand there will be for relatively low-cost cars, again enhancing competitive focus on the A-C segments.

But a new consideration in market segmentation, touched on in the introductory part of this chapter, is the growing idea that segmentation by engine size (cubic capacity) is too crude a measure, conflates customer categories, and does not adequately reflect user needs and wishes. Now it will take some time for this new view of segmentation to be worked out in practice, but one criterion mentioned by some of our interviewees is the utility versus leisure time distinction, seen as cutting across mere engine size considerations.

An extension of this idea also emerged in the discussion with car manufacturers. This is that if the old A-H segmentation of Table 5.5 is superseded by new criteria, there are likely to be more models rather than fewer models. In other words, non-traditional segmentation criteria lead to more niche marketing. And to the extent that new segments are rightly identified, there should be more global niche opportunities.

Finally on the segmentation issue, manufacturers selling to the luxury and/or performance segment expect to benefit from 1992 in terms of tax harmonisation opening up new national markets. As a British manufacturer put it there are some areas (of the EC) where taxation renders the national market 'highly restrictive for high-powered cars'.

How to Manage the Company Network

As suggested in the previous section the relationship with suppliers is seen as increasingly important as a lever to achieve quality, cost control and continuity of supply. There was a feeling among the interviewed managers that suppliers are generally stable these days in terms of their profitability and financial structure. An interesting qualification, however, was raised by one of the British manufacturers who argued that:

> I am always concerned for this increase in the suppliers' profitability, not because I think they must not have any margin, but because I do not have any significant proof that a sufficient portion of the profits is re-invested . . . I do not see an increase in their investments in technology and equipment to maintain a good level of competitiveness in the long term.

The managers are unanimous in wanting long-term relationships with suppliers, and in the conviction that supplier performance has to be evaluated on a long-term basis. There is also a view that suppliers constitute an asset, to be managed, and if necessary re-capitalised. There was talk too among manufacturers of inter-competitor agreements for the rationalisation of component purchasing. These considerations are important when one remembers that the end product in large measure results from the organised and partly robotised assembly of externally manufactured components: the suppliers contribute over 60 percent of the value of the completed car. In this context it is not surprising that the relationship between manufacturers and suppliers in this industry often takes the form of a quasi-vertical integration, with the supplier dedicating technology and specialist resources to the needs of the manufacturer.

This manufacturer–supplier relationship achieved a new importance in the early 1980s in the context of the recovery of the car industry. This importance has continued into the 1990s, but with the emphasis now on the suppliers' contribution to product quality and thus to customer satisfaction. And quality itself is taking on new meanings. Where formerly quality was understood primarily in terms of vehicle durability and reliability, and these are still important, quality is now increasingly seen as involving also:

– enhanced safety, sometimes by means of the 'de-responsi-

bilisation' of the driver referred to at the start of the chapter
- a greater harmony between vehicles and the environment
- an enhanced 'quality of life' for drivers in their 'third accommodation'.

All this means that the car is becoming, as a German manufacturer put it, 'a special object both with regard to the Community and the individual'.

Distribution Channels

The view of our interviewees is that customers will have an increasingly good deal, being offered better products, probably at lower prices, with more guarantees, and more favourable means of payment. All this is 'delivered' via the distribution system, which is thus seen by manufacturers as being of increasing importance.

Furthermore, the European manufacturers see differences between dealers in different parts of the world. Not only is there some apprehension regarding the 'showroom' or 'supermarket' models of dealership in the USA, referred to at the start of the chapter, but there is also a conviction that dealerships in Japan are qualitatively different. The Japanese dealers seem to the Europeans to be much less aggressive: they are not looking for customers but waiting for them.

But more than this Japanese dealers are seen as being extraordinarily faithful, such as to constitute an entry barrier to the European. As one of the British manufacturers put it: 'A Toyota dealer will always remain a Toyota dealer, as, on the other hand, it is difficult to find a Japanese willing to buy a European car.' Or again it is difficult if not impossible to distribute European cars in the Japanese market: 'because the distribution channels are controlled by the banks, the latter offer loans on special conditions to the whole distribution network, owned by the big groups' (British car manufacturer).

It should be added that manufacturers of luxury cars seem to attach rather less importance to the distribution in overall terms and focus more on specific skills possessed by dealers. One of the British manufacturers formulated this idea:

> Significant strategic changes will take place in distribution but the real problem is that the dealers must acquire more professionalism in the managerial operation of their sales points . . . The strategic objective is to concentrate on the high segment of the market, the whole marketing must be built on that basis, as well as the distribution, which must necessarily be exclusive and one make. This is the first step to build a corporate identity.

The Need for a New Style of Management

There was a feeling among the motor executives that the industry needs a new style of management, an interesting view considering how established the industry is. Indeed for many people the car factory is the archetype of rational industrial organisation, with a high division of labour and strong reporting lines. Our interviewees see a move away from this archetype, at least in its simple form. They believe, that is, that the European companies are going through a stage of transition from efficiency-oriented management (1980s) to quality-driven management (the spirit of the 1990s), with a correspondingly greater emphasis on management training and development.

It is the executives from what we have called the Euro-Latin countries who urge this development most forcibly, the northern European view being that this transition process started earlier. Generalising the views across the countries, however, the desired profile of the new managers is that they should:

- be younger
- exhibit a willingness to take risks
- be able to operate in a *less* proceduralised environment
- have a questioning attitude to management practices and choices
- not to be scared to take decisions
- be able to communicate, at all levels and in all directions.

All this is seen as desirable in a situation where there will be less bureaucracy and less emphasis on co-ordination through hierarchy. As an Italian executive expressed it: 'We feel sure that the necessary change of the managerial profile passes through a more general stage of de-hierarchisation of the whole organisation.'

Or to put it another way, in the efficiency stage the emphasis was on strict definition – of programmes, objectives, and behaviours. Now in the quality stage the demand is for multifunctionality, plurality and proaction. Again an Italian executive commented: 'We want an intellectual contribution from management, facilitated by a participative style. We give a lot of room for discussion, but then we want speed of execution.'

Another strand in this formulation is the emphasis on exchange of experience, and especially international experience. One of the German executives argued the importance of: 'internationality, of being able to take a European viewpoint in terms of the market, of having the means to adapt management systems and a pan-European management orientation.' This perceived need for a new style of management crosses with the opening up of Eastern Europe. It is felt that a response to this challenge can only be achieved by a better use of management resources, and a stronger emphasis on 'international-ised management', in the middle as well as at senior levels.

A new twist to the thesis is provided by one of the French executives who argues for an increase in the complexity of management roles to correspond to the decrease in organisational complexity: 'The process of structure simplification, the de-bureaucratisation of the organisation, must be balanced by deeper knowledge and skills regarding human resources.' And the enhanced emphasis on communication skills is fuelled by the greater perceived importance of both suppliers and distributors, discussed earlier. One of the Italian executives went even further, suggesting that the whole operation is suffused by a need to communicate the brand image, the identity of the trademark, and to evoke a response in the public mind.

To sum up, the car manufacturers feel they need teams which are creative rather than efficiency-minded, younger rather than vastly experienced, but above all international in outlook and versatile in management performance. In this context management development is seen as having a strategic nature, as a way of achieving competitive advantage.

The Dynamics of Change

There is clearly more agreement than dissension among our interviewees, though we have tried to represent the shades of opinion and emphasis among them. It may be helpful to round off with some propositions that supplement the testimony of the practitioners.

First we would like to argue that while the industry is a mature one, the various engine size (cc) segments have different life-cycles. The more flexible technology of the early 1980s facilitated the widening and deepening of the product ranges. In fact this has been applied at the small end of the range, and is working up to the D and E segments (Table 5.5) where gains are still to be made. So the small car end of the range is more mature, more competitive, and the Euro-Latin manufacturers that have been strongest there have more to fear from Japanese competition and are more hostile to it.

An alternative yet overlapping explanation of the different attitudes to the Japanese hinges on the degree of globalisation. Although from the outset motor manufacturers have been open to international competition, the individual companies are marked by different levels of globalisation, often reached at different times. So that manufacturers of prestige cars – in our study Jaguar, Porsche, Mercedes, BMW, and in part Rover – have been the first to seize the opportunity to pursue global niche strategies, while the companies

focusing on utility cars have a corporate history and culture dominated by national values – typically Fiat, PSA and Renault. Only more
recently have these companies formulated global strategies, at least
for some of their products. This latter group depend more on
Europe, more on their home countries, and more on keeping out the
Japanese.

In this dimension of global versus non-global (or late global) there
are also manufacturers occupying an intermediate position. VAG's
(Volkswagen) posture of global competition can be traced back to
the international success of the Beetle. Or again Lancia, and even
more Alfa Romeo, offer the Fiat group the opportunity to compete at
a global level in the segments of high-powered cars, albeit only
recently.

The more globalised manufacturers in terms of the above sketch
not only attach less importance to the Japanese threat, but are also
less likely to see 1992 and the Single European Market as having a
major impact. These manufacturers, of course, incline to the view
that their niches are more defensible than are the operations of the
generalists: the Single European Market may widen their scope and
facilitate the organisation of distribution, but it is not expected to be a
major event. These assumptions may, however, be undermined by
the opportunities presented by new flexible technology to engage in
multi-niche strategies. The essence of this is that one starts from a
fairly homogeneous set of components, still uses mass production
techniques to a degree, but is able to offer different products, each
focused on a specific market niche.

We have tended in this discussion of reactions to the Japanese to
concentrate on the two poles – the prestige car manufacturers and the
Euro-Latins. For the manufacturers in the middle ground – Ford,
VAG and GM/Opel – two other factors probably serve to determine
attitudes. The first is that these are companies accustomed to global
competition for a long time, while the second is that they have their
bases in countries which have already experienced a fair degree of
Japanese penetration.

Towards a Scenario

In any attempt to construct a scenario for the industry we would like
to suggest that the following elements are 'musts': the role of
Japanese competition; the basic conception of the car business; and
managing suppliers.

We have already discussed the how and why of Japanese penetration and the European reaction. No one doubts that Japanese
competition will continue but the question for the would-be scenario

builder is: in which countries and segments is the Japanese presence likely to be more substantial?

The view is that the Japanese are likely to be more successful competing in the utility car segments than in the leisure segments; that they will have most difficulty competing against European luxury cars. And approaching the issue by country rather than by market or segment, the Japanese will be most disadvantaged in countries which attach most importance to vehicle shape and style, and where these preferences reflect something in the national culture.

A further consideration with regard to the Japanese is that the competition they offer is usually evaluated on a product-to-product basis. This is entirely sensible, but another factor may give the Japanese a competitive advantage. If European market shares are eroded by Japanese competition then the distributors of European makes are likely to suffer a decline in profitability. This would make them very responsive to Japanese overtures, so that the Japanese may win over greater market share through the dynamics of distributor loyalty.

The second scenario consideration must hinge on the basic conception of the car business. The two counterposed conceptions are standardisation and microsegmentation. Traditionally standard-isation has been viewed as the key, but increasingly microsegment-ation appears to offer competitive advantage, and flexible technology may offer the means to reconcile these two approaches. But we are speaking here of possibility rather than of *fait accompli*.

The relationship with suppliers is important for a variety of reasons already canvassed – continuity of supply and security of operations, control, the initial contribution to quality, and so on. To this may be added the fact that both manufacturer preference and Japanese pressure are likely to lead to concentration among suppliers, through agreement or merger and acquisition processes. This in turn is likely to lead to a departure from the system of national networks of suppliers. Component supply is already international, but the development envisaged here would make it global, with a concomitant challenge for supplier management.

People and Culture

At an earlier stage we reported the views of the executives concerning a desirable transition from efficiency management to complexity management. The management style that emerged from the restructuring of the 1980s embraced rationality and efficiency within a rather short-term orientation. The complexity/quality management challenge of the 1990s calls for a management that is international, entrepreneurial, creative, interfunctional and communicative. All this has major implications for change in corporate culture. What is more, a lead for this change must come from the top with senior management itself demonstrating an ability for innovative thought and action.

6

European Developments in the 1990s: Managerial Views and Implications

Roland Calori

The four previous chapters took the perspective of each of the four industries that we have studied. Each industry has specific dynamics and of course the industry level is one at which it is appropriate to formulate strategies.

Now we will try to analyse the dynamics of the European market across industries, and some forces and perspectives common to several industries will be discussed. The important differences across industries and European countries will also be highlighted. At each step we will try to draw out the practical managerial implications regarding:

- diagnosis: how to assess the forces of internationalisation at the industry and at the segment level
- strategies: how to design an international strategy in Europe
- organisation: how to organise and manage an international firm at the European level, and how to reconcile synergies and local responsiveness.

Practitioners, however, should not expect any simple success recipe, because there is no simple recipe. What we will propose here will be ways to tackle the problems.

This chapter and the next are organised around ten themes, not all of equal importance. The first four themes are common to all industries, most managers agree about them, but there are also some differences that are worth mentioning.

The Themes

First, the dynamics of the competitive system may be different across segments in a given industry (by segment we mean a subset of products or customer groups, for instance luxury cars, F, is a segment in the car industry; high net worth individuals is a segment in the retail banking industry). So the segment level is the most appropriate one at which to analyse and formulate a strategy.

In the 1990s, a sort of bi-polarisation of all these industries will occur, with companies having to choose between becoming one of the major competitors (reaching an overall critical size in several segments) or focusing on one or a few niche(s). In both cases differentiation and international scope will probably be the main source of competitive advantage.

The concentration of the industry, which has been strong in the 1980s, will go on in the 1990s (with varying intensity between industries and countries). The forms of concentration will evolve and diversify: from mergers and acquisitions to various forms of alliances. As a result of these three forces, more federative forms of organisations should develop. In all cases the competition will be worldwide (even if it is not global according to a strict definition of the term). North American and Japanese competitors are expected on the European market in all these industries at different degrees and time horizons. Managers should assess globalisation and localisation forces, and look for 'loose bricks' to plan or to foresee entries and exits.

The next four developments are shared by some of the industries that we studied: they will be discussed in the following chapter. The first is, considering the political changes in Eastern Europe, managers are planning and some are implementing prudent moves towards Eastern European markets. But there are several Eastern Europes. The West German investments in East Germany (in the context of reunification) are different from the 50/50 joint ventures in Russia.

Secondly, international competitors (small ones as well as large ones) care about the development of their future 'European marketing': branding, advertising, and pricing across countries (however, the retail banks seem to be less concerned for the moment).

Thirdly, southern Europe will offer the biggest potential for growth in the EC, in the four mature industries that we studied. Fourthly, the personal development of managers will be a crucial source of competitive advantage, and in particular, training is becoming a strategic weapon.

These eight fundamental forces are presented in Table 6.1, which gives the perceived importance of each competitive force in each industry and mentions the countries where managers have the corresponding opinion. One might be surprised that we did not mention the Single European Market (1992) as one of the driving forces of industry dynamics in the 1990s. The reason is simple: for most of the managers, the Single European Market (SEM) will not be a crucial force in the evolution.

Table 6.1 *Industry profiles on the main driving forces*

Driving forces	Car manufacturing	Brewing	Retail banking	Book publishing
Segments in the industry have specific dynamics	FR-GB-SP-IT-FRG[1]	FR-GB-SP-IT-FRG-NL[2]	FR-GB-SP-IT-FRG-NL[3]	FR-GB-SP-IT-FRG-NL[3]
Reach a critical size or focus on a niche	FR-GB-IT-FRG[1]	FR-GB-SP-IT-FRG-NL-DK[2]	FR-GB-SP-IT-NL-DK[2]	FR-GB-SP-IT-FRG-NL[3]
Concentration by mergers, acquisitions and alliances	FR[2]-GB-SP-IT-FRG?[1]	FR-GB-SP-IT-FRG?-NL-DK[1]	FR-GB-SP-IT-FRG-NL-DK[3]	FR-GB-SP-IT?-FRG?[2]
Competition is worldwide	FR-GB-SP-IT-FRG[3]	FR-GB-IT-FRG-NL-DK[1]	FR-GB-FRG-NL[1]	FR-GB-SP[1]
Prudent moves towards Eastern Europe	FR-GB-IT-FRG[2]	FR-FRG[1]	FR-GB-FRG[1]	FR-FRG[2]
Growth in Southern Europe	FR-SP-FRG[1]	FR-GB-SP-IT?-FRG-DK[2]	FR-GB-SP-FRG-NL-DK[2]	FR-GB-SP[1]
Developing European marketing (for international competitors)	FR?[2]-GB-IT-FRG[1]	FR-GB-SP-IT-FRG-NL-DK[3]		FR-GB[1]
Training becomes a strategic weapon	FR-GB-SP-IT-FRG[1]	FR-SP-FRG-NL[1]	FR-GB-SP-IT-FRG-NL-DK[2]	FR[1]

[1] minor evolution of the industry
[2] major evolution of the industry
[3] fundamental evolution of the industry

FR: France
GB: Great Britain
SP: Spain
IT: Italy

FRG: Federal Republic of Germany
NL: the Nethe`lands
DK: Denmark

Fifthly, the impact of the SEM will be 'psychological', 'marginal', or 'indirect'. There are some exceptions: for some managers in the car industry the impact of the harmonisation and of the foreign policy of the EC will be important. In the retail banking business, the SEM (which had already started in 1990) will intensify competition and facilitate acquisitions and alliances abroad. The perceived impacts are different across countries, low in liberal ones (such as the UK and the Netherlands), high in more protectionist countries (such as France and Italy).

The last theme of the following chapter is the most important one; it has been developed by the interviewed managers and our cross-country comparisons confirm it: the diversity of Europe will still be very high, diversity of industrial structures (in a given industry), diversity of consumer behaviour, cultural traits, zones of attraction. So how is one to deal with such a patchwork?

Europe *is diverse*; on the other hand, the SEM contributes to the harmonisation of the European system. How can we reconcile diversity and harmonisation, how can we be European and world-wide? These are the important paradoxes which emerged from our study. Now we want to give some answers.

Market Segmentation

The segments of a given industry have different dynamics, and industries are more and more segmented. Managers agree on the increasing diversity of the segments in a given industry. It implies that *firms will increasingly have to differentiate* their strategies between segments, and that there will be *opportunities for focusing on particular segments*.

In the retail banking industry for instance, the segment of high net worth individuals is certainly the one which will become more international. It will be an opportunity for foreign banks, German, British and later on Japanese, to take a position in Europe and several of the bankers mentioned this as 'a war aim'. High net worth individuals can easily be reached by selective implantations in some major European cities:

> 1992 is important for banks but again you have to divide the market into several segments. In my opinion, if you want to specialise . . . everybody knows that a high net worth individual in general is more profitable for a bank than just a blue-collar worker in any factory! . . . And the top of the market is an opportunity to become more international (the Netherlands, retail banking).

Investment funds, which can be sold through direct banking and may take advantage of an international network will also quickly become

more international. Already, the most European financial institution
– ROBECO – is selling investment funds across Europe. In general,
all the financial services which could be sold through direct marketing
are opportunities to extend across frontiers without investing in a
network.

On the other hand, payment systems, the supply of credit,
consulting for shopkeepers and self-employed tradespeople, and
financial services to low-income customers will probably remain
regional or national markets; they require proximity or have a low
value added.

This segmentation trend is so strong that several banks in a variety
of countries are specialising their branches: it will be a major change
in the 1990s:

> We must begin to think in terms of different types of branches, depending
> on the place and on the targeted segment. So, from the universal branch to
> the minimal branch (fitted with cash dispensers or ATMs) . . . with a
> range of possibilities in between . . . It will depend on the segment of
> customers we want to serve (Italy, retail banking).

There are also differences in the dynamics between segments in the
car manufacturing industry; the top segment (the upper segment
starts at a price of about 50,000 DM, the luxury segment starts at a
price of about 75,000 DM, at summer 1990 prices), is growing faster
and will be more international. Jaguar, Porsche, Rolls Royce,
Mercedes cars sell all over the world, including Japan.

Worldwide competition does not affect all segments in the same
way. For instance, Japanese car manufacturers started to compete
with middle-range cars in most European countries and with four-
wheel drive vehicles in France. They may compete with luxury cars in
the longer term, but probably not before the end of the 1990s:

> In this luxury industry (luxury car segment), for some while, for some
> years, there will be quite some tussles as to how long it takes the Japanese
> to learn our tricks. But certainly for the volume industry (the mass car
> segment), there has been no question that they are well in advance of
> everybody else, technologically and managerially (Great Britain, car
> manufacturing).

On the other hand, opportunities in Eastern Europe are likely to be
limited to lower segments for the duration of the 1990s.

In the beer industry there are several ways to segment the market,
the most common being based on quality and image. The top of the
pyramid: 'specialities' and *bières spéciales* (the higher value-added
products) became more and more international in the 1980s, and this
tendency will continue in the 1990s. 'Specialities' offer many niche
opportunities for smaller competitors. The segment of non-alcoholic

(or low-alcohol) beers which need high marketing support will become an international business too. The growth in Europe of big food retailing chains will reinforce this trend.

A market segment may correspond to a country (or a region), when a country has very specific competitive rules. The German market is an exception in the beer industry, with limited import–export sales and a regional speciality orientation (pure beer): 'The regional orientation of the German market will certainly remain strong . . . It is coherent with the development towards specialities . . . Just the specialities' (Germany, brewing).

The book publishing industry belongs to a wider sector defined as 'communication media' where some major international groups already compete. The most common segmentation of the book publishing market differentiates mainly between literature (pocket books, general literature, youth books), 'heavy products' (art books, encyclopedias, and so on), school books, and scientific, technical and management books. Each of these segments has its own dynamics regarding, for instance, growth and scope (national versus international). At one end of the spectrum are the 'heavy products' which will become more and more international:

> If there is to be a European market in book publishing, it will be in the domain of heavy products – or products having a high profitability threshold. On the other hand in general literature groups do not have any European strategy, it is a more risky and fragmented business where small firms can be effective (France, book publishing).

The segment of scientific, technical and management books is also more open to internationalisation.

> Especially in science, technical and medical, you have to be able to sell around the world. Your national market is not big enough. The specialist author in that field will want access to international readers. So if you are small, you have to be in a network. If you cannot, the big publishers will attract the authors (Great Britain, book publishing).

On the other hand some segments are, and will stay, nationwide; for instance school books and most of the general literature business (when the language is not multinational): 'There is a typical national market, I mean one type of books hard to export: the market of school books. The language barrier excepted, all school books are dependent on politics, programmes and pedagogues which are different across countries' (France, book publishing). In addition, the pressure of substitutes such as computers, CD-ROM, video, is also very different between segments: high in encyclopedias and dictionaries for instance, negligible in literature.

The potential of international development of a segment is often

Table 6.2   *Differences between segments considering scope*

Still room for national scope	⟶	more and more international scope
Consulting for shopkeepers	ATMs	high net worth individuals
BANK		
payments for low income customers	direct banking	investment funds

		Luxury cars
CARS	small, medium, large cars	

Specialities (regional)		Specialities (international)
BEER		
middle and low end segments		special beers
	non-alcoholic beers	
restaurants, bars		food stores

School books		encyclopedias
BOOKS		
	literature, youth books	art books
	scientific and business books	

Note: All segments are not presented.

linked with two characteristics of the business: high sophistication of clients and high investments. Figure 6.2 shows the great differences between the evolutions of the scope of some segments in a given industry.

Marked differences also exist on other competitive characteristics, such as growth or the degree of concentration. This leads to statements such as: doing business in encyclopedias and art books is closer to doing business in investment funds than to publishing school books. Some industrial economists or practitioners may be surprised by such a proposition based on strategic characteristics.

The practical implications for firms in the 1990s are clear. Managers should define specific strategies at the segment level, which is the most accurate. And the strategies of a firm involved in several segments should be clearly differentiated. As the rules of the game are different, companies should organise by segment (product market) in order to fit with specific strategic projects. For instance, the question has been raised in the car industry:

Does the recent acquisition of Jaguar by Ford, and GM effectively taking control of Saab, does that herald the end of the two sectors of the industry: volume and specialists . . . No, I think that what will happen is that the owners of the specialist marks will try to keep them utterly independent and won't try to merge them. I think that would kill the market if you try to merge them in with the rest (Great Britain, car manufacturing).

The second consequence is that some competitors will find it easier to focus on *one* or *a few* segment(s) of an industry.

The tendency towards *microsegmentation* will increase the heterogeneity of the competition. In the beer industry for instance non-alcoholic beers have created a new segment and several microsegments such as whisky malt beer, aphrodisiac beer, morellos beer, panachés, beers with fruit juice, and so on, have added a number of new niches in the market.

In the car industry too, proposing several versions and presentations of the same model is becoming the rule, and the leisure versus utility dichotomy is increasing: 'One thing is helping us, the market is definitely becoming more sophisticated and segmented . . . If you analyse the market, it has moved down into much smaller segments. It also gives us the chance to pick up the niches we want to be in' (Great Britain, car manufacturing). These comments touch a second aspect of the major trends expected in the 1990s in Europe: a kind of bi-polarisation of these industries between big competitors with a critical mass in several segments and companies focused in one or a few niches.

Reach a Critical Size or Focus on a Niche

In the 1990s a sort of bi-polarisation of these industries will occur, and companies will have to choose between becoming one of the biggest competitors (reaching an overall critical size) or focusing on one (or a few) niche(s) or segment(s) to reinforce their competitive advantage. In other words, the medium-sized 'generalists' will be in difficulty. This phenomenon is the result of two combined trends: (a) the rise of technological and marketing investments, and (b) the tendency towards a stronger segmentation of the market (cf. the previous section).

When it becomes harder and harder to differentiate (the four industries that we studied are mature) and when some barriers to free competition are taken away, companies have to strengthen their competitive advantage.

Some will strengthen their advantage by reaching a critical mass and serving the whole market; they will exploit economies of scale (reduced unit costs thanks to higher volume), economies of scope (economies from sharing resources and skills and from synergies between businesses) and will exploit their high bargaining power with clients and suppliers. But as the market becomes more and more segmented, as strategies have to be differentiated between businesses, and as quality is becoming more and more important on the sophisticated European market, these firms will have to change from being 'generalists' to a position of 'differentiated generalists' (both playing volume *and* differentiating their strategies across segments, both trying to have competitive costs *and* a high level of quality).

Some other companies will strengthen their competitive advantage by focusing on one (or a few) niche(s) and serving it (them) with perfectly adapted products and services, but *also* with 'acceptable' costs (which means they will have to reach a critical size on the given segment). So they will enjoy a sort of total advantage on a given segment: favourable position on both differentiation *and* costs. Companies which focus on a *few* segments will be called 'multi-specialists'; companies which focus on one segment will be called 'niche players'.

The traditional dichotomy between low cost and differentiation will become less relevant; the relevant dichotomy will be between 'differentiated generalists' on the one hand, 'niche players' and 'multi-specialists' on the other.

The book publishing industry in Europe already has very different competitors: big international communication media companies such as Bertelsmann, Hachette, Groupe de la Cité, Pearson and Reed; and smaller book publishers more or less focused on some segments. The bi-polarisation of this industry will certainly become accentuated in the 1990s:

> Our target is to get within the top six companies because we think there are going to be six major players, and then a lot of minnows swimming around the edge. We think that is the place to be successful; the time of the middle ground has been and gone . . . There will be no middle ground players any more.. You have either got to be investing heavily in major schemes, production and marketing, or you have got to go for little niche markets (Great Britain, book publishing).

Or again:

> There will always be large and small publishers, but the middle-sized companies are being increasingly acquired by big publishers operating at an international level (the Netherlands, book publishing).

Some segments will be more hospitable for small competitors, for instance specialised literature (with many possible niches). Niche does not mean necessarily a national or regional market; on the contrary, the best niche players in the 1990s will be international. The international scope will help companies reach a critical size in the niche and raise barriers to competition. The strategy of the Dutch publisher Elsevier which focused on scientific and professional books and developed worldwide is a good example of an international niche strategy.

The same bi-polarisation is predicted in the retail banking business, but it is going to be a new phenomenon in the case of this industry:

> I do not think that the universal bank, such as BNP, will be more successful than specialised banks such as La Compagnie Bancaire . . . I think there will be six to eight universal banks in Europe by the year 2000, three French banks, two British ones and a couple of German banks . . . The other ones will have to specialise (France, retail banking).

The changing attitude of customers is one of the driving forces of the polarisation:

> More and more, the customer will not take all his or her services from the same bank. The higher net worth individuals or the small businesses are more and more likely to take specialist services from niche players who deliver that particular service better than anyone else does (Great Britain, retail banking).

The banks which will focus on a precise product/customer group should try to become international to strengthen their particular competitive advantage: 'Some financial institutions which focus will try to be European in their business, for instance the Compagnie Bancaire (strongly relying on direct marketing) or the best example – ROBECO – a truly European competitor focused on investment funds' (France, retail banking).

There seems to be an exception to this opinion on bi-polarisation in retail banking; some German bankers believe that the model of the universal bank will continue in the 1990s. The evolution discussed above may also take longer in southern countries, where the geographical proximity of the branch is still extremely important for the average Italian or Spanish customer.

As most of the retail banks will start with diversified activities, there should be a lot of transfers of businesses between competitors and most of the resulting institutions may look like multi-specialists (Bryan, 1988). Or to put it another way, each bank is diversified at the present time, and some of them will probably have to specialise.

In the car industry which is already more concentrated, further bi-polarisation will not be so marked. Some independent German car manufacturers demonstrate now that a company that is focused on the top segment and/or luxury cars and selling worldwide – an international niche player – can be effective with an output of around 0.4–0.5 million cars a year. But recently, several focused competitors have been taken over by large 'generalist' groups: Alfa Romeo and Ferrari have passed to Fiat, Jaguar has passed to Ford, and Saab has passed to GM. In these cases at least, it seems that the groups are going to preserve the autonomy of these taken-over companies.

So will there still be independent international niche players in the car industry by the year 2000, in a pure bi-polar system? No one can really predict the outcome, but there are some developments which could help independent focused car manufacturers to persist: alliances on R&D could help them to keep at the technological forefront, the market for luxury cars is growing (especially in Japan), luxury car manufacturers feel the need for exclusive distribution channels with superior service, and new manufacturing technologies could enable shorter series of vehicles. If independent international niche players survive, they will be pushed up to the top of the luxury segment (BMW and Porsche have already started to position themselves higher).

In the brewing industry the bi-polarisation – size/niche – is much more predictable:

> The first phenomenon is the phenomenon of size. I think that for breweries, the intermediary size will not exist any more. Either you are a small brewer, not in direct competition with the big ones, and you install yourself in market niches which are too small to interest the big companies, or you have to be big. This logic leads to two poles, on the one hand very large companies, and on the other, small focused dynamic companies. I do not believe in middle-sized companies between these two extremes (France, brewing).

To make profit out of a brewery, a minimum capacity of 2 million hectolitres a year is needed, except for very special beers. Capital and marketing expenses are getting higher and higher, so there will be only two alternatives to the international size strategy: (a) to keep a regional niche after having reached a sufficient regional scale with a strong enough image and a focus on bars and restaurants, and (b) to focus on the top of the pyramid: specialities, exporting to some foreign markets (as the value added of the product will be high enough to cover transportation and marketing costs).

The niche concept must not be misunderstood, there is a niche when there exist some real barriers to competition (exclusive product/service, image, captive distribution channel). Mere geographical proximity will not be a barrier if production costs are too high compared to the major competitors.

The best niche players will take an international position:

> I think that in the 1990s, for the big ones, there will be more possibilities, up-scaling. I also strongly believe in the small niche breweries, either on a specific segment of the beer market, or on a specific area selling to bars. Medium-sized breweries must make choices: either they must become big, or they must aim at some precise segment(s) of the industry. We are a European niche brewery. We aim specifically at the premium segment in the various geographical markets (the Netherlands, brewery).

Even German brewers, most of whom believe that the very fragmented German market will remain fragmented, predict the first stages of a bi-polarisation in the 1990s: 'There will be further concentration. But the growth of the big firms will give the small flexible firms an opportunity to differentiate' (Germany, brewing). The practical implication for managers can be summed up as follows: in the 1990s, your company will either have to become one of the biggest 'differentiated generalists', or a multi-specialist, or a niche player; in most cases it will be important to have an international scope.

The generalists who would lag behind the leaders in size or in quality of products and services will have problems; so rationalisation strategies, and merger and acquisition strategies, will be in vogue. The share swap and alliance between Renault and Volvo, for instance, is an interesting case of the formation of a 'differentiated generalist' in the car industry.

Medium-sized competitors will have to choose between huge investments to become bigger, or to refocus their portfolio of businesses on a few market segments (or niches) to become multi-specialists. And the second option may have more going for it. A company like Elsevier succeeded in recent years in such a turn-around:

> Until a few years ago, Elsevier was the largest book publisher in Holland. We have now virtually withdrawn from the Dutch book market . . . Not big enough to generate long-term profit growth . . . We did a turnaround, focusing on the segments at the top of the pyramid worldwide: scientific and professional books. Sales did not grow for some years but net margins trebled. Elsevier currently derives two-thirds of its trading result from markets outside Holland, approximately half of the profits from foreign markets comes from America and the remaining half from Europe and Japan.

The small businesses will only have one solution left, that of focusing on a 'real' niche; so they will have to strengthen their competitive advantage in their territory in order to dominate it and deter entries. There will be many opportunities for that, at least in banking, book publishing and brewing. The alternative will be to sell the business before it is too late! And this selling of companies will create opportunities of acquisitions in Europe.

Concentration: Mergers, Acquisitions, Alliances, Agreements

In Europe the rate of mergers and acquisitions has much increased during the last years; this tendency will strengthen in the 1990s. Forms of quasi-concentration – alliances, agreements – will develop particularly in industries like retail banking and book publishing.

Acquisitions and alliances will be the quickest way to gain market share and to become international in the four mature industries discussed in this book. The speed and intensity of the concentration process will vary according to the present level of concentration of each industry: it will be higher in the retail banking business (the most fragmented now) and lower in the car industry (now the most concentrated).

Everyone knows that the hardest thing in acquisition is *after*; managing the acquired firm, matching companies' cultures and styles. A new form of *federative* organisation may well develop as a result of market diversity (across businesses and countries) and of the acquisitions and alliances. *Federations* will be more structured than pure holding company forms, in the sense that they transfer skills and develop synergies between the companies of the federation. On the other hand, they are less structured than traditional multidivisional groups in the sense that they preserve a high autonomy for the subsidiaries and business units forming the company. The emergence of this new organisational form will be discussed later; it is one of the major challenges in the 1990s, as the failure rate for acquisitions is still high. In principle, alliances and agreements are fine but their success also requires some particular management skills.

Figure 6.1 gives a synthesis of the present degree of concentration on the European market (measured by the approximate market share of the first four competitors in Europe). Another dimension

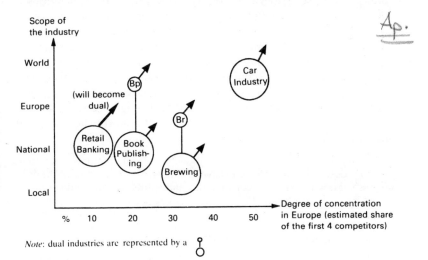

Note: dual industries are represented by a ○

Figure 6.1 *Predicted evolution of the degree of concentration and scope*

has been integrated to consider the existence of a number of small competitors behind the leaders. This shows that the brewing industry is already a 'dual' or 'bi-polar' industry with a few major competitors and a high number of small ones. Four competitors, Heineken, Kronenbourg (BSN), Carlsberg and Interbrew together hold about 30 percent of the European market but there are still a multitude of small breweries (about 1500), most of them in Germany. The book publishing industry is also bi-polar with some 15 major competitors (Bertelsmann, Hachette, Reed, Pearson, Mondadori, etc), and a high number of small companies. This is schematised by two separate circles in Figure 6.1. A third dimension has been crossed with the degree of concentration: the scope of the industry, from local to global (based on a rough estimation of the share of the national competitors in their home country and European competitors in Europe). Arrows in Figure 6.1 show the direction and the intensity of future concentration (predicted by the managers) as well as the evolution of the scope of the market.

In the brewing industry (in overcapacity now in Europe), two forces drive the concentration of the business: heavy investment in production and growing investment in marketing under the pressure of the food distribution channel. In brewing, a lot of consolidation at the European level has taken place during the last 20 years. But two important markets remain fragmented: the UK and above all Germany. In the rest of Europe, the leaders, Heineken, Kronenbourg (BSN), Carlsberg and Interbrew have dominant positions in their respective countries and together hold about 80 percent of the home markets. The case of the UK is particular in the sense that the decisions of the Monopolies and Mergers Commission concerning the limitation of the number of pubs owned by brewers may create new opportunities for acquisitions and new entries in the European market. It is also particular because major continental lager producers are already on the British market through production under licence, and the future of these licences is not clear (the licencees may become subcontractors one day):

> What is happening again is, with the swing to lager, you have got a trend towards the big battalions who have got the brands. The whole of the drink business, whether it is beer or wines and spirits or soft drinks, is going global . . . In the structure of the industry we forecast changes at the production end, quite significantly for surplus capacity to come out, for production to concentrate on fewer units, which will tend to be owned by the big global brand operators (Great Britain, brewing).

In Germany, the concentration of the 1200 breweries serving a 70 million hectolitre market is likely. The uncertainty is about the speed of the concentration process, and German brewers do not agree on that.

Non-European competitors, especially the Australians, may enter and develop in the European market by acquisitions or reciprocal agreements. Some of them are already here (Elders of Australia, Labatt of Canada). A foreign competitor buying a few breweries in diverse countries could get access to the distribution channels; the UK, Spain, and tomorrow perhaps Germany offer interesting opportunities. More spectacular 'intercontinental' acquisitions and reciprocal alliances might also take place:

> I think there will be global or international beer portfolios. If you went to market in the world with an Australian lager, a German pure lager, another continental lager and an American lager there is hardly a country in the world that you could not carve up, one way or another, through balancing your portfolios (Great Britain, brewing).

In the car industry further concentration is also foreseen, albeit for other reasons: the pressure of the Japanese competition discussed in detail in Chapter 5 together with the rise of investments in technology. But opinions diverge on the form of concentration; some managers envisage more mergers and takeovers, whereas some only forecast alliances and agreements among existing competitors. In fact, two scenarios should be considered when thinking about further concentration: whether the EC decides in favour of free competition with the Japanese car manufacturers (starting from 1993), in which case takeovers are probable, or whether the EC accepts the idea of maintaining quotas on Japanese imports in southern European countries during a transitory period, in which case alliances are more probable. We are inclined to opt for a middle hypothesis of looser quotas for a short transitory period.

Alliances and agreements are likely to range from collaboration to develop for instance a 'clean car' and pre-competitive research (such as the Prometheus project) towards stronger alliances and share swaps such as the one between Renault and Volvo announced in 1990, a range indicated by some of our interviewees:

> Alliances will be on motor development, the clean car, distribution network or building mutual factories (France, car manufacturing).

> Today everybody talks to everybody. Collaboration will be on joint research and development or joint manufacturing to reduce the cost of developing cars together, to be sold under different brands (Spain, car manufacturing).

Some of these alliances will be done with Japanese car manufacturers. Right now Toyota is having vehicles manufactured at the Hanover plant of Volkswagen. Honda has vehicles manufactured by the Rover Group. Ford has announced a joint venture with Nissan to make utility vehicles at the Motor Iberica plant in Spain. Such associations may put off the need for mergers and acquisitions. But alliances are a slow process and if the Japanese pressure increases with free competition there is likely to be a quicker rationalisation in the industry resulting in far fewer companies.

Moving up the distribution–production chain the equipment manufacturers will also concentrate and become more international. Moving down the chain to the distribution end, the number of dealers will be reduced, but the North American-style mega-dealers may not be successful in Europe.

In the retail banking sector high concentration is expected in the 1990s. At present this business is still very fragmented in Europe, where the market share of the biggest bank is under 3 percent. But as it is extremely expensive to create a network of branches from scratch, the international development of European *retail* banks is likely to be done by acquisitions and alliances (reciprocal agreements). The greater importance of technological investments (computerisation), the development of telecommunication technologies, and the opportunities offered by recent deregulations are the driving forces of the concentration:

> We are busy renovating our computer system; it is an investment of about 600 million FF (this also goes for an international computer network). We think that most of the banks in Europe cannot invest so much . . . They will have to share factories and anyway they will have problems with such investments (France, retail banking).

Automatic teller machines (ATMs) today, telecommunication and on-line home banking tomorrow, will allow a geographical extension of banks but they will require high investments, which will be a barrier to small competitors.

So the concentration by acquisitions and mergers is likely to develop *first* within the frontiers of each nation:

> The Deutsche Bank already bought up a network in Italy and they want to do the same in other European countries. But there will be very few competitors with such a strategy. Most of the mergers and acquisitions will take place at home, the French in France, the Italians in Italy, the British in the UK (France, retail banking).

The recent wave of mergers in Denmark is an extreme illustration of this trend: number one, Den Danske Bank, number two, Handelsbanken, and number six, Den Danske Provinz Bank all merged to form the Den Danske Bank; number three, SDS, number four, Privat Banken, and number seven, Andels Banken, again merged to form the Unibank. These two groups now hold 55 percent of the Danish market.

Big banks taking over small banks will be the most frequent form of such acquisitions: 'Small banking institutions are increasingly under pressure. They lean on big competitors or are acquired by bigger ones. This trend will continue in the retail banking sector' (Germany, retail banking). With regard to international acquisitions, some countries appear to be particularly attractive: the UK, Spain and Italy are the ones most often cited by our interviewees; in most of the cases the acquisitions will be friendly: 'When buying a bank, its management is an important factor, so hostile takeovers seem improbable to me in the banking sector' (the Netherlands, retail banking).

The most common way to internationalise the retail banking business will be alliances and reciprocal agreements. There are already some agreements at the European level between institutions like the Dredsner Bank, the BNP, Allianz (insurance) and the Bank of Santander, for example, or between the Crédit Lyonnais, the Commerzbank, the Banco di Roma and the Banco Hispano Americano.

Some managers believe this will be the most viable way to internationalise:

> You won't see NatWest buy a major French or German bank, you won't see any institution in the UK doing that. What you will see (and what you have seen) is joint ventures, reciprocal agreements, share swaps; that's the way to get into a market (Great Britain, retail banking).

> European-wide services could not be done by a wholly owned international network; it will require co-operation with foreign networks of foreign banks in the other European countries (Germany, retail banking).

Exchanges of networks between two banks from different countries will certainly increase even if the bargain is difficult (for instance the exchange of branches between the BNP in France and the Bank of Bilbao in Spain has taken more than a year of negotiations).

The savings banks which cannot extend their territory have already started some co-operation agreements with other savings banks in the EC. Alliances will probably include insurance companies; for instance a contract between a French retail bank and a British insurance company would allow all kinds of interesting complementarities.

Besides this, many retail banks also have a corporate banking business which is already more international and can be a bridgehead in some countries. So, combining acquisitions of small banks, alliances and agreements of all kinds, some European retail banks will progressively internationalise and concentrate the market.

In the book publishing industry the concentration process may be expected to take two forms: (a) the strengthening of the big (multimedia) groups by acquisitions, and (b) more and more intensive *networking and agreements* between smaller competitors.

We had comments from France and Spain:

> Whether the small book publishers will reach some mutual agreements and form stronger networks, more competitive, or, if they do not agree, they will be eaten by the big ones.

> The Spanish market is very much fragmented. Last year 44,000 books were published by 250 publishers, among which only 20 are structured. In four to five years, with the new laws on public companies and the pressures on the market, the only ones to survive will be these 20.

Three forces drive this concentration process: the optimisation of the cost of distribution, the strategy of the big media communication groups which acquire book publishers (who are in contact with authors who are a main source of creativity), and the growing pressure of retailers (supermarkets, book/hi-fi/video retailing chains), especially if one day the regulation on the set price of books is abandoned.

Acquisitions are the quickest way to achieve international development and to jump over language barriers. Spain and the UK are certainly attractive countries for acquisitions as they give access to a world market in these basic languages. On the other hand, publishers are often strong personalities and they do not like to be eaten up (even if the buyer preserves their autonomy) so networks and joint ventures are likely to develop among the small and medium-sized competitors.

Book publishers have a long habit of networking with authors, with printers, with distributors and with other publishers, at the Frankfurt bookfair for instance where copyrights are sold abroad. Stronger networking and agreements in the 1990s will probably give birth to many more co-editions: 'We see opportunities for co-operation in economic science and in training. To develop jointly in different countries, have a book written simultaneously in several languages' (Germany, book publishing). Or again: 'I think one of the main changes will be the development of co-editions. For instance three of our collections which came out in 1989 are international co-editions, and they have had a considerable success . . . One of them has been co-edited in six countries' (Spain, book publishing).

While it seems that acquisitions and agreements are the best ways to overcome language barriers, the identity of the acquired/partner should be preserved, especially in the case of book publishing. This is a common view regarding the concentration process in the four industries that we studied in Europe: *big groups seek to preserve the identity and brands of the companies they acquire.*

Brands have value and, as the market is more and more segmented by product or country (as argued earlier), multi-brands are a way to differentiate between the businesses. After some acquisitions, a company is advised to keep such a variety. Fiat, Lancia, Alfa Romeo, Maserati and Ferrari for instance are names which correspond roughly to market segments, even though they all belong to the Fiat 'federation'.

This principle goes beyond marketing effectiveness. *The companies which grow through acquisitions on diverse markets and/or countries should be managed in a federative way.*

> In the Hachette group, there is Hachette but also Grasset, Le Chêne, Lattès, Stock, Fayard, Livre de Poche in France, Salvat in Spain, and so on, the image of the company should not disappear; if you consolidate too much, the team will disappear, and if you lose the team, you lose the substance (France, book publishing).

In a *federation* each member keeps its autonomy and identity but members share *some* things which are sources of competitive advantage (it may be some suppliers, or some R&D, or some production facilities, or logistics, or marketing) and each member benefits from the overall power of the federation. Federations are somewhere between pure holdings (with financial links) and multi-divisional structured groups. In a federation the headquarters staff are slim and act as specialist consultants for the product market units (or subsidiaries). Top managers in our study also pointed out that the roles and responsibilities of organisational units should be differentiated, with various degrees of decentralisation across the federation. In this sense, what managers called 'federations' are not far from the integrated network form described by Bartlett (1986) in the case of transnational companies.

Our differentiated federations would be much like Bartlett's decentralised integrated networks. The slight difference between the two can be explained by the development through acquisitions and alliances which seems to require a preservation of the identity of each new member in the federation.

Some giant firms, like General Motors in the automobile industry, are organised as federations in Europe (and worldwide). But so may be smaller ones, as long as they have been involved in acquisitions, in several businesses in Europe. A federative form reduces the risks of cultural clashes between the buyer and the acquired and it makes it easier to add newcomers to the structure.

Two other practical implications for managers should be underlined. As alliances and agreements seem to develop (forms of quasi-concentration), managers should think more in co-operative terms: what are the opportunities of agreements and alliances? They should start to assess *the strengths and weaknesses of their network* (compared to those of their competitors) as a complement to the good old SWOT analysis of the single company.

Mergers, acquisitions and alliances are ways to reinforce competitive advantages, to extend in other countries, as a way to enter and develop in Europe for American and Japanese firms. But they can be offensive strategies only for companies which already have some sort of competitive advantage. In this context weak competitors should prepare themselves to be sold in good condition, before it is too late. In both cases you have to be quick in the mergers and acquisitions game; it is just like at the college ball, the prettiest girls (and the most handsome guys) are picked up first. The game is not simple because boys and girls from other colleges also compete, the North Americans, the Japanese, the Australians . . . Their role in this concentration trend is important, and we will look at it in the next section. They create pressure on the Europe-based companies and sometimes take position by acquisitions or shareholding (as Honda in Rover, Elders in Courage). Extending the metaphor there are fewer reasons to close the doors if these guys/girls are attractive and have good intentions!

Steps towards Worldwide Markets

As soon as one competitor takes a position worldwide the rules of the game start to change. In the car industry the first movers were General Motors and Ford many years ago. In the beer industry Heineken was the first. In book publishing some companies started to move to a worldwide scale, especially in scientific and management books and encyclopedias. No world player has emerged yet in retail banking, but some experts think that one day Japanese banks will move to Europe as they have started to do in the USA. The broadening of geographical scope is linked with economies of scale and concentration, and then other competitors have to follow the first movers.

We would like to consider here international moves from third countries towards the EC, and from the EC towards the rest of the world, both under the form of establishment (investment) and import–export relationships. Figure 6.1 showed that the present geographical scopes of the four industries that we studied are different:

- Retail banking is still national (or even local) for most of the competitors, even if some major retail banks have some foreign subsidiaries and branches.
- Book publishing is national for most of the competitors and European or global for a few giants.

- Brewing is national for most of the competitors and European for some leaders (among whom one is trying to extend worldwide).
- Car manufacturing is European for some of the competitors and global for the others.

So, these four industries offer a complete spectrum of geographical scopes of the competition. The more the scope broadens, the more pressure and threat there is on the European market coming from third countries. But, even in the most national business – retail banking – the threat of foreign entries (Japanese in this case) influences the strategies of some firms.

The expected international pressures are different between industries: high in the car industry, lower in brewing, retail banking and book publishing.

The three forces of the triad – Japan, the USA and Western Europe – will meet on a new ground: Eastern Europe (including the USSR), where they will be relatively prudent in the short term; East Germany is already a case apart with the reunification of Germany, which issue we take up later.

Western Europe is an attractive market and will experience the growing pressure from the Japanese firms (and to a lesser degree from American firms):

- European industry is more fragmented than its US and Japanese counterparts (for instance, there are two major brewers with 80 percent of the market in the USA, compared to four of them with 35 percent in Europe)
- the European market has good potential with over 320 million people
- the problem is solvable
- in spite of differences among customers which will persist for some time, regulatory barriers between countries will fall and this will ease access
- Western Europe can be a bridge to Eastern Europe.

Foreign companies (American, Japanese or others) that are planning an entry on the European market, and European companies which are planning to extend in other European countries should 'look for loose bricks' (cf. Hamel and Prahalad, 1985). There are two kinds of loose bricks:

- a country (or region) which is open to foreign investment or to imports and which is attractive (for its domestic resources or demand, or for its access to other attractive markets). The openness of the country to foreign investments may come from a belief in free trade or from a need for foreign resources and skills

- weak points in the spectrum of possible competitive advantages in the business; these may be in costs (cost of capital or manpower, scale, processes), in technology (product innovations, manufacturing, quality of products and services), in marketing (logistics, communications) or in management.

Most of the Japanese companies do not need any lesson on this basic rule of strategy. For instance, they took their position in the UK car industry by exports and transplants, counting on the openness of Great Britain and its weaknesses in the car business (manufacturing and management). The United Kingdom is and will be a bridgehead to Europe for Japanese companies. Recent events in the computer business are a further demonstration of this simple strategy. It is sometimes also true for North American and Australian companies. Companies of European origin should follow the same principle to extend in other European countries or worldwide: look for the loose brick.

This implies a previous careful analysis of the conception-production-distribution chain (the so-called value chain in the theory of business strategy) in several possible countries, and of the barriers to imports and foreign investments. It relies on a careful analysis of the evolution of the sources of competitive advantage (costs, synergies, differentiation, proximity of the customers). Later we will propose a simple method to *assess the globalisation forces* and the *localisation forces* of an industry and of a segment in order to inspire competitive international strategies, and apply it to the businesses we have studied in this research.

In the retail banking business future Japanese entries in Europe are expected by several managers whom we interviewed:

Our real competitors in the future will be the Japanese. In the hit parade of the 15 first world banks, the first 12 are Japanese. They will enter the retail banking business in Europe one day; just like they have done in the USA – in California; they will buy up networks in Europe (France, retail banking).

The Japanese are already present in wholesale banking activities. Several European banks already raise money in Japan and borrow from Japan. Besides the Japanese, the Australians, the North Americans and the Swiss are expected to take a position in the British market. Some managers believe that the German market is also attractive to the Japanese and that now German banks are strengthening the control of their capital to deter Japanese entries.

The main force from the EC will be Western European banks going east, prudently, with measured risks. For the moment West European banks give loans, some sell banking technology, some open a few branches which have more to do with wholesale banking (although the case of East Germany is now different).

In the book publishing industry a few competitors are already competing globally, especially in the English-speaking world. British groups seem to be more interested in the English-speaking North American market than in the continent; they have a worldwide perspective. For instance, Penguin sells only one-third of its books in Great Britain, and more than half of Penguin business is in the USA:

> Americans now own a very large part of the British publishing industry. The Canadians with International Thomson have worldwide interests. On the other hand Maxwell and Reed have major interests in the United States. Even the Germans and the French have made major investments in the US and the UK . . . So it has come down at most to maybe a dozen major publishers throughout the world that control the book publishing industry (Great Britain, book publishing).

Four main expected strategic moves worldwide should be pointed out: European publishers taking a position in both the North and South American markets, the printing of books partly moving to South East Asia, and Western European publishers going east:

> Until now we discussed Spain which has 40 million inhabitants, whereas in Latin America there are 300 million in the 21 Spanish-speaking countries. This is a fabulous market. But it has a very bad economic situation . . . We must print over there . . . It is obvious that the big multinationals which have come to Spain are also aiming at the South American market (Spain, book publishing).

Publishers may also save money in having their *expensive* books printed in South East Asia (Hong Kong or Macao), and some already do it for printing artbooks. Book publishers from Western Europe, especially the French and the German, have a special interest in Eastern European markets, and they will probably strengthen their positions there.

Drinking a nice beer while reading a nice book should be appreciated in most of the countries of the world. The competitors in the beer industry are still mainly continental European (except a few of them having a small share in another continent). The Americans are powerful but they are still American; they only started to be interested in Europe and in Japan five years ago. In Europe Heineken and Carlsberg traditionally have export markets worldwide mainly because their home market was so small (but their share in other continents is still small).

Americans and Australians are likely to strengthen their position in Europe, especially the Australians who are very active competitors:

Elders is one of the most active foreign competitors in the world. They have Skerch, they have taken over Courage in the UK . . . They approach Europe from the UK. They hardly ship any beer from Australia to Holland. Fosters are one of those who might do some major acquisitions in Europe . . . They are working the way we do, with one exclusive partner in a certain country; they know Europe is a multi-local market (the Netherlands, brewing).

The Japanese could also come to Europe, the Japanese leader Kirin have publicly declared that they would like to buy a brewery. It will be harʌl anyway for these foreigners on the European market: the demand is relatively conservative, it is stagnant, and there is overcapacity.

Acquisitions are the only way to get access quickly to distribution channels and then to add one's beer to an existing portfolio. The evolution of the British and of the German market will be favourable to such strategies. The other way round a few European brands like Heineken and Carlsberg export worldwide (but there are fewer opportunities for acquisition for instance in North America). Some European specialities from smaller brewers (like Grolsch in Holland or Abbaye de Leffe in Belgium for instance) will go on having success in countries which appreciate good beer: Canada, USA, Japan, Australia, New Zealand, Indonesia, South Korea, Taïwan, Singapore and Hong Kong.

Some more spectacular intercontinental changes could happen if one of the big European brewers demands to sell or if an alliance of reciprocal distribution and production under licence were to be concluded between companies from two or three continents.

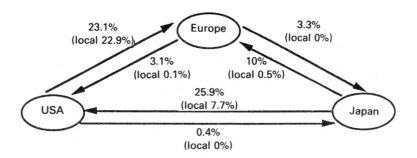

% Market share in the corresponding zones.
(local %) Share of local transplants.

Figure 6.2　*Respective shares in the triad (car manufacturing industry, 1989)*

It is banal to say that the car manufacturing industry is getting more and more global. But one should know that in the EC (which as we have seen is the first market in the world with about 13.5 million cars per year) the Japanese car manufacturers only have 10 percent of the market and the North American companies only have about 23 percent. Even more, the shares of European competitors in the USA and in Japan are still very low (about 3 percent). These exchanges are depicted in Figure 6.2.

There are still about 28 car manufacturers in the world. So the industry is not, properly speaking, global yet. Rover in Great Britain and Fiat in Italy have more than half of their sales in their home country; so *there is still much room for interpenetration of geographical markets*. This slack is likely to be taken up by the end of the 1990s.

The first driving force in this globalisation process is the rise of technological investments; the second one is the aggressive strategy of some Japanese car manufacturers (who have a strong competitive advantage); and the third one is the Single European Market (1992) which is reducing internal barriers to trade in the EC and external barriers such as quotas limiting imports of Japanese cars in southern Europe.

The quotas to limit Japanese imports in France (about 3 percent), in Italy (about 1 percent) and in Spain are being questioned right now in Brussels. The Japanese car manufacturers now have about 28 percent of the US market, so the Americans turn to Europe and give signs of collusion with the Japanese in manufacturing small cars. The Japanese have taken a position in the UK (with the share of Honda in Rover and with two transplants: Nissan and Toyota, and there are rumours about Mazda with Ford). Within five or six years these transplants will produce about 1.5 million cars, and Japanese exports will represent about 1.5 million more cars in Europe (a bit more than today). So together the Japanese could take about 22 percent of the European market in the mid-1990s, more than that if the quotas protecting France, Italy and Spain are not maintained during a transitory period. In all scenarios the Japanese car manufacturers will profit from their strong competitive advantages: in product development programmes (quicker), in manufacturing (more efficient), and in management (transferable to the USA and Europe): 'Whereas European car makers are planning a total quality system, the Japanese who already have quality are going to fight again on costs' (Italy, car manufacturing).

Europeans have some strengths in design and distribution, but the Japanese could very well get more dealers by offering them higher percentages. Even if southern Europe is protected for a transitory period, they will put pressure on northern Europe which in turn will put pressure on southern Europe and they will be able to export cars manufactured in their British or American factories, so whatever happens the Japanese will be the winners by the end of the 1990s: 'The objective is to survive, the main issue for everyone is not to get a bit more, it is to hold the existing' (Germany, car manufacturing).

On the other hand the new Eastern European market will soon bring opportunities for some West European firms. The European superiority for the top segment cars (class E and luxury cars) will probably last for some years (one and a half generation of cars); during this period the Japanese market will be *the* one for exclusive cars. The Japanese already import a high proportion of German luxury cars. But by the end of the 1990s the competition from the Japanese will put pressure on this segment too:

> The Japanese exclusive cars such as Lexus, Infinity, will be in Europe within two or three years. If you look at the content of the car, they are eight cylinders, which cost 50,000 to 60,000 DM. Their characteristics are equivalent to Mercedes S class or BMW 7 which cost 70,000 to 80,000 DM; that will be real hard competition (Germany, car manufacturing).

In this worldwide battle as most of the European car manufacturers are still European it will be even harder for them to develop worldwide.

Considering these trends, a first practical implication for managers is to assess the forces which are favourable to international development – globalisation forces – and the forces which are favourable to domestic strategies – localisation forces. This general model has been put forward by Bartlett (1986); and we operationalised it and applied it to the four industries that were studied. An evaluation of globalisation versus localisation forces can be carried out by scanning a few of the parameters.

Some economic forces have the effect of enlarging the geographical scope of a business:

- High, increasing capital intensity, i.e. the ratio investments (marketing, R&D, production) to sales.
- High, increasing optimal production–distribution scale of the business compared to the world market (ratio: optimal scale to world market).
- High, increasing pressure of the clients (international clients) and/or suppliers.
- High, increasing value-added of the product/service compared to the transportation/communication costs.
- High, increasing importance of costs as a competitive advantage and importance of economies of scale on costs.

- More international strategic moves of some competitors (new entrants in a zone or new movers abroad).

Some economic forces on the other hand tend to focus the geographical scope of a business:

- High, increasing differences between local customers' preferences rooted in cultural, physiological or technical differences (and sometimes just chauvinism!).
- High, increasing importance of the physical proximity to the client as a key success factor, for instance for delivery in time, for people-intensive businesses, for some services.
- High, increasing differences in technical norms.
- High, increasing protectionist measures (quotas, taxation on imports, subsidies to national champions, barriers to foreign investments, and so on).
- High-growth large sophisticated domestic markets, attractive enough to keep national champions busy.
- High, increasing importance of differentiation as a competitive advantage.

An analysis of these globalisation/localisation forces will give a picture of the present situation and of the changes to expect in the geographical scope of the industry, and the geographical scope *of each segment.*

Figure 6.3 gives a simplified view of the result with (1) the four industries studied and (2) a few segments in the book publishing industry. A 'global' industry has high globalisation characteristics and low localisation ones. A 'multidomestic' industry is high on localisation forces and low on globalisation forces. A 'transnational' industry is high in both globalisation *and* localisation. The fourth category low in both globalisation and localisation forces can hardly be named (something like stalemate). A dynamic analysis of these forces will help to identify the trends.

The Single European Market will reduce localisation forces in Europe: it will make differences in norms acceptable (mutual recognition of norms) and it will reduce protectionist measures. It will also increase globalisation forces by its indirect effects on international strategic moves and on cost reductions. According to the situation and to the expected evolution of the segments, strategic moves can be designed.

● In a multidomestic industry/segment (now or in the future) a company may have two main strategies according to its competitive position: stay national or buy foreign companies in attractive foreign markets (and manage them in a federative way).

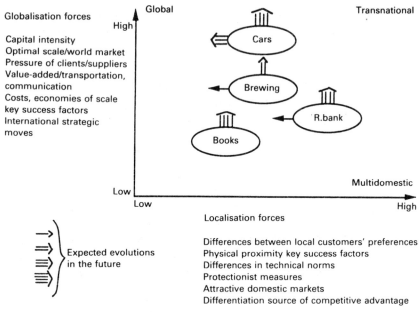

(1): Industry level

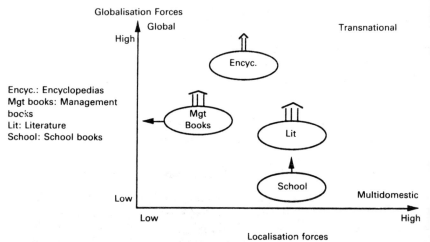

(2): Segment level

Note: The positions of industries/segments can be evaluated with a system of scores on each parameter of each dimension (one score for the present situation, one score for the expected evolution).

Figure 6.3   *Globalisation/localisation forces*

- In a global industry/segment (now or in the future) competitors should increase volume, share resources with other segments, and homogenise strategy across countries. The international development can be organic or by acquisitions. In the case of acquisitions, the strategy formulation and some elements of the value chain should be centralised and synergies between units should be exploited.

- In a transnational industry/segment (now or in the future), the international development should be done preferably by acquisitions and/or alliances. In the case of organic development, the creation of a relatively autonomous subsidiary will preserve local responsiveness. The transnational business should be managed as a 'federation', especially in the case of growth by acquisitions. In the case of organic growth, the 'integrative network' mode could also fit a transnational business.

- In a diversified company, involved in several different segments (global, transnational and multidomestic) – such as a book publisher involved in encyclopedias, school books, management books and literature (there are some that fit this description), the international strategy should be differentiated; once again a federative form would be appropriate.

- In the case of transnational industries or industries which are 'in the middle' a company may choose to accentuate co-ordination and concentration (manage the business in a more global way) *or*, on the other hand, chose to accentuate autonomy and dispersion (manage the business in a more multidomestic way) *according to the* company's specific skills.

The second implication for managers (cf. Hamel and Prahalad, 1985) is to *look for 'loose bricks'* and be selective in the international development of the firm.

Looking for *loose bricks* can be done *in a defensive manner*: a company asks itself, are there some geographic areas in my territory which are open and attractive enough for new entrants? Are there some weak points in the conception–production–distribution chain which could allow a new entrant (strong in this domain) to succeed on my territory (Porter, 1990)? Such an analysis can also be done at a country level. For example here are *some* of the (many) loose bricks we could find in the four industries studied:

- the manufacturing cost of German luxury cars
- the logistics and distribution of books in Italy
- the production costs of many British breweries and the brewing/ owning pubs dilemma in the UK

– the fragmentation and the relative technological lag of the Spanish retail banking system, with too many branches.

Eliminating such loose bricks can be a strategy for a company on its home market. When this elimination of the loose brick appears to be too difficult, then the last solution may be to welcome foreign competitors on to one's territory (as the British did in the car industry).

Symmetrically, *loose bricks should be exploited by outsiders, in an offensive strategy*:

– compete with German luxury cars on costs and price (and be as good as they are on the main key success factors: harmony of the car and best service to clients)
– enter the Italian book market on the distribution side
– buy a British brewery, modernise production capacities, get the distribution channel, add brands
– exchange a network of branches with a Spanish bank and put technology in there.

A systematic search for loose bricks, both at home and elsewhere, usually generates good ideas. This principle is also worth applying to Eastern Europe, and one can find a few loose bricks there. This will be the first focus of the next chapter.

References

Bartlett, Christopher A. (1986) 'Building and managing the transnational: The new organizational challenge' in M.E. Porter (ed.), *Competition in Global Industries*. Boston: Harvard University Press, pp. 367–401.

Hamel, Gary and Prahalad, C.K. (1985) 'Do you really have a global strategy?', *Harvard Business Review*.

Lowell, Bryan (1988) *Breaking up the Bank*. Homewood, Ill: Dow Jones-Irwin.

Porter, Michael E. (1990) *The Competitive Advantage of Nations*. New York: The Free Press.

7

Markets and Managers

Roland Calori

Prudent Moves towards Eastern Europe

Eastern Europe represents a potential market of 140 million people and of about 350 million including the western (European) part of the USSR. Purchasing power is low in these countries, especially in terms of foreign currency. But this global picture is misleading: there are several Eastern Europes.

- The German Democratic Republic as it was until October 1990 (16.5 million people) had a GNP per inhabitant a little higher than that of Spain; the area is industrialised and does not have much debt. The reunification with West Germany (monetary since 1 July 1990, full union since 3 October 1990) makes East Germany a rather attractive market with low risk, but one dominated by West Germany even before reunification. In fact East Germany has now become a part of Germany, and thereby a part of the EC.
- Czechoslovakia and Hungary are two small 'tigers' (together 27 million inhabitants) very close to Western Europe; their political, economic and social situation is favourable to trade development with Western Europe.
- Yugoslavia is a case apart: its market of some 26 million inhabitants has been more open to the west for some years, prior to the opening up of Eastern Europe in 1989.
- Poland is even more a case apart with 39 million inhabitants and a huge amount of debt (about $35 billion).
- In Bulgaria and Romania, political tensions between parties and minorities make for a rather unstable situation.
- Finally the USSR, with a strong core – Russia – and some turbulent republics, is politically also very uncertain, but on the other hand an enormous potential market.

When European managers think about the east they mainly consider the GDR as was, Czechoslovakia and Hungary, which are 'neighbours', and Russia which is a big but risky market.

West Germany certainly has advantages, based on culture and/or geographical proximity across what was the GDR bridge. France has some cultural links with Poland and Romania. Among EC countries, Germany, Italy and France have the strongest experience of previous business with the East. Everyone among our interviewees agrees that Eastern Europe is an opportunity for European development but in general, *the moves of Western European firms towards the east still are very prudent.*

> Don't we have a memory? Six months ago, newspapers wrote about the enormous debts of most of the eastern countries, their low purchasing power. The recent political changes will not transform the economic situation so quickly. Of course things will happen but it will be slow (France, car manufacturing).

Among the four industries studied, brewing will probably be less concerned with Eastern Europe. The demand for premium price western beers will be rather marginal, as will the demand for technology transfer. Some West German brewers will find an extension to their domestic market. In East Germany there is a potential of 25 million hectolitres, the breweries are obsolete, some will doubtless close, and there will be opportunities to reinvest (buy a brand) and to sell West German beer.

In the book publishing industry, the French and Germans see an opportunity for future developments. The Germans are turning to the former GDR to exploit a new market and publish new authors: 'The biggest and newest orientation for us is towards the GDR, that is what we are concerned about; the problem which we discussed at length with the executive board this last month' (Germany, book publishing).

Or again:

> We start to examine the market of Eastern Europe cautiously . . . . We recently created two subsidiaries on a 50/50 basis with one of the main Russian publishers – Progress – one in Moscow and one in Paris. We are careful, France has an important audience in Romania, Hungary and Poland, but there is the problem of repatriation of currencies in these relatively poor countries . . . . The weakness of the Russians is distribution, and we are going to help them to set up a network like ours (France, book publishing).

Joint ventures seem to be the best solution in order to take a position. The part of publishing concerned with 'heavy' products is the most concerned with these opportunities.

British publishers seem to have enough to do with the English-speaking world, and observe that it is about time that Far Eastern publishers set up laws to forbid copying. Spanish publishers find Eastern Europe rather distant and are more interested in South America.

In the retail banking industry, once again the Germans and the French will probably be the more active Western European actors in Eastern Europe. The German banks are in an exceptional situation as a result of German reunification (economic *and* monetary). They are establishing networks in what was East Germany. From this position it is likely that they will extend retail banking to peripheral countries.

Corporate banking with regard to Eastern Europe will grow with the increase in industrial and commercial activity. But *retail* banking will probably be limited to technology for some years:

> Talking about Eastern Europe, it is too soon to draw conclusions from what is happening there . . . too unstable still. There will be liberalisation in the financial industry but we do not know if those countries will let us take positions. I would say that we would rather conclude partnerships in transfers of knowhow, in selling turnkey factories. These countries have archaic systems . . . . For instance one day they will need automatic payment machines, so there is an opportunity . . . . We have signed a contract with a Russian bank for which we will take care of the computerisation of credit cards (France, retail banking).

British managers seem to be less enthusiastic, 'too risky still'; Spanish managers think these countries are too far away.

The opportunities and the expected strategic moves in the car industry are the most significant. At present, in proportion to the population, people in Eastern Europe buy ten times fewer cars than people in the EC. Table 7.1 gives a comparison of the consumption of cars between Western and Eastern European countries.

It is hard to forecast the future demand in eastern countries for 1995 and for 2000. The experts say that it should grow considerably and that it will depend on the growth of income per capita (it will also

Table 7.1 *Consumption of cars in Western and Eastern Europe*

1989 Figures (number of new cars bought every year)			
West Germany	2,820,000	USSR	975,000
France	2,350,000	Poland	250,000
Italy	2,320,000	GDR	200,000
U.K.	2,310,000	Yugoslavia	180,000
Spain	1,150,000	Hungary	130,000
		Czechoslovakia	125,000
		Bulgaria	70,000
		Romania	25,000
Total	13,400,000	Total	1,955,000
Population	320,000,000	Population	420,000,000

depend on political development and on the price of oil). In countries like the former GDR the present demand is certainly higher than 200,000; East Germans used to wait for several years to get their car because of production shortages. In the short term the former GDR is the targeted market: 'The annexation of the DDR (GDR) brings substantial growth potential but this will not be realised fully for new cars for a couple of years. In the domain of used cars, the impact will be quicker. . . . This is favourable to the West German manufacturers anyway' (Germany, car manufacturing).

The Volkswagen Golf will be produced at Dresden, Opel (GM) is already in the area of the former GDR, and some other European car manufacturers set up networks of dealers. Opel (GM) now has a joint venture in Hungary to produce the Opel Kadett. Fiat is already established in some Eastern European countries, targeting the biggest markets: the USSR, Poland and Yugoslavia. Ford is taking a position in Czechoslovakia and now in Hungary to produce spare parts to be exported:

> I think that people are going to be reluctant to invest a lot of money in Eastern Europe in manufacturing facilities so long as the currency situation is what it is. One inexpensive way to set up in Eastern Europe might be component manufacturing to start, with a view to exporting those components to Western Europe to use in carshare to generate hard currency so that you can sell new vehicles in. That will be a step, followed by manufacturing industry (Great Britain, car manufacturing).

In the next ten years the issue is smaller cars (as well as trucks), but later on the market may open up for the top car segments.

Among Eastern European car manufacturers, Lada (mainly in the USSR), Zastava (in Yugoslavia) and Skoda (in Czechoslovakia) have started some exporting. The production of the Eastern European countries has stagnated at around 2.5 million cars. With the involvement of western car manufacturers, local production could increase to up to 3.3 million cars in 1995 (USSR 1.8 million, Poland 0.38 million, Czechoslovakia 0.19 million, and GDR 0.36 million, an 80 percent increase). This would leave a share to exports from Western Europe.

But the Japanese car manufacturers have to be taken into account, for they are also aiming at Eastern Europe, including the USSR. Suzuki, for instance, is interested in Hungary, and projects are expected in Poland. Anyway the opening of Eastern Europe is like a ray of sunshine on the somewhat dark horizon of European car manufacturers:

> If you leave out the word western and say the European car market, it is 18 million potential units, that is to me a major dramatic change . . . . It will

not be a quick kill, the economies are not sophisticated enough, they do not have hard currency, and it will be a struggle, but it will happen and it will be much more dramatic than 1992 (Great Britain, car manufacturing).

We believe that simple exportation to Eastern Europe is a limited, short-term and arguably short-sighted strategy. As for all developing countries, local investments will be necessary, most often in joint ventures. In the car industry, the local development of component and equipment manufacturing will also be crucial in the first phase. As with all investments *selectivity* will be required. Some managers dream of a scenario similar to that which recently occurred in Spain; but there are two major differences: first, political instability in some of these countries and secondly, a lack of hard currency. The political and financial support of western countries for Eastern Europe may of course reduce such uncertainties.

But southern Europe is another growth opportunity.

Growth in Southern Europe

Southern Europe, including Spain and Portugal, a large part of Italy and Greece (although we conducted no interviews in Greece), is another area for growth right inside the EC. The late accession of Spain and Portugal to the EC followed this growth logic, and there were also cultural links between these countries and the rest of the continent.

One needs to recognise that Spain's economic situation is not much better than that of the former GDR. The GNP per capita in Spain is about $US12,000, hourly salaries are about $US2.4, industrial production represents about 30 percent of the GNP and the external debt is about $US34 billion. With 40 million inhabitants, Spain still has real potential for economic and social progress. The situation is similar in the south of Italy; in Portugal and Greece the need for development is even more acute. Before considering Eastern Europe, some of our managers prefer to go to southern Europe for growth opportunities (and sun).

In the beer industry the consumption is going down in the north of Europe (minus 1 percent a year on average), whereas it is going up in the south. In the 'garlic belt' (as some British people call it) during the last ten years, growth was about + 10 percent a year. The consumption per capita in Spain is now superior to that of France (60 litres per year compared to 45 litres per year), and the growth is slowing down. Growth has also slowed down in Italy which still has a low per capita consumption (24 litres per year). In the southern countries the substitution of beer for wine, and fashion, were the causes of this development: 'The present trends in growth of demand should continue for some years; that is to say stagnation or little regression in northern Europe and a relatively high growth in southern Europe (about 5 percent a year) in countries like Spain, Italy, Greece and Portugal' (France, brewing).

In Spain, in Italy and in Greece all the major European brewers, Heineken, Kronenbourg, United Breweries already have a stake; but there are still a few opportunities for acquisitions and reciprocal licences: 'The market is developing quickly, the introduction of foreign beers has boosted it. Carlsberg and Heineken have made an effort at the right time, and there are still very good prospects' (Spain, brewing). French, German, Dutch and Danish brewers agree on this.

In book publishing the French are planning to work more in the south:

> We sell to a big subsidiary in Spain called Salvat; they joined the group two years ago. Salvat is involved in all our businesses. Their turnover is about 600 million FF a year; it has developed in Latin America as well . . . . Another subsidiary in Europe is mainly based in Italy – Grollier Europe (France, book publishing).

Spanish people read more and more, and Spain is also a bridge to South America: 'The only language which is any kind of a serious competitor to English is Spanish . . . . We do also publish in Spanish and we have co-publishing ventures in other languages' (Great Britain, book publishing).

In this context, the biggest European groups are buying in Spain. Bertelsmann acquired Plaza y Ianès, Hachette bought Grisalbo, and there are other groups like Maxwell, Mondadori and Agostini working in Spain; they buy Spanish publishers and sign agreements. The Italian market may be less attractive for foreigners in the domain of general literature; but it often has growth potential in particular segments such as heavy products and scientific, technical and management books.

In the retail banking business northern Europe is saturated, whereas there is potential for development and technological innovation in the south. For instance only one Italian in two has a bank account: 'For French banks, Latin countries are most interesting, Portugal, Spain, Italy. Then, we will go to the UK . . . . The German market is too much protected for us' (France, retail banking). The major British competitors are also in Spain, where they found a 'loose brick': 'We are in Spain. Spain is a very profitable market, it is backward in terms of technology. We have the ability, therefore, to bring our expertise into that market and that is a market we will continue to develop' (Great Britain, retail banking).

Now international banks have taken up positions in Spain with large networks; including Barclays, Banque Nationale de Paris, Citibank (USA) and Deutsche Bank. They will clearly try to develop these positions. The economic development of Spain started 15 years ago with a real boom from June 1986 when Spain signed the integration agreement with the EC. When the standard of living rises, people borrow money (and pay it back). The establishment of new banks is now more controlled (as it was in Italy) but the economic and social development era is not finished yet. Transitional states like Portugal and Greece will also be attractive.

In the car industry, several car manufacturers have built factories in Spain, including Renault, PSA (Peugeot), and Ford, among others. A new competitor has also emerged in Spain: SEAT, formerly Fiat, is now under the control of Volkswagen. The Italian market has always been occupied by Fiat, of course, holding about two-thirds of the home market, so entry to the Italian market is difficult. Because of very high purchase tax on cars in Greece that market is limited to small cars or used cars; it will not really open up unless these taxes are dramatically reduced.

Considering all four industries in our study, and many others on the basis of wider knowledge, southern Europe has a significant potential for growth, with relatively low salaries for the moment and relatively good labour productivity. This may well attract companies from other countries looking for a bridgehead into Europe, and also of course European companies looking for growth or trying to relocate manufacturing.

The Emergence of European Marketing

Europe is a highly diverse cluster of countries: there is cultural diversity, differences in consumers' behaviour, technical diversity (norms), differences in taxation systems and in regulations.

This has led the majority of internationally based companies to differentiate their market strategy between countries or regions within Europe. Even when the *brand* is the same – international – the advertising themes may be different, the prices are different across countries for the same product (according to the competitive position of the firm and the level of taxes), and the distribution channels may be different.

The Single European Market is going to eliminate some of these differences: harmonisation of the value added tax, mutual recognition of technical norms and standards and so on, but certainly not all of them. On the other hand, international mergers and acquisitions lead to multi-brand groups or federations, highly diverse and at the same time trying to create some synergies. It looks as though marketing managers are going to have to work hard in formulating and implementing European market strategies that will reconcile unity and diversity!

In retail banking, European marketing is not a crucial challenge yet, simply because there is not yet any really pan-European retail bank. Some focused competitors such as ROBECO in investment funds are starting European advertising campaigns. In the case of acquisitions abroad, banks are faced with the dilemma of whether to keep the name of the acquired bank or not. There is in fact a tendency to keep the name. But keeping the name may be a barrier to changing the image when it is necessary. Direct marketing techniques and parallel distribution networks are likely to develop. European banks will need to improve their skills in these domains. With deregulation and increased competition, the managers will have to be more aware of future pricing problems.

In book publishing too, the rule is to keep the names of the publishers that 'join' a group. Various forms of direct marketing and sales by mail are expected to develop in the 1990s. For instance the leading German publisher Bertelsmann came to France by sharing a book club, France Loisir, together with Le Groupe de la Cité. These forms of distribution demand high investments but they will surely gain importance in the next few years, requiring particular marketing skills. Anyway, the traditional Frankfurt fair will remain the marketing centre of the book publishing industry.

British publishers which are more European already are concerned with the competition of US editions of their books sold in Europe. They are also concerned with the question of a more homogeneous pricing policy control. Some, like Longman, Penguin and Heinemann, have sales forces on the Continent and have begun to treat Europe as their home territory.

In the car industry the European marketing problems are pricing and distribution. At the moment, car manufacturers sell their cars at different prices throughout Europe. The price in a given country depends on the competitive position of the company and on the level of taxes (VAT and others). If the position is strong and taxes are low, the price is high; if the position is weak and the taxes are high on an attractive market, the price is low. In the 1990s the VAT should be progressively harmonised, and European car manufacturers will try more and more to sell Europe-wide (they are still mainly national). So the prices in turn should harmonise to avoid the development of parallel international distribution channels, and pricing policy will be critical, especially when margins get thinner.

The second marketing development will be in logistics. International strategies will require a reorganisation of distribution, more efficient Europe-wide; the Single European Market will facilitate it:

> 1992 in itself is going to change distribution. Because at the moment, for instance, we have a national sales company. We have a warehouse for parts, we have an office, a managing director in Belgium, in Holland and in Germany. And it is so because they are different countries. If you say there is a 13 million car market and I don't have to worry about national barriers . . . then you can get rid of half the parts, you don't have to keep them in strategic places, you can reorganise your sales coverage and you would be able to reduce dramatically the cost of distribution (Great Britain, car manufacturing).

European marketing will certainly be a key success factor in the beer industry, for leading European brands and for international niche players. Differences in consumers' habits, tastes and representations, and differences in distribution channels across countries will have to be managed.

On one hand there will be some European 'homogenisation': 'The most important change will be the need for increased skills in European marketing, pricing, distribution, packaging. Brands will become more and more European; we are busy co-ordinating our packaging at the European level. We already do it for non-alcoholic beer . . . Our advertising is becoming European (the Netherlands, brewing).

European brands are positioned as good quality beers in their original home market and they enter new markets with a position of speciality (premium price). In the 1990s, high differences in image and pricing (for the same beer between European countries) will have to be reduced; otherwise parallel distribution channels will develop (taking profit from these differences). The changes in image and price will need to be monitored carefully, as the general tendency would probably be a fall of prices and 'thinner' margins. These changes in strategy could come with changes in organisation:

> In the past, we had one organisation per country. This year (1990) we became a European organisation. The marketing will be organised with a European scope, product policies will be decided at the European level. Then the decisions will be demultiplied in each country served by the company: Belgium, France, the Netherlands, the UK, Italy and Spain (Belgium, brewing).

But it will not be so simple (the ambiguity is in the word 'demultiplied'). First, some companies growing by acquisitions are keeping the local brands (alongside their international brands), and this of course means differentiated marketing strategies. Moreover, for a given brand, some managers would recommend differentiating the advertising across countries where European consumers' behaviours are different, as in beer consumption. According to this differentiation principle a company could build its communication on, say, humour in the UK, freshness in Portugal, friendship in France, luxury in Greece, and sensuality in Italy. Even if some marketing costs are in this case duplicated, we believe that diversity should be managed by diversity.

We also agree on the future need for international competitors: (a) to concentrate and/or co-ordinate the European marketing strategy (mainly product and price), and (b) to co-ordinate distribution, sales force and communication policy. But operational marketing such as advertising (creative expression and media allocation) and sales should be decentralised at the country level (or at the level of a cluster of homogeneous countries). These suggestions are coherent with the ones of Takeuchi and Porter (1986) who claim that international marketing should *simultaneously* standardise and differentiate across countries.

But we leave the conclusion to a German manager in the car industry:

> We want a unified orientation, a unified corporate identity. But the market leads implementation. Implementation includes a part of national marketing. We do not follow the idea that the advertising strategy should be the same in France and in Germany. The advertising is something that is localised. We can help our subsidiaries, but there is so much national mentality and uniqueness . . . . We cannot feel it at the corporate level so we do not want to take care of the implementation (Germany, car manufacturing).

Some other elements in the value chain, the sequence of activities that companies configure to enhance value, will probably gain more from concentration; we have already mentioned in this connection logistics (in the car industry, in beer, and in book publishing); in some cases manufacturing too (for instance for high value-added beers). Diversity will slowly decrease in the 1990s; for instance when European TV will be common and when some major retailers will have European positions, when the rules will change for those selling foodstuffs. All this implies a need for international marketing skills.

Training: A Strategic Weapon

To formulate and implement international strategies, to succeed in international marketing and development, companies will need managers who can deal with intercultural problems. To strengthen the competitiveness of the firm and use new technologies fully, the workforce will have to be more effective (especially in industries like car manufacturing and retail banking where new technologies are key success factors). So, after all, it is not surprising that European top managers believe in human resources development as a strategic challenge in the 1990s. Recruitment of high potential multilingual managers is already considered a major challenge. With regard to the broader categories of personnel, training will again be more and more seen as a strategic weapon.

In the brewing industry pan-European brewers are clear that they need international managers:

> People must change jobs in the company, across functions and across countries; today we must be generalists, effective in different countries. For instance, I had to go back to school to improve my English. We should not recruit any manager who is not at least bilingual and mobile. When we have an international meeting for instance, we cannot afford any language problems. Interpreters are not a solution . . . . Recently we had a meeting where eight different languages were represented, English speaking was the only way to do it (France, brewing).

Or again:

> We have a number of international management programmes, where we get people together from all over the world, different operating companies, different cultural backgrounds, and put them into our management training programmes for some weeks. We have that at three levels: junior, middle and senior management. You need to work along the same lines with corporate brands . . . . The people can tell each other about their respective experiences. So you have cross-fertilisation between operating units (the Netherlands, brewing).

International publishing-media groups train international managers, but smaller book publishers have a different challenge, that of implanting management techniques and marketing in a business which was not much open to such things in the past.

International experience and training will also be conditions of success in the car industry as was argued in Chapter 5, but other specific questions have to be solved: cross-fertilisation between functions and teamwork, involving middle managers and people on the shopfloor: 'Understanding that the power comes from the 40,000 people of the company, and not from the board of directors, is a penny that has dropped here' (Great Britain, car manufacturing). The Japanese style may have inspired British managers. Now most European car manufacturers include among their priorities training the mass of underqualified workers (some immigrant workers in the motor industry do not even know how to read and write). The workforce of the automobile industry is turning to a new style.

Retail banking is in the same situation in that training is a priority at all levels of the hierarchy. The quality of services depends on the quality of the personnel. As consumers are more and more demanding and technologies are more and more sophisticated, retail banks have to 'transform' their employees. Personal training in part was mentioned by most of the interviewed managers in retail banks as a key success factor (up to 7 percent of the salaries are spent in training in some banks).

> There are still steep differences between managers in our network, differences in training level. We are making a particular effort in this domain. The personnel should be trained to face the future and strengthen the bank culture. The concept of best service to clients should be based on getting the most out of computers, but also on well-trained employees (Spain, retail banking).

A message echoed in Italy:

> I believe that customers are quite concerned with the quality of services and on the way they are sold, and so with the quality of the people in the bank. We have to be professionals and, for this reason, the training of our front office staff is a priority, as they are the first contact with the potential customer . . . . Last year 4000 employees participated in our training courses (Italy, retail banking).

The content of training will be more and more a mix of technical and management skills, where previous training emphasised the technical and procedural aspects of bank work. Training will be increasingly mixed with other means of personal development – participative management, periods spent abroad, job rotation – in order to change competences *and behaviour.*

Such practices show the move towards integrated and 'strategic' human resource management. Industries have specific needs but a common one: the development of managers who can work internationally and deal with intercultural problems (at least for the companies which have an international strategy).

Business schools know there is a pressing need, and most of them proclaim the international nature of their programmes, which in fact are all too often superficial (a couple of practice periods abroad are not enough to learn to deal with multicultural problems). International companies could organise so as to satisfy their own needs, perhaps in partnership with business schools. They have to improve the strategic management of people, give more seats on board and executive committees to the human resource managers, and to recruit and promote more foreign managers. The EC has some programmes to stimulate European training – such as Erasmus and Comet – but only one manager mentioned them in our study.

Impact of the Single European Market (1992)

Many studies of the impact of the Single European Market on the economy of EC countries have appeared in recent years (see Chapter 1). The date of 1992 (31 December) has become a symbol, the eve of a new era in European history. Most studies agree on the importance of the Single European Market as a driving force in the dynamics of European industry. Some three years after the signing of the Single European Market Act (1986), and still two years before 1992, our study among managers in four diverse industries suggests that the impact will be more modest.

Broadly, the impact of the Single European Market is very different across industries, and for most of the businesses it is just an accelerating force among others in the dynamics of internationalisation. While most of the managers speak about the psychological, indirect impact of 1992, many of them think it is a non-event.

The political changes in Eastern Europe, thought to herald major economic changes, are perceived as at least as important as the Single European Market. Considering also the growing number of special agreements with some other countries (mainly those in the European Free Trade Association), it looks as though the frontiers of the EC are getting less and less clear.

The foreign economic policy of Brussels is defined by some vague rules or recommendations such as 'reciprocity', and the attitudes of the member states often diverge (for instance divergences between

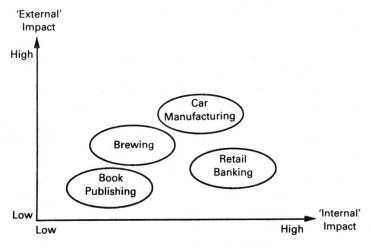

Figure 7.1 *Summary of the impacts of the Single European Market on the four industries studied*

Table 7.2 *Impact of the Single European Market, managers' perceptions*

	Book publishing	Brewing	Retail banking	Car manufacturing
No significant impact	It will change nothing at all because it cannot cross the linguistic and cultural barriers (FR, GB, IT, NL). It will change nothing at all in educational publishing, except for leading to more books about Europe!	It will not change much, nothing will be happening (NL, GB, FR). Because beer consumers are conservative in G, NL, DK. Other forces such as the growing pressure of the food channel and the MMC decision have much stronger impact (NL, GB, FR, G).	It will not change much because retail banking is by nature a domestic, proximity business (IT). Because cultural differences are high (NL), national currencies are all strong in the EMS; and some countries are already very liberal (GB, NL).	For many managers 1992 is a non-event.
Some companies already are European/ international	Big companies are already European (at least) (FR, G, NL, GB). Many have experience of agreements and co-editions (FR). The Frankfurt fair exists; it is a way to internationalise even for small companies.	The major brewers have already taken position in Europe (except Germany) (NL, FR). Foreign competitors already dominate markets like Italy (IT).	Banks already have experience of the other EC countries, they always had to deal internationally at least with their correspondents (GB).	Some companies are already European, e.g. Ford of Europe (GB). Big international companies will not be affected.
Psychological impact	It creates a dynamic prompting companies to look outside (DK). It will widen our frame of reference (SP). Authors now think about adaptations of their work for other countries (F).	It raises consciousness rather than having a direct impact (GB). It will change mentalities (NL).	It had and still has a psychological impact on executives, on their strategies (FR).	The impact has been more psychological since 1987.

Indirect impact	The need for training will increase and so will the need for books (GB).	It will have an indirect impact through increased competition (DK). It will have an impact on the customers more than on the banks (G). Our clients will go abroad and we will follow them (G, DK).	Indirect impacts could be important in retail banking.
Accelerator of market forces		Sensible measures will accelerate market dynamics (GB). Firms have to do things faster (DK).	Strengthening a process already going on (NL).
Progressive impact	It will start in 1993 but changes will not be perceptible before 2000 (GB, FR).	It already started in 1990 with the free circulation of money. It will be a reality in 2000, 1992 is just an episode (FR).	1992 as a progressive accelerator.
Harmonisation of VAT	The minimum rate of VAT is applied everywhere but there are still differences. It is a chance for publishers to align the rate on the lowest – 0% in UK – to stimulate demand (FR, SP, GB, G). The International Union of Publishers is lobbying for that (FR, SP, GB, G).	The harmonisation of VAT (let us say between 14–20%) will have a positive impact on demand and quality (FR, IT). It will stimulate the luxury car market (GB).	Positive impact of the harmonisation of VAT.

	Book publishing	Brewing	Retail banking	Car manufacturing
Harmonisation of excise duties		It will stimulate demand in countries where excise duties are high now. But the positions of the member states are opposite, and the wine lobby is strong; so probably nothing spectacular will happen (FR, GB, SP). In 1996 beer could be taxed in the *exporting* country; if taxes are high, some exporters will be disadvantaged (DK).		It will stimulate the luxury car market (GB). (ex: 230% taxes in DK now)	Harmonisation of excise duties could stimulate the market but it is uncertain.
Harmonisation of regulations	Harmonisation of copyrights will simplify the market (G).	On the protection of health and environment, the EC will take measures: − impact on the product − impact on the packaging (ex: reuse bottles) (NL) − impact on advertising on TV now forbidden in some EC countries (DK, GB). What will be decided in Brussels?	Home country control; in 1993 a bank will have to follow its home regulations in all EC countries. It will be advantaged or disadvantaged depending on what these are. Competition will cause a move towards minimum requirements.	Anti-pollution regulations will be a new constraint (FR). If speed limit for all Europe is decided, it will affect German cars (G).	Companies should contribute to health and environment protection.

Harmonisation of norms, standards	The Germans lost their battle on the purity law on 12 March 1987, but it did not change the behaviour of German consumers and brewers (FR, G).			To a large extent this has been done already, but further harmonisation is going to make things easier. Unique Reception Certificate will save time and money (FR). Harmonisation of standards will lower production costs (G).	Harmonisation of norms is on its way; depends on the industry.
Reduced barriers between EC countries	Should have a positive but limited impact on the opening of the German market (FR, G, NL).		You are able to set up foreign money accounts and circulate money abroad, buy investment funds (starting from June 1990 anticipating January 1993) (SP, GB, FR).	Residual import taxes in Spain will be abolished by 1 March 1993. It will be favourable to exporting and investing in Spain (SP).	Crucial in the retail banking business.
Subsidies		Subsidies for the translation of books should be maintained if not increased (FR).		(no manager mentioned the EC contribution to R&D pre-competitive programmes)	Few subsidies.
Prices	Now foreign beer brands are sold premium in foreign countries and cheap in their home country. Differences in prices will be reduced under the risk of parallel distribution channels (GB, IT). Risks of re-imports will homogenise prices (G).	The system of the set price of books could be abolished, no one knows (NL, GB, FR, G). If so the pressure of big retail chains on book publishers will increase. The system could be harmonised (for instance aligned on the British Net Book Agreement. Tougher competition on prices (SP).	Prices of banking services are very different now. Increased international competition will lead to a harmonisation and a diminution of prices (FR, SP, IT).	Prices will be homogenised throughout Europe (FR, GB). Prices will go down at last in the UK where they are high at the moment.	Harmonisation of prices will be a crucial consequence of 1992.

	Book publishing	Brewing	Retail banking	Car manufacturing	
Harmonisation of demand, supply			Harmonisation of demand and banking practices (NL, FR, SP).		
Distribution system	New channel will open up and it will facilitate the reallocation of distribution (G). German wholesalers may supply French bookshops (FR). Foreign distributors will be able to enter the Italian market more easily (IT).	It will make it easier to reallocate the logistics network in a more rational way (NL). It will facilitate the international development of big food retailing chains and reinforce their pressure on brewers (GB). Transportation costs and time will decrease (NL).		It will open up opportunities to restructure distribution (fewer frontier problems) (GB). It will improve the delivery of spare parts (G). The 12385 regulation which gives European car manufacturers the control of car distribution may be questioned (FR). Transportation easier (G).	Opportunities to rethink the distribution system and establish abroad.
Production system		It will ease the relocalisation of production (NL).		It will stimulate investments in factories abroad (F, G).	Big companies may relocalise production.
Mergers Acquisitions Alliances	There will be less protectionism towards foreign buyers in the EC (NL).		Alliances will be eased (FR). Acquisitions of big national banks will become possible (GB, G).		Less protectionism towards EC buyers.
Entries and development of foreign competitors				The entry and development of Japanese competitors will be eased. The future of the European car industry	The threat of Japanese competitors in Europe is a key

Not much impact on the book publishing industry, some uncertainties on the position of the EC.		
Not much impact for major brewers. Health questions to follow. Pricing and international distribution to consider.	Barriers have been removed, but habits are strong. Financial products and prices will harmonise. Cross-frontier acquisitions and alliances will become easier.	Norms are harmonised. Prices and international distribution to be determined. But first of all how to resist the Japanese and define an external policy at the EC level?
	is very dependent on the position of EC towards quotas. French, Italian and Spanish car manufacturers are protected now, but would be exposed without quotas. They ask for a ten-year transition period. They lobby for that. The decision is not taken yet. A compromise is probable so it is likely that the Single European Act will intensify the pressure from foreign competitors (sooner or later) (FR, GB, IT, SP). The principle of reciprocity is too vague.	issue in the car industry and one of the key questions at Brussels.

British liberalism and French protectionism). This makes it all the more difficult for managers to foresee what will happen.

We would like to consider two broad dimensions which are tightly interrelated: the internal impact of the SEM on the strategies and performances of Europe-based firms, and the external impact on the strategies and performances of third countries' firms in Europe. This aspect of the dynamics of the four industries that we studied is presented in Figure 7.1. By 'external' impact we mean mainly that the SEM may prompt foreign competitors, such as US, Japanese or Australian firms, to enter Europe.

This is likely in the sense that the SEM will reduce barriers to free trade, so it will stimulate international development strategies, which will accelerate mergers, acquisitions and alliances. The SEM is a major liberal step towards free trade and market forces. A more precise analysis of the implications is presented in Table 7.2. Consequences are presented in rows and reading in columns gives a picture of the combined influence of the SEM on each industry.

As the Single European Market did not aim to remove cultural and linguistic barriers, the book publishing industry will not be much affected by 1992. The main impacts expected by managers in the three other industries studied are diverse.

The main impact in the beer industry will be on the harmonisation of prices (combined with the harmonisation of taxes and probably of TV advertising). So the SEM will contribute to a basic market force: the development of European marketing.

In the retail banking sector the SEM deregulation will facilitate mergers, acquisitions and alliances between banks from different countries. In this domain, it has (already in 1990) had a determinant influence on the concentration process in Europe.

Quotas or no quotas against Japanese imports during a transitory period, one day the liberal policy of the EC towards third countries will influence the future of the car industry in Europe. (Under the pressure of the French, Italian and Spanish car manufacturers and in spite of the initial liberal position of the EC towards third countries (and the liberal position of the German and British car manufacturers), it seems that a compromise will be reached: a transitory period of five years (starting in 1993) during which the increase of Japanese exports to Europe will be monitored.) Besides, for a few years now car manufacturers have progressed in the harmonisation of norms. This is a contribution to the international (EC and worldwide) development of markets.

So it looks as if the SEM policies have been well designed to *amplify* market forces and the opinion of a liberal British manager we interviewed sums up our conclusions perfectly: 'I see it really as a bit of a sideshow to the real market pressures that are taking place. You cannot alter the market. If the measures that are taking place are sensible ones, I think they will tend to accelerate market forces. It is the marketplace which decides, it is not legislation'.

Managers and policy makers are agreed on this liberal thesis. But an important divergence between the point of view of managers and the point of view of the EC Commission should be underlined. Brussels insists on potential cost reductions, economies of scale, critical mass (see Directorate-General, 1988); on the other hand, managers do not talk much about cost reductions thanks to the SEM (for them cost reduction will come from technological innovation). Managers expect price reductions! They insist on the diversity of the European market and the trend towards quality which will require innovation, segmentation of the market and differentiation strategies.

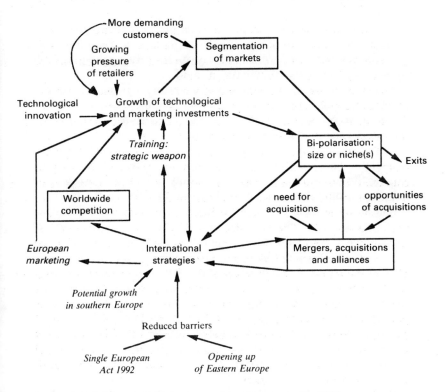

Figure 7.2 *Dynamics of the competitive systems in the 1990s: managers' cognitive map*

The potential for scale economies in Europe due to the SEM should not be overestimated; harmonisation will take place but diversity will be strong in the 1990s: '1992 will be an explosion of diversity and differences more than of homogenisation'.

The *combination* of the Single European Market *and* the opening up of Eastern Europe certainly increases the attractiveness of Europe for companies from other developed countries. The two events happening at about the same time do reduce trade barriers, and inspire more international strategies. North American firms rediscover Europe and the Japanese companies now take a position.

In this context all competitors should have an international strategy (including the ones who will stay in their small national niches and who should have a defensive strategy to face new entries). Ninety percent of the managers we interviewed are planning to extend the boundaries of their geographical market. Since not everyone can be a winner in the relatively mature markets that we studied, no new entries (in the industry) and several exits are expected and *cooperative forms of international development should flourish*.

Based on the executives' perceptions on the dynamics of these industries in the 1990s, we drew the managers' cognitive map presented in Figure 7.2, which is a way of summarising their views. It shows the main forces they have in mind and their interrelations.

As we believe that managers' cognitions will determine the strategy of their firms, which in turn will shape the evolution of the competitive system, this is the way things could happen in the 1990s in Europe (at least in the four diverse industries that we studied). Taken together, the perceptions of managers look particularly relevant and articulate. This is not such a surprise if we consider that they are among the foremost experts in their competitive systems (and that expert consultation is one of the best ways to predict the future).

The differences in perceptions that we found between industries are *normal*; by definition an industry has a particular set of technologies, competitors, customers and a specific history.

But one point should be raised here; when looking at individual perceptions (individual cognitive maps) we noticed that a manager generally has a partial perception, probably *biased* by the history of his or her firm, his or her present strategy and by the particularities of the industry *in the home country*. For instance, two German managers in the brewing industry have a very different view of the competitive system. One believes that the German market will concentrate quickly and that German brewers will export more and more, whereas another believes that the market will remain fragmented, local and dedicated to pure German beer. The differences can be explained by the differences in strategies between the two firms (one has grown by acquisitions, sells to the food channel and exports, the other is local and tries to hold a niche). Altogether the perceptions of German brewers are different from the perceptions of French brewers because of differences in market structures between the two countries (fragmented market with high share of bars and restaurants in Germany, concentrated market with high share of the food channel and international activities in France).

We also noticed that managers in companies which are already international have a much more complete and relevant view of the future of the business. This may sound trivial, but in fact it has a major practical implication. As most of the managers want their company to go international, they need to change their frames of reference; they need to understand all the dimensions of the problem and the diversity of foreign countries or regions if they want to turn their wishes into successful realities. Several means should be combined to change frames of reference: more systematic information on foreign markets, travelling abroad, international seminars, training, job rotation in foreign countries, and above all recruiting foreign managers and having some of them on the executive committee or board of directors. From what we learned in our interviews, a few international companies actually follow the above precepts, and some of them are starting; this is the way to manage the diversity of the European market.

The European Patchwork

First, it should be noted that in each of the industries that we studied, there is always a country in the EC which is very different from the norm. For instance, the United Kingdom car industry is unusual in Europe: the Japanese have already taken a position there (a share in the Rover Group and transplants of Toyota and Nissan). For the British, the Japanese threat may be, in fact, an opportunity. In the brewing industry, the German market is very different from the other EC markets, with hundreds of small companies brewing a 'pure beverage'. Retail banking in Spain is still regulated, with a particular system of re-financing, and with the highest density of branches in Europe and high profitability. Book publishers in the United Kingdom (publishing in English) serve the whole world market much more easily than, say, Danish publishers with their five million potential readers.

These are just some extreme examples of the high diversity across countries in a given industry. Table 7.3 gives a more complete picture of the differences between countries. It is limited to the four industries and the seven EC countries that we studied; adding

Table 7.3 *Synopsis: Differences across countries in the four industries studied*

	Brewing	Book publishing
Denmark	• Mature market (slow decreasing demand) • High level of consumption • Concentrated • Re-use bottles only	• Protected and limited by the language • High level of consumption • Distribution relies on the post
Federal Republic of Germany	• Mature market (slow decreasing demand) • High level of consumption • Very fragmented (1100 regional and local breweries) • Low profitability • 'Pure beer'	• High level of consumption • Some strong dominating multi-media groups • Strong in logistics • Distribution relies on the post
France	• Mature market (decreasing in the north and increasing in the south) • Low level of consumption • Concentrated (1 company holds 50%) • High share of the food channel	• Low level of consumption • 2 strong dominating multi-media groups (international and many small focused publishers)
Great Britain	• Mature market (slow decreasing demand) • High level of consumption • Breweries integrated downwards in pubs • Fragmented • Lager/ales, stouts	• High level of consumption • International market definition (world) • Some strong multi-media groups and small focused publishers
Italy	• Growth market but limited by the consumption of wine • Low level of consumption • Concentrating under the pressure of international competitors	• Relatively low level of consumption • Limited by the language • Some strong multi-media groups and many small publishers
Netherlands	• Mature market • High level of consumption • Concentrated (2 international competitors)	• High level of consumption (including English) • Rather concentrated • International competitors
Spain	• Growth market but reaching a high level of consumption • Concentrating under the pressure of international competitors • Still regionalised	• Growth market • Still fragmented and regionalised but concentrating under the pressure of some national groups • International market definition (South America)

	Retail banking	Car manufacturing
Denmark	• Concentrating	• No national champion • Market limited by high taxation • Open to Japanese imports (30% of the market)
Federal Republic of Germany	• Three strong competitors going abroad • Concept of universal bank still valid • Bank + insurance • German banks much involved in industry (and vice versa)	• Demand for D, E, F categories (Chapter 5) • Several strong competitors differentiated in the higher segments • Low VAT • Liberal towards the Japanese
France	• 4 strong competitors going abroad • Still a strong involvement of the state • High level of technology in retail banking	• 'Average market' • 2 French competitors holding a high share • Relatively high VAT • Lobbying for quotas against Japanese competition
Great Britain	• Three strong competitors • International positions • Less frontiers between corporate and retail banking • Overbanked • Particular institutions such as building societies	• 'Average market' • One national champion • Open to foreign investments and technology (including Japanese shares, imports and transplants)
Italy	• Fragmented market • Underbanked • Traditional attitude of the clients (proximity . . .) • Still believe in the model of universal bank • Still regionalised	• 'Average market' • Dominated by a national competitor in all segments • Lobbying for quotas against Japanese competition • Relatively high VAT
Netherlands	• Some strong competitors • Fewer frontiers between corporate and retail banking • Overbanked	• No national champion • Open to Japanese imports
Spain	• Growth market • Still profitable • Still fragmented and regionalised • Too many branches • Protective regulations (to be abolished in 1992)	• Growing market • Demand for categories A, B, C, D • One newly founded national champion under control of foreign owner • Several factories of foreign competitors • Would prefer protection against Japanese invasion

Greece, Ireland, Belgium, Luxembourg and Portugal would doubt-less increase the diversity of market structures. For instance, in the beer market, two countries only – Denmark and the Netherlands – have similar market characteristics, whereas all the others have particular structures and consumption habits.

In book publishing, the United Kingdom and Spain are two particular cases, considering the international scope of their potential market. The Germans read a lot, the French do not.

In retail banking, the Germans still believe in the model of the universal bank, whereas the French believe in multi-specialisation. Italy is underbanked and Great Britain is overbanked.

In car manufacturing the Germans are well positioned on the top segments. The British have welcomed Japanese manufacturers, whereas the Italian and the two French companies are trying to maintain barriers to protect their business against Japanese invasion.

The strategic implications are clear when one considers such differences across EC countries: a competitor aiming at several countries in the EC market should tailor its strategy according to the market structure of each country.

Another way to look at differences across Europe is to try to understand consumers' behaviour. The following characteristics of the consumers' behaviour have been identified and proposed by one of the companies which participated in the study:

- the German consumer is 'chauvinistic' and 'cold',
- the British consumer is 'price-sensitive' and 'takes profit',
- the Dutch consumer is 'thrifty' and 'critical',
- the Spanish consumer is 'extremist',
- the French consumer is 'impulsive' and 'likes novelty',
- the Italian consumer is 'impulsive' and 'takes care of the look',
- the Scandinavian consumer is 'quality minded' and 'critical . . . even more than the Dutch!'.

Finally, it is hard to characterise Belgium consumers: 'Wallons' behave like the French and 'Flamands' behave like the Dutch (except in the eyes of the Dutch themselves).

This last point suggests that regional differences may be as important as national differences. Italians from the north and the south are different. In Spain, Catalonians, Basques, Castilians and Andalusians speak different languages. One can also find important differences between the regions of France, between regions of Germany and between regions of Great Britain. The barriers of language are clear manifestations of these cultural differences (which are often combined with industrial and economic differences).

One of the managers we interviewed argued that the Single

European Market might have an indirect influence on the resurgence of ethnic local identities across Europe.

> Since we started to talk about united Europe, the regional cultural movements have developed! The Catalans speak Catalan, the Basques throw bombs, the Sardinians want to learn Sardinian at school, the Lombard league is developing, and so on . . . . Could there be something like a fragmentation of national entities induced by the European project? . . . I do not know (Italy, book publishing).

The interest in regional cultures may have a marginal direct effect on the book publishing industry. But what should be noted here is the necessity for managers to understand these microcultural differences in order to be more effective in negotiations and working life with foreigners in Europe. Differences between ethnic groups or regions are probably more discriminant than national cultures (Hofstede, 1980). From what we know, no systematic study at this level has been published yet (though one such study has been carried out in 1989 by the Centre de Communication Avancé, Paris).

Combining differences in market structures and differences in customers' behaviour leads to a simple characterisation of the seven countries that we studied. The attributes may sound simplistic but we believe they can be helpful to managers who will have to deal with several of these European countries.

Germany is the country of *differentiation* and *regionalisation*, at least in the four industries that we studied; among the European leaders in these businesses several are German (Volkswagen, Bertelsmann, Deutsche Bank). Especially in *industrial* businesses, German firms have succeeded in *differentiating* their products. Mercedes, BMW, Porsche and to a lesser degree Audi; most of the differentiated car manufacturers in Europe are German. Through the purity law, and the habits of the German customers, German brewers are also differentiated. Efficient logistics (speed of delivery) and cultural commitment are characteristics of the German book publishing industry. In service businesses, such as banking, the regional federative structure of Germany dominates and quality of service is a rule. *So, to succeed in Germany, premium products and a multi-regional approach are needed.*

France also has strong competitors at the European level (Hachette, PSA, Renault, Crédit Agricole, BNP, BSN). French companies and consumers seem to be *more innovative than the average* (at least they have this reputation). They demonstrated it in the retail banking business with the high degree of automation and the emergence of home banking based on the minitel network (of the post and telecommunication). The 'aphrodisiac beer' recently launched by a French brewery is anecdotal but it is one of the many symptoms of innovativeness. France also is a country of *strong state intervention*, even if it is changing slowly. Two of the major French banks are nationalised and the state is the majority shareholder in Renault (the status of Renault had to be changed when the alliance with Volvo was instituted).

Great Britain is the *champion of liberalism* in the EC; this has been one of the reasons for the international development of the financial sector (London). The liberalism and international scope of the UK led to a strong position in the banking sector and in book publishing (NatWest, Barclays, Maxwell, Reed, Pearson, etc). Linked to this liberal position, the UK has become the *bridgehead* of the developed countries in the European market. North American car makers, publishers and banks in the past, Japanese car manufacturers and banks, Australian brewers and bankers more recently established themselves in Europe through Great Britain. The bridge could also be used the other way round, EC countries using Great Britain as a bridgehead to the English-speaking world and to the world financial markets.

The Netherlands is also liberal; the limits of the home market have created the necessary pressure for international development. So the Dutch became *the champions of internationalisation*. Companies like Heineken and Grolsch in the brewing industry, Wolters-Kluwer and Elsevier in book publishing and ABN in banking are among the most successful in their international strategies. Related to that is the ability of the Dutch to speak several European languages.

Denmark has been outside the big battles for some time, because of the small size of its market. If we except a few major competitors such as Carlsberg, one way to qualify Danish companies would be 'small is beautiful'. But this is changing now with the important mergers in the banking sector, for instance. Another characteristic of Denmark is the *high level of taxes* of all kinds which are at the origin of a national sport: transborder trade (for books and beer for instance).

Italy is *a dual country*. The traditional duality between the north and the south is reproduced among companies. The most modern banks compete with archaic ones. The most modern breweries compete with others in obsolete plants and the distribution channels are over-complicated. On the other hand, the restructuring of the automobile industry gave birth to a powerful group at the European level, with some prestigious names (Fiat, Lancia, Alfa Romeo, Maserati, Ferrari).

Spain appears to be a *regionalised* country still, with regional leaders for instance in the brewing industry, in retail banking and to a lesser degree in book publishing (at the distribution level). Regionalisation also means fragmentation. Except in the car industry, national leaders are emerging *now* in a wave of mergers and acquisitions. Managers mentioned another interesting characteristic: the Spanish lifestyle (which was very particular) is changing and becoming 'more and more European'. This change has already had an impact on the four industries that we studied.

Another dimension helps us to understand the diversity of Europe: namely the historical *zones of influence* of some of the bigger EC countries. In other words, the place of some European countries in the world.

The United Kingdom has historical – economic and cultural – links with North America and with the Commonwealth countries (stronger links for instance than with the French or with the Germans). Spain has historical – economic and cultural – links with South America. France has the same kind of links with many African countries. Finally, Germany has built strong economic relationships with Eastern Europe.

These particular zones of influence or attraction could be considered as centrifugal forces; they are in a way. But, when adding up all these zones, one will discover that Europe is at the crossroads of the western world and that *EC countries complement each other on the world map*, excepting of course East Asia, which is under the influence of Japan and China, and which is still a case apart.

Managers around the world will draw strategic and practical conclusions themselves from each of these characteristics, such as that there are opportunities to take positions and transform the market in Italy and Spain, that the UK is a perfect bridgehead to start serving Europe (besides all people speak English there and it is easier to be understood!), and that there will still be room for national niche players in some industries, as long as they reach a sufficient scale and are differentiated.

We would like to offer here a more general conclusion on the necessity to deal with European diversity; in fact, *to reconcile unity and diversity* in a Europe-wide strategy. Three types of actors should be directly interested in this question: European companies which already do business across Europe, non-European companies in the same position, and national European companies which aim to take a position Europe-wide (this question has already partly been addressed in the earlier section on 'European Marketing').

Companies will have to reconcile the progressive and indirect harmonisation of the European market (under the pressure of international competition and of some policies of the Single European Market) and the high diversity of this market (across countries).

First of all, there will be several profiles of effective pan-European competitors because the profile will depend on the specific sources of competitive advantage and on the balance between globalisation and localisation forces in a given business in Europe.

The first characteristic of an effective pan-European competitor will be to *assess* the diverse sources of competitive advantage (across segments and countries) and the globalisation and localisation forces (by product segment), considering each element of the value chain of the business. Such a systematic analysis will suggest specific formulae for the configuration and co-ordination of activities (see Bartlett and Ghoshal, 1987). For those who are looking for a simple profile we might suggest the following.

Some elements in the value-enhancing chain activities in which companies engage *could be centralised* to improve economies of scale and efficiency: mainly production and logistics. Production should be located in countries which offer a competitive advantage in production (skills or costs) and a sufficient potential of consumption (in a reachable circle around the point of location).

Flexible technologies could allow final variations of the product or service to adapt to specific country demands (for instance in packaging). *The logistics* (inbound and outbound) could be (re)defined at the European level and also be more centralised by zones. On the other hand, some of the 'downstream value activities' could be decentralised by country to deal with diversity. In short, marketing and sales should have national or regional perspectives: (a) keep the identity of national names in case of acquisitions, (b) adapt advertising to each country's specificities, and (c) for some time, accept price differences between countries, then be ready to standardise pricing at the European level.

This decentralisation of marketing and sales should not mean a complete autonomy of national sales subsidiaries; these diverse policies should be *co-ordinated* at the European level to avoid inconsistencies and to seize any opportunity of pan-European action to improve costs. In the beer industry Heineken, for instance, is a good example of such a European strategy.

In some industries which are ready for that (high globalisation forces, low localisation forces), a strong competitor could try to play a completely homogeneous Europe-wide strategy. Maybe one of the Japanese competitors will try it in the car industry in the future. Paradoxically, ignoring European diversity may be a key force in forming a really *single* European market.

But we do not believe that such an extreme strategy of standardisation would be effective in the short term, at least in the industries that we studied, although it is probably different in purely global industries such as consumer electronics.

Of course the level of centralisation/decentralisation of a company in Europe will depend on the balance between globalisation and localisation forces (cf. Chapter 6). Centralisation goes with high globalisation and low localisation forces, decentralisation goes with the converse. A more subtle alchemy is needed when both globalisation and localisation forces are high. The profile of the European competitor that we suggested above could fit in such a context.

Europe-wide companies, especially when they grew by acquisitions, could take more and more the form of *federations* of business units (by product–market and/or by country).

Federations conciliate co-ordination and synergies *with* a relative autonomy of the business units and slim headquarters. Some federations like Volkswagen–Audi–Seat, or Fiat–Alfa Romeo–Maserati–Ferrari in the car industry, and Hachette or Pearson in publishing, illustrate such new organisational forms. Smaller companies can also take federative forms when their businesses and locations are diverse; we found some of them in the beer industry (Le Pêcheur), in book publishing (Poeschel Verlag) and in retail banking (Lyonnaise de Banque).

To reconcile synergies and diversity and to manage an international federative company, top management will have to be more and more international. It means that *several nationalities* should be represented at the higher levels of management, and that the managers should have *international experience* (and language abilities).

These principles are valid also for companies of third country origin – north American and Japanese for instance – which aim to develop in the European market. Some multinationals follow these principles, but not all of them do. The new pan-European companies emerging now still have much to learn in this domain.

References

Bartlett, Christopher A. and Ghoshal, Sumantra (1987) 'Managing across borders: New organizational responses', *Sloan Management Review*.

Directorate-General for Economic and Financial Affairs, Commission of the EC (1988) 'The Economics of 1992', *European Economy*, No. 35.

Hofstede, Geert H. (1980) *Culture's Consequences: International Differences in Work Related Values*. Beverly Hills: Sage Publications.

Takeuchi, Hirataka and Porter, Michael E. (1986) 'Three roles of international marketing in global strategy', in M.E. Porter (ed.), *Competition in Global Industries*. Boston: Harvard University Press, pp. 111–46.

8

Countries, Cultures and Constraints

Jean-Louis Barsoux and Peter Lawrence

Throughout the book differences between countries have been mentioned. But for the most part this has been a matter of specifics, of saying that Italian brewing has this or that characteristic, that representatives of retail banking in Britain express distinctive opinions, that the car market in Denmark is different from that in Germany, and so on. The purpose now, however, is to talk about the differences between countries in a more general way, even if reference is made back to the same countries and industries that have figured in the study for illustrative purposes.

In brief the argument we would like to develop here is that there are differences between countries which are significant for the way companies operate. These differences are likely to persist beyond 1992. That nationality is thus a variable in shaping or 'contexting' corporate strategy, and that national differences impinge directly, and indirectly, in that they sometimes shape the mental maps that managers have of their industries and markets. Hence in the first instance our emphasis in this chapter will be on heterogeneity, on differences between countries interesting from the point of view of business. And our *point de depart* will be how that heterogeneity manifests itself in terms of the different business philosophies they espouse.

The 'Level Playing Field' and the Anglo-Saxon View of Business

The English with their partiality for sporting metaphors like to speak of the Single European Market initiative as aiming at the establishment of a 'level playing field' for business and trading within the EC, one in which all 'players' will compete equally. Is this likely to be achieved? In all sorts of administrative and well-documented ways it clearly will be achieved in the form of the much-vaunted abolition of non-tariff barriers. But from an Anglo-Saxon viewpoint there is an important sense in which the level playing field will not be level enough.

Since the mid-1980s, the UK has served as the training ground for hostile takeovers. Britain, following in the footsteps of the US, has seen corporate raiding develop into a fine art. In the Anglo-Saxon scheme of things the freedom of companies to engage in business manoeuvres of the merger–acquisition–takeover kind is fundamental. This in turn is entirely consistent with the predominance of equity financing, 'short termism', and the priority given to shareholder value. A Single European Market that does not institutionalise this freedom, and equalise as between member states the possibility of initiating or resisting takeovers, is seen on the British side as incomplete. And it does not seem likely that the playing field will be level in this matter by 1992. As things stand, would-be foreign takeovers are not well received in mainland Europe. The chairman of the Deutsche Bank, Alfred Herrhausen, is an outspoken but otherwise fairly typical critic of takeovers conducted in an aggressive US style. He simply states that: 'such conduct has no place in our economic culture' (*Director*, June 1989: 100).

Cross-border Acquisitions after 1992

First there is the question of the small countries in the EC. Big companies in small countries tend to become national institutions, at least in a metaphorical sense. Would, for example, the Danish government allow a foreign brewer to buy Carlsberg? Or would a foreign publisher seeking a Scandinavian bridgehead be allowed to acquire the Gyldendal Publishing Company, owned by a foundation that also owns, and links in perpetuity, Gyldendal and the Louisiana Art Museum north of Copenhagen, and whose CEO is a member of the Danish prime minister's 'think tank'?

Or if these Danish examples are thought to be a special case in that the organisations have *fond* (foundation) status then consider the Netherlands. The shares of KLM are not government-owned; in theory it could be bought. Nor is this a preposterous suggestion. Airlines are bought and sold. KLM itself has a 20 percent stake in Sabena, Belgium's national airline (and British Airways owns another 20 percent of Sabena). And KLM also has shares in Transavia Holland, Martinair Holland, Air UK, and a much-publicised stake in Northwest Airlines in the USA. But could anyone imagine either the Dutch government or the Dutch business community allowing KLM to be bought?

Or again, would it be possible for an outsider to buy a Dutch bank? In theory it ought to be possible in terms of the relative size of Dutch as against certain non-Dutch banks. Yet again one has reservations in practice. As one of the British bankers put it:

On the continent there are so many poison pills! In Holland, for instance, it is a common tactic to issue massive share options. So as soon as you go along and bid aggressively for a bank the share options are triggered and you end up paying three times the price. That is a big disincentive to go and buy a Dutch bank.

Nor is it simply a question of the small countries. There was a general agreement in the sample of interviewed managers that it would be difficult to effect takeovers in (West) Germany. First, a lot of the equity of German companies is in the hands of the banks (for example, Deutsche Bank's 28 percent share of Mercedes-Benz), primarily a result of the hyperinflation in Germany in the 1920s and banks' recapitalisation of many manufacturing companies on the basis of an equity stake. Secondly, there is an interesting twist in the German scenario in that manufacturing companies also commonly own bank shares, thus having a stake in their masters! Again this is an insight that came to light in the interviews with British bankers. Thirdly, and although intangible this may be the most important consideration, there is something of a patriotic emotional bonding among German banks and companies, deriving from their role and solidarity in the post-war reconstruction period: they were re-born partners in the time of the *Wirtschaftswunder*, again making it difficult for foreigners to 'break in', disposing German firms to 'close ranks' in the face of a hostile (foreign) takeover attempt.

The French Connection

Finally in this connection is the fact that independent of the size of nation states, the government–industry relationship may vary. This is not a *pro forma* point. The French/British comparison is particularly striking. At the strong end of the continuum we have France. In France more companies are owned by the state since the immediate post-Second World War period, and a further spate of nationalisation occurred during the period of France's socialist government, 1981–6. And it is not just a quantitative thing.

Many of France's most conspicuous industrial successes – from railways to telecommunications, aeronautics to energy – are state initiatives, even though it is often private sector companies that are doing the development and manufacture. It is an important feature of the French system that government is more active in shaping industrial policy. It is also the case that many firms in France have a relationship with government that is qualitatively different from that existing in Britain (or America). It further follows that the phrase and fact of 'nationalised industry' has connotations in France that are different from those in Britain. For anecdotal evidence of this, we need simply look at the way the Renault headquarters on the banks of the Seine announces in huge letters that it is *Renault – Régie Nationale* – under state tutelage. It is unthinkable that any British state-owned industry should similarly trumpet that fact. In France to be a public sector firm means to bask in the reflected glory of the French state – it is image-enhancing, not image-demeaning.

Clearly, the threshold between the state and industry in France has always been lower; there is more common recruitment to top positions in both (from the *grandes écoles*), and more exchange of personnel (*pantouflage*), and more co-operation via state-sponsored *planification*. In France's highly politicised corporate scene the heads of the private companies may well identify their jobs with the national interests of France itself. Jacques Calvet, chairman of Peugeot, epitomises the view:

> Remember the celebrated formula of a one-time head of General Motors that what was good for GM was good for the US? Well I consider that what is good for France is good for Peugeot. I cannot see how the French car industry can fight for interests contrary to French interests (*Financial Times*, 21 May 1990: 32).

The reversal of the GM slogan in the French case is especially poignant. It reflects the desire to do right by France (*la gloire de la France*). Calvet's is symbolic of the attitude instilled in members of the French establishment who can move between the top public and private sector jobs with aplomb. The choice of company heads, the structuring of industries and the orientation of activity where the largest French firms are concerned has always been tied up with national ambitions. And although the 1980s did much to lift the administrative tutelage, French companies are still not fully exposed to the rigours of Anglo-Saxon-style business manoeuvres.

This idea of an asymmetrical relationship between Britain and some of its neighbours has been developed at some length not simply as a piece of special pleading for Britain by British-based writers. There is a general feeling that British waywardness within the Common Market derives simply from wrongheadedness. It is suggested here that part of it is that Britain is the representative in the EC of a different business philosophy, one more influenced by American adventurism than by notions of continental solidarity.

Management Style

These countries also encompass differences in management style. A cursory look at some of Europe's leading industrialists reveals big differences in style. If we take again France's Jacques Calvet, head of the Peugeot group, for example, we see an embodiment of the 'French dream'. First Calvet is a graduate of the Ecole Nationale d'Administration, the elite civil service college, he was head of the personal staff of former President Valery Giscard d'Estaing while Giscard was Finance Minister, and Calvet later headed the Banque Nationale de Paris, the largest state-owned bank – before 'changing codes' and joining the privately-owned Peugeot.

Not surprisingly, this itinerary has left its mark on his management style. Calvet himself has admitted to being sometimes, 'too Cartesian' in his management approach: 'I have a fault from which I suffer greatly. I am too logical, not sufficiently directed by intuition' (*Financial Times*, 21 May 1990: 32). Now, although Calvet's background is exceptional, he is representative of a French tradition which puts a premium on educated cleverness and intellectual rigour. Contrast with this Britain's traditional emphasis on social skills and pragmatism. Is it any surprise that Britain's best-known industrialist is probably the former head of ICI, Sir John Harvey-Jones? And consider his views on management:

> The manager has to be extremely sensitive – I know this, of course, makes people fall about – but nevertheless, actually management is a very sensitive job. You need to be a master of every single club in the golf bag, but the art is to continuously choose the appropriate club for that particular day in that particular situation ('Take it from the Top', Video Arts, 1990).

We see in Harvey-Jones' style a concern with interpersonal skills and persuasion. This is what British managers think management is about, both for real and in the image they like to cultivate.

Or consider the archetypal Italian industrialist, Fiat's Giovanni Agnelli. He is Europe's most powerful businessman. Like Henry Ford in his time, Mr Agnelli lives in a country that places few limits on corporate power. Along with a number of Italy's leading corporate lights, Mr Agnelli has a nickname, *l'Avvocato* (the lawyer) – some of the others include Olivetti's Carlo de Benedetti who is known as *l'Ingegnere* (the engineer); Silvio Berlusconi, owner of the TV-to-supermarkets conglomerate, is *Sua Emittentza* (his 'emittence' – a pun on a cardinal's honorific); and Ferruzzi-Montedison's Rual Gardini is *il Contadino* (the farmer). This profusion of sobriquets (shades of Mussolini's *il Duce*) reflects a very personalised view of management. Italian business is marked by the cult of the personality and the accompanying penchant for flair and charisma. Could this be why the Italian economy encompasses so many small businesses – each one headed by an aspiring Agnelli?

Or again what about the Netherlands? Here one might take Freddy

Heineken, chairman of the famous Dutch brewery. How does he incarnate the values of Dutch management? The answer is simple. Heineken is the third largest brewer in the world, behind Anheuser Busch and Miller of the USA, claiming 4.2 percent of the world market. But Mr Heineken is not satisfied with this. He talks of growth potential and eschews talk of saturated markets. He asks, 'Why can't we get to 8 percent of the world market?' (*Financial Times*, 24 July 1989: 34).

In this attitude he reflects the internationalist bent of Dutch management as a whole (Lawrence, 1991). As a country with a small domestic market, the Dutch were obliged to look outside early – Heineken, for instance, was the first foreign beer allowed into the US in 1933 when Prohibition ended. But this early export orientation was merely an extension of centuries of mercantile tradition. The Netherlands has been a spectacular overachiever in international transport and freight; it has the largest harbour in the world (Rotterdam); an enterprising national airline (KLM); and a disproportionate number of the world's leading multinationals. Its managers also display what, by Anglo-Saxon standards, is uncanny linguistic ability.

Each of the leaders cited above then, arguably represents different national preoccupations, either in terms of managerial background or outlook. Now the differences in style we have outlined will mainly inform differences in managerial behaviour, which is not the primary focus of this book. But differences in style may also affect strategic choice and problem formulation. They will colour managerial perceptions and will determine what managers think of as being natural, possible and relevant. For instance, the Germans would conceive some things as possible because they are technically minded and they know that technical understanding is widespread among German managers. The Dutch might regard certain far-flung countries (Heineken have a brewery in Chad and a stake in a brewery in Shanghai) as natural markets to cultivate because of their seasoned adaptability abroad and the fact that Dutch managers, unlike some of their French counterparts, are not overawed by the prospect of going abroad.

And of course, when it comes to strategy, formulation is only part of it: it has sometimes been said that effective strategy is 10 percent inspiration and 90 percent implementation, so that differences between countries in terms of management style may give rise to different behaviours, and that will affect implementation. For instance, French management with its *esprit de planification* formulates strategy in all its intellectual plenitude, but rather assumes implementation will follow naturally. British managers, on the other hand, will devote less effort to perfecting the abstract plan, and pay more attention to implementation using their social and political skills and their ability to 'muddle through'.

Industrial Democracy

Some of the EC countries in our study have co-determination systems, and some do not, and there were occasional references to this in the interviews. While a full consideration of the industrial democracy question would be inappropriate here, it may be helpful to make two points.

First in popular discussions of industrial democracy and the Social Charter there is a tendency to dichotomise: there are the 'good guy' countries such as the Netherlands and West Germany with very credible co-determination systems, and the 'bad guys', among whom Britain is pre-eminent, who do not have such systems. Now Britain probably deserves to be singled out as shamelessly hostile to industrial democracy, the one country where even the trade union movement is ambivalent to this development. Our point is simply that it is not black and white. There are a lot of half-way houses. Between Britain and West Germany there is Italy, whose post-war constitution is lyrical on the subject of industrial democracy, but where nothing much exists in practice. Or France which has a recently (1981–6) enlarged body of industrial democracy legislation, but where its principal organ, the *comité d'entreprise*, is much inferior in the power it exercises compared to a German *Betriebsrat* or a Dutch *ondernemingsraad*.

The second point relates to our earlier discussion of the 'level playing field', Anglo-Saxon style. There is no shortage of explanation for Britain's hostility or lukewarm attitude to co-determination – it has to do with the class system, adversarial industrial relations and so forth. But we would like to suggest a further reason for that position.

Co-determination runs counter to the easy buying and selling of companies. Simply having some works council or other body that has the right to be informed, consulted, and express its wishes takes the speed, secrecy and unfettered market initiative out of take-overs. A recent Anglo-Dutch study, for instance, has shown the 'deterrent effect' of worker democracy in a clash between Dutch and American business cultures (Wenlock, 1990). So that the industrial democracy variable as between countries has wider implications – for strategy and business philosophy. And in Britain's case, there are business policy reasons for corporate reluctance to embrace co-determination.

Special Interests

The special interests that the various countries have is revealed time and again in our interviews. For the most part this is a simple point, yet one that seems all too easily forgotten (or repressed) in the 1992 euphoria. One or two examples may be helpful.

The most obvious example is West Germany, as it was at the time of the research interviews. Everyone has confidently assumed that West Germany will 'clean up' East Germany in every sense of the phrase. Certainly, West Germany has an interest in East Germany that is unrivalled to the point of being exclusive. Yet perhaps more interesting, and more momentous, is the question: will a unified Germany come to exercise the same cultural, political and economic dominance in Eastern Europe that it did in the nineteenth century and indeed right up to the time of the Third Reich and the Second World War, when peaceful influence was exchanged for military subjugation. Clearly this wider German influence is possible, but without being predestined. Whether or not it happens will depend as much on the expectations of the countries involved as on the economic realities.

Or consider the case of Spain. A recently acceding member of the EC, seemingly putting its past behind it, with a rapidly developing economy that has attracted a lot of interest from the other countries, a fact documented at company initiative level in our interviews. Yet Spain is 'locked in' to one of the world's top four languages. No other country in the world, let alone in the EC, has the same linguistic and cultural link with the greater part of Latin America. Relations between Spain and Latin America are historically strong, with many family and educational ties. And this fact emerges as a business reality in our interviews, with Spanish publishers for example speaking of their representation and market interests in South America. And although outside the scope of our study, there is the interesting case of pharmaceutical companies. The South American connection is useful to them because it saves having to go through complicated, slow and expensive drug registration procedures. Most South American countries will accept Spanish certification.

The challenge of Japan gives us another line of cleavage within the EC. With one exception no one actually welcomes Japanese economic penetration in Europe, though responses vary from indifference tinged with concern to downright hostility. The smaller countries such as Holland and Denmark tend to the view that they are too small to attract much Japanese attention (with the exception of Philips in the Netherlands). West Germany tacitly inclines to the view that they can for the most part beat the Japanese at their own game of product quality and manufacturing efficiency. The 'Euro-Latin countries', especially France and Italy, are much more explicitly hostile to Japanese export penetration, and in the case of the automobile industry this hostility is quite implacable. For instance, Peugeot boss Jacques Calvet is not just in favour of introducing an EC-wide quota on Japanese cars, but he believes that quota should also include European-built Japanese cars.

The 'odd man out' country yet again, is Britain. Not only is Britain, as usual, lacking any sense of European solidarity – it was dubbed 'Japan's fifth largest island' by Jacques Calvet – but other considerations are also at work. Paramount is the view that Japan may help Britain to achieve a favourable trade balance in manufactured goods. Let the Japanese have their bridgehead in Britain, and with a bit of luck cars made in Sunderland, then Derby, will flow to continental Europe in a way that indigenous British cars have not since the 1950s.

Side by side with this gross consideration is something more subtle and qualitative. It is the view that it will be good to have Japanese companies in Britain because they will set a good example and one which will hopefully have 'knock-on' effects for British industry. The Japanese, that is, are newly considered to be the exemplars of best practice in such matters as workplace discipline, employee commitment, the minutiae of manufacturing organisation, quality standards, and the organisation of suppliers. If all this passes down to British industry in general on a 'drip-feed' basis, Britain might become the economic 'holy terror' of Europe.

And there are sometimes more esoteric historic associations for those prepared to dig diligently. One of the things which has resulted from the opening up of Eastern Europe recently is the re-emergence of the Baltic republics – Estonia, Lithuania, Latvia – which have a little-known Swedish connection. They are all on the coast facing Sweden. They all have Swedish-speaking minorities in them and Swedish settlements. And they all used to be part of the Swedish sphere of influence in their 'younger days'. Thus, they would all regard Sweden as their natural trading partner. Estonia in particular had the same sort of place in the Swedish psyche in the inter-war period that Paris did for Americans in the 1920s – Estonia was somewhere to go for fun and sin. Indeed a regular ferry service has now been started from Stockholm to Tallinn, the capital of Estonia, which leaves from the same terminal as boats to Finland.

Over Space and Time

Most of the special interests referred to in the last section, and others less prominent – the Netherlands–Indonesia, Denmark–Greenland, Italy–Libya – are a legacy of history. But there are other ways in which the past shapes the future, or at least there are continuities of disposition and expectation. Again a contrasted example from among the countries in the study may help.

The French think big; says the CEO of a French bank: 'The major European banks will open offices in the major cities in France and Europe, which will increase competition. French bankers must set a lead to stay ahead in the globalisation game.' But that is not a sentiment echoed for the most part by the German or Italian, British or Danish bankers. More representative of the other camp are the remarks of a British banker: 'We can see no advantage in entering Europe, except very tentatively, focusing on the mortgage or insurance market.'

Another British banker gives a new dimension to this relative caution, arguing that it is regarded as a plus if another country is so regionalised that you can acquire a presence in a region, for example Catalonia in Spain or the Suisse Romande in Switzerland, without having to aim at a national presence. This strategy means one avoids the expense of acquiring a national stake, one is less likely to provoke a hostile response by local banks, and one does not fritter away one's energies having five branches in every European capital but nothing to go with it. These considerations are all perfectly sensible, of course, but is it not an interesting contrast? The French see challenge and big stage drama: the British when offered international scope 'go shopping' for sub-national regions!

Throughout, the responses of the French executives were the most 'bullish' in the sample. They invariably take 1992 seriously, they say it does matter, they see threats and opportunities there. Many of the French companies whose executives were interviewed had cross-border alliances in place, or were looking for them; often they had subsidiaries or 'implantations' in other EC countries, especially Spain and Italy. This in turn is consistent with French enthusiasm for the Channel Tunnel linking France and England, that contrasts with British apathy. Or again French acquisitions in Britain, of companies such as Metal Box, have attracted comment in the British financial press and have also been seen as evidence of France's European demarche.

This posture is historically consistent. For France this is Act Two of an exciting production whose Act One was in 1957–8 with the signing of the Rome Treaty and the inception of the Common Market. It is clear from testimonies of that period that this was regarded as a major step for the French *patronat*, the occasion for modernising French manufacturing in response to direct European and especially German competition. And now looking back, 1957–8 was a milestone on the road to greater prosperity, an indisputable part of *les trentes glorieuses*, the 30 years of economic advance following the Liberation of 1944.

All this contrasts with the British orientation. British entry to the EC was born out of the realisation of national economic under-performance, driven by a hope that somehow or other EC member-ship would give Britain the dramatic economic growth rate enjoyed by, say, Italy in the years after 1958. At best a *mariage de convenance*, with questions raised about the burden of the dowry.

Nearly two decades later the British orientation does not seem to have changed so much. A common theme cross-nationally in the interviews (excepting France) is that the importance of 1992 has been exaggerated, that it will not make that much difference. This view-point is especially marked among the British executives who would offer often sensible and closely reasoned arguments as to why little would change. The British are not uninterested in the Single European Market, but it does not for them have the status of a *rendezvous avec l'histoire*. The British orientation is pragmatic, and focuses on the tangible. British publishers ask what will happen to the net book agreement, British brewers yearn for a harmonisation of VAT rates on alcohol and are haunted by the fact that a can of lager costs 17 pence in the Pas de Calais and 40 pence in the supermarket in Dover. British bankers pursue niche strategies, look for particular things that they might do better in particular foreign markets.

Even if we take Britain as something of a stick-in-the-mud with regard to European unity, we can see in the response of other countries an enthusiasm born of different motives. We have already seen how France has seized on 1992 as a device to spur French industry to do what it needs to do anyway – become more self-reliant, internationally minded and responsive to market forces. In many ways France regards Europe as a vehicle for its ambitions to become once more *une grande puissance*. We can contrast this with the rather purer response of the Netherlands. Dutch keenness on European unification is merely the culmination of decades and even centuries of internationalist attitudes. And perhaps at the most altruistic end of the spectrum we have Spain which has embraced Europe, indeed democracy, with the fervour of a former exile. (All the buses in Spain bear the Council of Europe flag.) After decades in the wilderness, we see people relieved to find old friends.

The example of Spain brings us neatly on to another interesting point regarding history and heterogeneity. Simply stated, it is that countries may have significant experiences at different times. For instance, all the Common Market countries are parliamentary democracies. But that conspectus of countries includes some that have been democratic for over a 1000 years (UK), and others that have been ploughing a faltering furrow towards democracy since 1975 (Spain). And to drive home that point we have a whole new group of countries in the centre of Europe which have been parliamentary democracies only since the turn of 1989/90. Now some of these countries (notably Hungary and Czechoslovakia) are mooted as prospective EC members, yet it is clear they are not to be compared with France and Britain, Denmark and Holland, or even with West Germany in the matter of the establishment of democratic institutions.

Or if we take another criterion, those former COMECON countries are also free market economies, but we all know that they are radically different âs market economies from those prevailing in, say, Denmark or Italy. So it is not just a question of asking 'has it happened?'. *When* it happened has significant implications for economic life and in turn for the strategy of companies.

Now these rather gross comparisons can be refined and sectoralised. So that if we take the deregulation of banking as a criterion we could say, for instance, that Britain and Norway have similar systems. But in fact, Norwegian banking has only been deregulated since the mid-1980s, a decision which threw the Norwegian banking scene into upheaval. Banks switched from a very conservative, judicious lending role to being very keen to offer easy credit, discarding the usual controls and taking a rather cavalier attitude towards credit-worthiness. The upshot was that the banks lent too much, people reneged on loans, and 1988/89 saw a crisis with several banks going to the wall. If we look again at Norway in ten years' time there will no longer be a problem, but presently there is still confusion.

Or again consider publishing. Representatives of Spanish publishing say that theirs is a growth market because people are really keen to get hold of the books so long held back by the censor. There is an accumulated thirst which longs to be satiated. The example is even more striking in what used to be East Germany. What seemed on the surface to be a pretty emaciated market with poor collective purchasing power in fact turned out to be something of a goldmine for West German publishers. As it transpired, although salaries were low in East Germany, there was a high rate of savings; so when West German publishers peddled their wares in East Germany they found their books were snatched up with wild enthusiasm. Consumers even helped to unload the trucks bearing the formerly forbidden fruit!

Facts and Beyond

We have touched on a number of contrasts between the countries in our sample that emerged in the interviews and at the same time seem to structure the perceptions of our executives. Sometimes these differences are factual, or have some factual starting point; yet the merely factual is soon transcended by meaning and interpretation, by attitude and conviction. More important than the facts is what we do with them, how they become embedded in meanings that shape our view of things, condition our understanding.

Imagine a publishing executive in the USA thinking about Europe and wondering which would be desirable markets to enter. His thoughts light for a moment on one of the smaller countries of the EC – Denmark. Our putative American executive considers Denmark briefly – and dismisses it. A small country, tiny population (only five million, they have more pigs than people) and a minority language. What is more books in Denmark carry 22 percent VAT, hardly a force for market buoyancy.

Yet while in the USA 0.2 new titles are published annually per 1000 population, the corresponding figure for Denmark is 2.0. This is a fact, and a striking one. If one knew this one might think in book market terms of Denmark having a population of 50 million, or put it in the same category as France. What is more, of the two million households in Denmark, a quarter belong to one or more book clubs.

Our American executive may not know these facts but at least he will know that publishing is a business like any other, and it is all about the bottom line. This notion will clearly not be foreign to the Danish publishing world, yet a consistent strain of literary patriotism and idealism emerges in our interviews with Danish publishers, crossed on occasion with long-term vision bordering on the heroic. One of the publishers has an imprint devoted to young, undiscovered Danish writers: not only is this series unprofitable, but the magnitude of its unprofitability is a source of corporate pride. Yet in 15 years' time at least some of these loyally sponsored unknown writers will be bestsellers. This strand of idealism and professional conviction is nicely expressed by the CEO of another Danish publisher who claimed: 'I do not think I would publish something I do not somehow feel something for. Publishing is both a matter of business and of love!'

Together with the long-term orientation of Danish publishers, ready to sponsor youthful talent and wait for mature bestsellers, is a traditionally stable relationship between writers and publishers. Danish writers do not 'shop around', they are not bound to their publishers by contract but by natural loyalty. All our Danish publishers volunteered this testimony, and it was common in the interviews to use marriage-based metaphors to connote this stable relationship. On one occasion the interviewer asked a publishing CEO if he was not sometimes exasperated to find a rival had snapped up a writer/title he wanted. The reply is instructive: 'No. I have only felt that a few times. If we really looked at it in this way we would then go out and try to buy each other's writers, and we do not do that here in Denmark.'

From an American viewpoint there are other things which seem to be understood differently in Danish publishing. In an interview with a smaller Danish publisher the interviewer asked the CEO if he felt his publishing house had any advantage over a larger rival. This produced the modest response: 'I do not think we can do anything which (name of rival publisher) cannot do. Maybe we are able to react faster and get a manuscript through the system faster.' Now the USA is not included in our study, but there are some American executives in our interview sample who were heading up American companies in Europe. One of these American CEOs was asked in the interview about his company's strengths. This question elicited a vigorous and comprehensive answer. When asked the corresponding question about possible weaknesses, he listed a number of *former* weaknesses, all of which had been overcome, thereby yielding a second list of corporate strengths! Is this American–Danish comparison not instructive?

We began this little illustration from Danish publishing with contrasted facts about new titles per year per 1000 population. Yet interesting and relevant though the fact is, arguably more important are the differences in meaning, in what is expected, treated as usual, taken for granted. Yet successful business operations are built on this knowledge.

Countries with Maps

The Danish publishing example is simply taken as an introduction to a wider phenomenon. Throughout our study when executives speak of their companies or industries, it is clear that they have what one might call 'mental maps' in the sense developed by Johnson (1987). By mental map we mean the manager's taken-for-granted understanding of the way things naturally are. For instance, French publishers will take it for granted that it is their mission to be internationalist. Spanish publishers will take it for granted that it is their mission to publish in Latin America. Danish publishers will take it for granted that their mission is to publish young hopefuls. Mental maps shape managerial perceptions of what is possible in a business sense.

Now, nationality is only one of a number of factors that impinge on the construction of these mental maps, but it is an important one, it has not received much prominence elsewhere, and our study seems to highlight it. Some more illustrations, crossing various industries and countries may be helpful.

French Publishing Revisited

At an earlier stage we referred to the relative 'bullishness' of the French companies vis-à-vis the Single European Market. The French seem to see 1992 as potentially important: a source of threat and opportunity, as something that should be prepared for especially by alliances, and we added that this is quite consistent with the French response to the inception of the EC in the 1950s.

This general phenomenon is manifest in French publishing. Among our sample of six French publishers there were references to 'implantations' in France and Spain, alliances with publishers from other countries (in two cases even in Russia), and cross-border ownership of bookclubs. One of the French publishers spoke (British-style) of having over 50 percent of its business in North America, another had tried to buy the British publisher Collins. Even executives denying the importance of 1992 played up the need for internationalisation and cross-border alliances.

There is another angle, perhaps less striking. It is quite simply that the French publishing industry seems to be marked by more 'downstream' integration. One of the publishers has a distribution centre in Paris significantly mentioned by some of the others as a force in the industry; there were various references to owning bookshops, chains in some cases, and bookshops abroad, as well as to controlled distribution through bookclubs (or the desirability of having it). Like Danish publishing statistics, these are facts of business organisation, but more importantly they structure the understanding of an industry.

American Business and European Industry

In the earlier discussion of takeover activity it was suggested that Britain shares an American business philosophy which emphasises profits and performance while relegating all else to the status of a means to achieve the end. This view, of course, does not lack expression in Europe; there is no black and white contrast. Yet there is a diffuse alternative orientation in continental Europe that one concentrates on excellence in the particular industry and assumes that profitability will ensue. This rather intangible difference may be apprehended sometimes in focus and lack of focus in certain industries. Let us consider brewing.

The continental brewers are there to make beer. They may make soft drinks and mineral water as well, and perhaps have some supply contracts with cafés or retailers, but that is usually it. There is an interesting comparison with the British brewers, treated here as exemplars of this American business orientation. In the earlier chapter on the brewing industry it was jauntily remarked that British brewers do not seem to know whether they are in manufacturing, property, or distribution. Even more important is the fact that they do not care so long as they are making money. And to be fair they seem to make more of it, at least expressed as a proportion of turnover, than say the more product-focused brewers of West Germany.

With a more American business philosophy it seems perfectly normal to British brewers that they should make beer, and other things; that they should own public houses and manage a property portfolio, that they can move in (and out!) of hotel ownership, dance halls, budget accommodation, betting shops and off-licences. One of the British interviewees expressed this much broader focus by describing his brewery as being in the leisure industry. The company mission was to fight for its share of what he called 'the leisure pound'. German executives, to take a counter-example, do not say things like this.

Or again consider the unusual perspective of the Italian brewers. As in most countries, consumption of alcohol is on the decline. There is a vigorous anti-alcohol lobby. These are not obvious causes for rejoicing in the brewing community. And yet Italian brewers display an optimism not shared by their European counterparts. The reason is that in Italy, a traditionally wine-drinking country, beer is regarded as a low-alcohol alternative. It follows that Italian brewers see beer consumption picking up as the anti-alcohol lobby gains strength.

Foreign Chic or Foreign Rubbish

It was once observed that in Swedish vegetable markets Swedish produce is labelled as to region of origin. Non-Swedish produce is left unlabelled, thereby being tacitly consigned to the category of foreign rubbish (Lawrence and Spybey, 1986). We would like to suggest that countries vary broadly in their orientation to goods of foreign origin. Again beer is a nice example. Let us take Germany as a starting point.

The famous *Reinheitsgebot* is one of the world's oldest food laws and the Creed-cum-Ten Commandments of the German brewing industry. It was established in 1516 by Duke Wilhelm IV of Bavaria and decreed that beer should be made exclusively of four pure ingredients – malt, hops, yeast and water. Germany is the second biggest beer market in the world after the USA. Even this hard bold market fact hardly does justice to the seriousness with which the Germans, and in particular the Bavarians, take their beer.

Although the EC forced West Germany to abandon the *Reinheitsgebot*, at least as a requirement for imported beer, this has made little practical difference in the marketplace. No self-respecting German will commit cultural treason by drinking beer that has not been brewed according to the dictates of the *Reinheitsgebot*. Beer is not so much a way of life in Bavaria as a religious edict. There are festivals throughout the year, from the *Fasching* carnival in the first few months, via the *Starkbier* festivities at Lent, and *Biergarten* time in the summer, right through to the awesome consumption of the *Oktoberfest*.

Nor is beer patriotism the exclusive property of the Germans. This is also a Danish strength. Carlsberg of course has a large market share in Denmark, but there are other good Danish breweries and they are represented in our study. One Danish brewing executive summarised for us Denmark's record on foreign beers:

> Carlsberg attempted to market Budweiser. It was a big failure, and frankly I do not think they were really sorry about it. Brugsen (Danish supermarket chain) imported Holsten beer from Germany. That did not go either. Dansk Supermarked (another chain) tried with Beck's Bier (brewed in Bremen, West Germany). That was not a success either. Faxe (a Danish brewer) tried with Löwenbrau, but that did not go. Until now no foreign brewer has been successful in Denmark.

There is a further twist to the Danish story. Driving down to the German border, crossing over and filling the tank with cheap German petrol and the boot with cheap beer is a national pastime for Danes. It is not German beer they buy, however, but good reliable Danish beer thoughtfully placed just over the border for them by friendly Danish breweries.

For a contrast consider Britain. One of the present writers lives in the small English town of Melton Mowbray with a population of less than 25,000. In the town's supermarkets one can buy beer from East and West Germany, from Denmark of course, from Holland, Belgium, and Luxembourg, from France, Spain, Switzerland, Italy, Czechoslovakia and Poland. Beers from Canada, the USA, Japan, Australia, Singapore and Mexico are also on sale. One store alone offers products from four Dutch and seven West German breweries.

The fact that there is little in the way of indigenous British lager is of course part of the explanation. Yet this sharp contrast between Britain and some of its continental neighbours is suffused by a conviction that foreign is fashionable.

Fast Driving in the Car Industry

We will end on a note of quasi-surrealism. Germany is one of the few countries with no speed limit on its motorways. This is a source of immense moral and psychological satisfaction to the Germans. When a temporary speed limit was introduced during the first oil crisis at the end of 1973 it produced a public outcry, backed by utterly spurious arguments to the effect that the speed limit (about 70 miles per hour) would not allow German drivers to get into top gear and was therefore actually wasteful of petrol. This basic German freedom also enables the Germans to patronise others – the Dutch, for example, who are rather proud of their speed limits, or the Danes who come to Germany to 'refresh themselves on our autobahns'.

Fascinatingly this conviction finds expression in some of the German car industry interviews. One manager urges that a speed limit on German motorways would increase accidents since it would render the motorways unattractive to German drivers who would switch to non-motorway roads with higher accident rates. A beautifully logical argument of course, but not one that you would hear from a Dutchman.

But the German conviction goes further and enters the realms of competitive advantage and market positioning. We have further interview testimony to the effect that the absence of a motorway speed limit favours the quality and high performance segment of the German car industry. This is probably a fair claim: more fun to drive a Porsche in Germany than in Denmark. Yet the testimony goes further and urges that this is a competitive advantage abroad, that foreigners have greater confidence in German quality cars knowing that they have bean designed for and proven on the unrestricted *Autobahnen*.

Not an easy claim to confirm or disprove. But more interesting is the fact that it is not an idea one could readily come to in Tokyo or Detroit City.

Maps without Compass

We have explored various ways in which national differences may affect products, markets and business. We are not making any exclusive claim for nationality here. It is simply one of a number of forces which shape the mental maps that managers have.

There is a last point to be made. We are dealing here with paradigms that are specific to industries, to countries, or to both. These paradigms are not easy to apprehend if one is an outsider – to the industry, the country, or to Europe as a whole. Nor are they necessarily things that will be readily revealed by formal methods of market research and business enquiry. You can look up the population of Denmark in an encyclopedia, but there is no way that you can find out that Danish publishers are more patriotic than American publishers – not unless a Danish publisher tells you, and even he or she might not realise it. The idea has been expressed by the psychiatrist R.D. Laing with his observation, 'I don't know what I don't know'. This is not a simple imperative to 'master the facts', but an exhortation to engage in the subtleties of understanding.

Our final point is a subtle one. Simply stated, it is that Europe is differently perceived from without, especially from the USA. The US view of Europe will be different from the European view of Europe. Typically, what perceptive Americans will latch on to is that there is more heterogeneity in Europe, that the Common Market isn't really a United States of Europe, and that there are more differences between, say, Holland and Belgium than between Vermont and New Hampshire.

Americans who see that are right. The difference in manners, in social assumptions, in cultural attitudes and consequently in business *mores*, will always be more marked in Europe. And this is what most of this chapter has been about, drawing the attention of insiders and outsiders to that manifold heterogeneity. But there is more to it than that. Europe is also different from the USA because it is marked by more conditionality in business decision making. What do we mean by conditionality?

When American CEOs decide to do something, they do not need to ask anybody, they just do it. When Americans say, 'It's a great idea, okay let's go, let's do it now!' they are not just expressing a temperamental inclination towards positiveness and non-fatalism – although they are doing both of those things – they are also expressing what is institutionally possible for them. So that even the German, Danish or Dutch manager who has that same purposeful American temperament would not be able to act like this. The European reaction is more likely to be: 'This is a great idea. We will now discuss it with the supervisory board, then we'll discuss it with our trade unions. And we should perhaps let the worker representatives comment on it. And since we're a fairly big company we'd better consult government. In fact we're not just going to consult the

Ministry of Employment but the Environmental Ministry too, because what we're going to do has environmental implications.'

This is what we mean by conditionality. That European companies are much more likely to have two-tier boards, to require consultation with the labour unions which are inestimably more important than they are in the USA; and there will often be some form of dialogue with government. In the USA, on the other hand, talking to the government is for wimps and companies with defence contracts. To burlesque the situation, American firms do what they want to do; then hire lawyers to get them off the hook if necessary. The economy is a matter for businessmen; they know what is in the interests of America.

Conditionality, then, is something that distinguishes Europe – and it is something that is little recognised from the outside. It is perhaps as important as the heterogeneity we have been preaching in the chapter.

If we come back and take an intra-European view then again there are big differences in the degree of this conditionality with, say, the Netherlands – complete with co-determination, two-tier boards, government consultation, at the strong end of the spectrum – and Britain with relatively few of those things at the other end. Yet Britain would still be marked by greater conditionality in our sense than is the USA. So that European conditionality is both relative and variable.

References

Barsoux, Jean-Louis and Lawrence, Peter (1990) *Management in France*. London: Cassell.

Johnson, Gerry (1987) *Strategic Change and the Management Process*. Oxford: Basil Blackwell.

Lawrence, Peter and Spybey, Tony (1986) *Management and Society in Sweden*. London: Routledge & Kegan Paul.

Lawrence, Peter (1991) *Management in the Netherlands*. Oxford: Oxford University Press.

Wenlock, Heather (1990) *'The management of transfer of undertakings: A comparison of employee participation practices in the United Kingdom and the Netherlands'*, DPhil thesis, St Edmund Hall, Oxford.

9

Conclusions

Tugrul Atamer and Gerry Johnson

'L'Europe ne sera pas ce que nous en ferons. Elle sera d'abord ce que nous en pensons' (Debray, 1989). Managers will greatly influence the changing economic and social character of Europe and, clearly, their understanding of the future of Europe and the EC will influence their acts. Yet how they manage the strategic development of their businesses requires them to come to terms with a series of complex, even paradoxical situations. The most institutionalised manifestation of a changing Europe – the Single European Market and its chronology of 1992 – is seen as something of a 'non-event': however, there is little clarity among managers as to what does constitute a European market. The rationale for a European free market differs between Brussels technocrats and business executives: not least in the role of Europe as a trading bloc. Notions of what constitutes a European market also differ by country and, of course, by industry. Executives talk of global strategy development, yet emphasise the importance in Europe of local responsiveness. It is not even clear which countries constitute Europe any longer.

This chapter explores some of these issues and considers some of their implications for management.

What is Europe?

The most basic problem faced by anyone trying to understand Europe is defining what it is. Boundary definitions of a geographical or political nature, legislative bases, or the strategic views of executives, are all problematic. Apart from the countries in the EC and perhaps those seeking entry, we must now include what used to be East Germany: but what of other Eastern European countries? There are political pressures for the west to help close the huge economic gap with the east, not least to avoid political de-stability. There are also commercial opportunities for investment and co-operation between firms in west and east. And it is not only East Germany which has shown an internal readiness for change: so too have Hungary, Czechoslovakia and Poland. The future of Europe, then, can no longer be thought of in terms of the existing EC: but it is not clear how it should be defined.

Certainly legislative bases of definition do not greatly help the executive who is considering a European strategy for an organisation. Consider, for example, the regulations that will govern the Single European Market. Are there to be quotas or not in the car industry? Will TV advertising for beer be allowed across the whole of Europe? What rates of excise duty and VAT will there be on cars and beer from 1996? What will be the consequences of home country rules in banking? What are the reciprocity principles towards third countries? The rules of the SEM are too ill-formed for executives to be sure of their impact.

In any case, executives do not regard the legislative processes of defining the trading bloc of Europe as the most influential force in determining their strategies. They see much more important economic and social forces shaping the future of the four industries we studied, forces such as:

- in the beer industry, the stagnation of demand, the increasing power of the food retailing supermarket chains, the ever-growing marketing costs linked to the logic of transnational branding,
- in retail banking, the technological evolution which requires higher and higher investment and the training of personnel,
- in the car industry, the competitive gap between European companies and the Japanese on a worldwide basis,
- in the book publishing industry, the probable concentration of the distribution channels and the 'bestsellerisation' of the market.

In each of those industries, the developing European market is as much the result of changes in trading patterns and company strategies as the cause of such changes: yet the explanations for this vary in different industries and companies.

Managers in already international companies argue: 'we did not wait for the SEM, we already are European'. Others, for example in the car industry, see their market as worldwide anyway. The views here are that European issues are subsumed within wider, global strategic considerations. Such views do not, of course, always square with the evidence. For example even in the car industry, many European companies still have a high percentage of their sales in their home country.

In smaller businesses, views on the relevance and impact of Europe differ considerably. There are those who see increasing Europeanisation as having a high impact – particularly for businesses trying to compete at a national level rather than across Europe. There are others who see Europe as incidental to changes already under way due to internationalisation of markets at the European level or on a global basis: views common in retail banking and brewing for example. Still other managers in smaller national-based companies believe that they will survive in small national, or sub-national niches – for example in brewing or book publishing, although it is sometimes difficult to see just what they regard as a defensible niche.

Overall, for most managers the developing Europe certainly has to be taken into account but its formal constitution is hardly central to their deliberations.

Technocratic and Managerial Rationales for Europe

So, is the Single European Market just the invention of a band of Brussels technocrats? There are certainly some divergencies between their rationales and those of managers. Brussels argues for the creation of a homogeneous European market with harmonisation of norms, of taxes, and of regulations; this will come about by agreement, by legislation or by market pressures. It is necessary because there are potential cost reductions, economies of scale and the opportunity of critical mass and rationalisation – all good economic arguments which contributed to the reasons for the Single European Market (SEM).

However, managers do not talk much about cost reductions as a result of the SEM. For them, technological improvements will be the main sources of cost reductions; and these are necessary because marketing costs could rise and prices fall with increased competition across Europe. The benefits of a developing Europe for the managers arise in other ways. They emphasise the *diversity* of the European market: diverse customer behaviour and cultural norms, and diverse distribution channels for example. They also point to the increasing need for quality, with more sophisticated customers asking for more sophisticated products, requiring clearer market positioning but yielding opportunities for differentiation and innovation.

For instance, it has been argued in Brussels that the potential cost reductions resulting from the SEM are between 3 and 7 percent of the beer industry value-added, assuming the concentration of the German market after abolishing the beer purity law. However, executives in the industry do not see the German beer industry rationalising quickly because of the conservative German consumer. And, rather than cost-reduction strategies, they emphasise the opportunities of speciality beers and product innovations such as low-alcohol beer. They seek benefits from the diversity of Europe and its consumers, rather than through homogeneity and scale.

The forces at work in the developing European market are complex. They will certainly be influenced by the legislators, and by increasing harmonisation around such legislation, as well as growing cultural harmonisation in the long term: yet the diversity of Europe cannot be denied. It raises other paradoxes: how does the manager reconcile the harmonisation of Europe with its diversity, and the 'domestic' nature of the European market with growing global pressures on trade and industry?

Europe and Worldwide Trade

The growing internationalisation of trade has been demonstrated in terms of trade statistics over a long period of time. The formation of economic and cultural blocs has taken different forms: the Japanisation of South East Asia; the gap between developed countries and underdeveloped countries; and the treaties forming the EC. But how does this relate to the views of managers?

Many managers see a wider international basis of strategy than Europe itself: perhaps this is an encouraging sign in terms of world trade from Europe. On the other hand, the views of many managers are still nationally and sub-nationally rooted; and for some Europe is not so much an entity, but a series of 'export markets'. For most managers, however, world trends are more significant than the particular changes occurring in Europe: it is not their natural inclination to see Europe as the base for worldwide trading endeavours. This is borne out by past statistics. The share of Europe (including the EFTA countries, Yugoslavia, Turkey and Israel) in world trade in 1986 was 45 percent of the exports and 43 percent of the imports, including intra-community exchanges. This looks a great deal. But when considering Western Europe as a bloc (excluding intra-community exchanges) the share of world trade falls to 13.8 percent (of the exports) in 1986, a decrease from 15.3 percent in 1967. The share of Europe in imports also decreased from 17 to 12 percent during the same period (Herzog and Unal, 1988).

What we see is a decline in the impact of Europe as a trading bloc in world trade, with Europeans doing more and more business with other Europeans. Perhaps the best illustration of this uncomfortable position is the car industry. Whereas the Japanese are already in America substantially as well as in Europe, and the Americans are already in Europe, the share of European car manufacturers in the USA and Japan is very low – a problem acknowledged by European car industry executives. Moreover, the increase of the Japanese market share in Europe seems inevitable. Indeed, executives see it as central in the development of their strategies. However, the emphasis is more on how to defend against this entry than how to become a successful player on a worldwide basis. The Japanese pressure is driving managers in the car industry towards attempts to secure domestic and European markets *despite* their recognition of the increasingly global nature of the industry.

The picture should not be so gloomy according to Michael Porter's principles of worldwide competitive success (Porter, 1990). Competitive companies and industries develop in nations or areas where qualified human resources are abundant, production factors and the infrastructures are available, local suppliers and adjacent industries are effective, customers are demanding and sophisticated, and high rivalry stimulates innovation and progress. Europe surely has all these conditions to improve its ability to compete worldwide; companies and policy makers just have to stimulate these determinants. Moreover Europe has a diverse set of competitive advantages; so there ought to be the potential for synergy as the development of 'one Europe' allows competitive advantages to cross-fertilise. This suggests that rivalry between European countries and companies should not be avoided but encouraged; that acquisitions and alliances are beneficial in order to stimulate such pan-European development of experience and skills; and no doubt foster, in turn, a cadre of pan-European international managers with expertise to further reinforce such advantages. Further, to be more effective worldwide, European companies might stimulate the historical links European countries have with other parts of the world: France with parts of Africa, Spain with South America, the UK with the Commonwealth and the USA and the Germans with Eastern Europe, for example.

The potential for Europe, as a trading bloc, appears to be real enough: but it is questionable whether managers see this as the major opportunity for their businesses.

Gaining – and Resisting – Entry into Europe

Executives recognise that with 323 million customers, the EC cannot be neglected by American and Japanese companies; further penetration is inevitable. Though Europe is still relatively fragmented compared to Japan or even the USA, the SEM is likely to decrease this fragmentation and therefore increase the attractiveness of Europe.

The UK, Spain and Eastern Europe are the most likely bridgeheads to Europe. The UK welcomes foreign investments and is relatively liberal towards acquisitions by foreigners; besides the use of English, the financial infrastructure of London and the future

Channel Tunnel make it the more interesting. Spain has relatively low-cost, good quality manpower, and the Spanish and Portuguese markets are growing. The state of flux, and the need for inward investment, make Eastern Europe, especially Czechoslovakia, Hungary, Poland and East Germany, likely bases for establishing a European presence.

The likelihood of entry strategies by particular firms may well result from what has become known as the 'loose brick' approach (Hamel and Prahalad, 1985), by which an entrant exploits the weak strategic position of a European business or business sector. Historically, the weak point of Europe in the automobile industry was the UK, with problems of quality, manpower, manufacturing, reinvestment and management leading to a deteriorating domestic and an enfeebled international competitive position. The Japanese built their European entry strategies on initial penetration of the UK by exploiting weaknesses and gaps in that market, and building alliances. This early exploitation of weaknesses was followed by the widening of product ranges and investment in the infrastructure of manufacturing and distribution. A similar approach can be foreseen in other areas: the distribution of books or beer in Italy; assistance with the restructuring of industry in Eastern Europe; exploiting the relatively underdeveloped retail banking system in southern Europe; or exploiting the growing importance of global banking and building alliances with some of the European banks.

Managers in Europe recognise that a head-on entry strategy on a major scale may not be likely in all industries. Alliances and agreements are more likely ways of entering. This is not only because of the cost of direct entry, or acquisition; it is also because such alliances and agreements are means of gaining experience of markets, distribution, manpower and location strategies, especially in a diverse market.

The Japanese understand these lessons well and have demonstrated their ability to succeed through such strategies. The US has been less successful in the past. Whilst in the car industry General Motors and Ford succeeded in taking a significant position, they entered during a period of European reconstruction and consolidated after the EC was founded. American companies have been less successful more recently in other industries – Anheuser Busch have been notably unsuccessful in the beer industry, for example, and the Americans have not made a major impact in Europe in retail banking or book publishing. Their main pitfall may be failing to exploit the diversity of Europe, regarding it as a more homogeneous geographical area, and seeking cost-driven 'Euroglobal' strategies of dominance. Although such an approach may succeed in some markets, the likelihood of dominance in Europe on such a singular basis is unlikely, even given the SEM.

This further emphasises the dilemma facing Europeans. The SEM argues for a more homogeneous Europe with all its economic advantages; but, arguably, in so doing increases the ease of entry. Many managers see the diversity of Europe as a significant entry barrier to overseas competition and argue for the preservation of such diversity, not least because of their ability to manage it more successfully than non-Europeans. Yet the evidence is that such diversity can also provide the very 'loose bricks' that allow more sophisticated entry strategies. European companies may argue that entry is inevitable and choose to co-operate by establishing alliances with possible entrants as a means of controlling and benefiting from it. Governments may recognise the inevitability of such moves and negotiate inward investment arrangements rather than risk heavy imports and the loss of local jobs. An alternative for the European manager might be to seek to manage diversity better by ensuring that, while it is maintained, the competitive positions of its components are strong. This argument leads towards not state or European control, but pan-European companies, or alliances that can manage such diversity effectively; and thus, in turn, to the argument for acquisitions and mergers across Europe to establish strong Europe-wide firms.

The lesson for the entrant seems to be clear enough. Europe is a diverse geographical, cultural and market entity. Successful entry is unlikely through crude attempts of scale and dominance. It is more likely that successful entry will be achieved by knowing the markets sufficiently well to identify the weak areas resulting from diversity and exploiting those systematically, either through investment or through alliances.

Managing Complexity in Europe

We have argued that understanding Europe requires the recognition of the paradox of Europe; and managing strategically therefore requires the ability to manage complex situations. One implication is to question traditional 'wisdom' which argues that a company cannot be both competitive in costs and differentiated with high perceived quality corresponding to segment specific demands. The Japanese may be accustomed to managing such paradoxes; North American and European managers need to develop similar abilities.

Figure 9.1 shows the three major forces that influence complexity. The SEM, and its underlying rationale, is a formalised recognition of

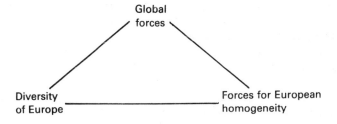

Figure 9.1

forces which may be under way in Europe: forces for an increasingly homogeneous Europe, perhaps the concentration of industries, and in the longer term, the homogenisation of buying behaviour. While such changes are recognised, and even welcomed by European managers, who see the opportunity for more truly common and open markets, they emphasise rather more two other forces. First, the diversity of Europe, in geographical, linguistic, cultural and market terms, as an enduring phenomenon. Secondly, however, increasingly global market developments and the requirement to compete on a global basis. These three forces provide managers with a complex strategic problem: strategic success somehow needs to embrace the recognition of local diversity, yet control the exploitation of global trends. The fact that no-one knows how fast homogenisation will occur or exactly what the scope will be for benefits of scale, cost reductions and synergies, adds to the challenge.

The starting point for understanding this problem is, perhaps, to recognise that markets in general are becoming more complex anyway: Europe is not unique in this but does provide an example. There have been at least two major long-term historical trends, neither of which is a product of the SEM as such. First the trend towards the homogenisation of lifestyle: the development of international communication media is a driving force of this long-term process. For instance the Spanish talk about becoming more 'European', which affects book publishing and the consumption of beer in a traditional wine region for example. An increase in tourism across Europe has also affected markets – in the provision of personal financial services, or the increasing price comparison of cars, or even beer – across boundaries. In parallel, another long-term trend is towards customer sophistication and hence required quality. This has to be understood not so much on the crude geographical or socioeconomic bases of segmentation, but more precise attitudinal and behavioural segmentation; and in consequence the requirement of more innovative product range planning and product design. The point is that these trends of increasing homogeneity, yet increasing market diversity, are under way in Europe notwithstanding the SEM or any other formalisation of markets. A high degree of market sensitivity is required to manage what appears to be a homogeneity/diversity paradox. This might be begun by analysis of homogenisation and localisation diversity forces at the product line level, as proposed in Chapter 6. The evaluation of forces of homogenisation at the customer level needs to be considered in terms of its implications for potential economies of scale, transport and communication costs, location of head offices or plant and so on. And the forces of diversity in terms of customer needs and buying behaviour need to be examined, similarly in terms of location policies, research and development needs, marketing policies and so on.

For instance our analysis in Chapter 6 showed that cars is a transnational industry becoming global with increasing homogenisation forces and decreasing localisation forces. Retail banking is a multidomestic industry becoming transnational again with decreasing localisation forces but increasing forces towards globalisation. Brewing is in the middle – some decreasing localisation forces and some increasing globalisation forces. In the book publishing industry localisation forces do exist – the cultural and language barriers for example; but globalisation forces are increasing. So in the car industry a company might pay particular attention to developing a transnational or a global strategy; whereas in retail banking, it should seek a multidomestic (or domestic) strategy: the same type of evaluation is even more instructive at the segment level (again as shown in Chapter 6).

Executives also need to consider issues of organisational design as it relates to products and services; particularly in terms of how to manage homogeneity through greater centralisation to gain synergies and reduce costs; and how to manage diversity through more decentralised operations to gain flexibility to meet different customer needs. Two major European brewers (Heineken and Kronenbourg) are examples of companies which manage homogenisation with a core product across countries and rationalisation of their product facilities and logistics across Europe. They also manage diversity by diversification of their product portfolios (bières speciales, bières de luxe, and low-alcohol beer), diverse advertising messages across Europe, and different brand names in some foreign countries, perhaps keeping the original brand after an acquisition (for Heineken: Dreher in Italy, El Aguila in Spain, for example).

The external forces for increasing homogeneity and yet diversity are real enough and organisations will have to learn to cope with them. However, faced with complex implications of analysis and organisation we might highlight one of the quotes from an executive in our study. Certainly homogeneity is an attractive trend in terms of the economics of business. However: 'Watch out for economies of scale: personally I never met any economy of scale in my life, I never met a synergy . . . . But I met people, products, clients.' If there has to be a choice, it is likely to be wise to recognise the importance of diversity, not least because it demands a closeness to market and customer needs and trends which are likely to lead to greater innovation, differentiation and thus a likelihood of greater competitive strength.

European Challenges and 'Managerial Wisdom'

Those who have studied strategic decision making in organisations have observed the way in which managers, faced with complexity, bring to bear simplification processes so that the situations can be handled. In effect they interpret the complexity they face through a frame of reference or mental map specific to themselves, or more likely to the group, organisation, or even industry in which they work. These mental maps are made up of beliefs and assumptions, often taken for granted, which amount to inherited 'managerial wisdom': and understanding them is therefore important in understanding how managers are likely to respond to changes in any industry. In analysing them for the managers we interviewed, some findings emerged which give useful clues to the development of managerial skills to face the challenge of Europe. For example, within the same industry and within companies of the same sort of size, the mental maps of managers could be very different across Europe. Examples of these differences are given in the previous chapter: they are not surprising given the different histories and cultures of each organisation. However, if the mental maps of the managers are aggregated so that all the different beliefs and assumptions, for example about Europe and its development, are brought together, the resulting frame of reference for the evolution of an industry, or the evolution of Europe, is extremely instructive. In other words the aggregate 'wisdom' of managers is a great deal richer than any individual mental map, and, of course, a good deal less organisationally biased.

Once stated this is an obvious point: however its implications for the development of strategies and the development of managers is significant. For example, almost all European brewers outside Germany take for granted the difficulties of penetrating the traditional German market; nor do any of the brewers outside Germany discuss very much the significance of the Eastern European brewing industry, although this is commonly discussed in Germany. Grounds for conceiving of entry strategies into Germany may, however, emerge from bringing together insights of the German brewers and skills taken for granted by other European brewers. For example, other European brewers are more sophisticated in dealing with retailers than the German brewers who may well be facing demands for concentration of supply in Germany. Or again, is it possible that the parochial UK brewers could benefit from the development of speciality beers on the continent? Perhaps in so doing, they could build a network of brewing alliances which could protect them from acquisition by major European or non-European companies.

This is of course just a partial example of the benefits of cross-fertilising between the different experience of managers. However examples exist in the other industries. Differences in the car industry mainly relate to the position vis-à-vis Japanese competition; differences in book publishing relate to views about books as cultural products or commodity products; differences in retail banking relate to location as a critical success factor, or differences in views about multi-specialised banking versus universal banking.

Bringing together these mental maps then, can, be a contribution to the understanding of a developing Europe and also the generation of strategic options. However, most firms in our survey are not seeking to achieve such cross-fertilisation. They are attempting to deal with Europe in terms of their historically formed view of the world. Arguably the companies that will succeed in Europe will be those that can break away from such constraints. But is this possible?

There is much evidence to suggest that the process of changing mental maps internally among the existing management team is highly problematic. Advocated changes in strategy are likely to lead to significant threats to the cultural and political systems of organisations and consequent resistance. In such circumstances the likelihood of change is low until the organisation faces either crisis or substantial perceived danger; or until some powerful 'outsider', often in the form of a new chief executive, is introduced into the organisation (Johnson, 1988). The potential dangers of inertia of strategy in a developing Europe are significant: it may be a prime task of those that see the changes to ensure that the potential of threat or danger to it is fostered internally within their organisation.

Given the benefits of bringing together conflicting mental maps of the developments which are occurring, this might be achieved in different ways: for example through acquisitions and mergers or alliances across Europe; through the recruitment of staff from other companies in different parts of Europe, perhaps at a senior level; from visiting other countries and talking with managers in other countries, and preferably in a language understood by both parties!

Such cross-fertilisation is, however, likely to be unhelpful unless the organisation is designed in such a way as to take advantage of this learning process. Earlier the importance of organisational design to take advantage of the different strategies in Europe was raised. Underlying the argument was the view that a greater allowance for diversity in the market needs to occur: organisational design also needs to take account of and encourage a greater diversity of view. More open systems in which challenges and questioning are common need to be encouraged: strategy development processes which are more reliant on strategic thinking and challenging and less reliant on procedural systems and budgeting, need to be more commonplace. Such approaches, designed to challenge and question assumptions and take account of contra-indicative evidence have been developed – for example by Mason and Mitroff (1981).

The overall message we take from the study is that managers cannot expect to manage strategic success in Europe by a reliance on 'proven' strategic formulae of the past. Europe is developing in ways which will challenge managers to understand and cope with the nature of this complexity and tune their management systems to cope with it. The victims will be those from within Europe, or from without, who cannot; who believe that they will not be affected by a developing Europe; or whose views as to how to construct strategy for Europe are blunt and over-simplified.

References

Debray, R. (1989) *Tous Azimuts*. Paris: Editions Odile Jacob.

Hamel, G. and Prahalad, C.K. (1985) 'Do you really have a global strategy?', *Harvard Business Review*, July–August, pp. 139–48.

Herzog, C. and Unal, D. (1988) 'Les deux visages de l'Europe occidentale', *Furtibles*, décembre.

Johnson, G.N. (1988) 'Re-thinking incrementalism', *Strategic Management Journal*, 9: 75–91.

Mason, R.O. and Mitroff, I.I. (1981) *Challenging Strategic Planning Assumptions*. New York: John Wiley & Sons.

Porter, M.E. (1990) *The Competitive Advantage of Nations*. New York: The Free Press.

Index

Index compiled by Meg Davies (Society of Indexers)